MW01623555

Firelei Báez
Ian Cooper
David Kennedy Cutler
E.V. Day
Melvin Edwards
Natalie Frank
Jane Hammond
Jim Hodges
William Kentridge
Jon Kessler
Glenn Ligon
Suzanne McClelland
Arlene Shechet
Kate Shepherd
Molly Smith
Do Ho Suh
Mary Temple
Richard Tuttle
Ursula von Rydingsvard
B. Wurtz

The Ruth and Elmer Wellin Museum of Art's programs and publications are made possible, in part, with funds from The John B. Root '44 Exhibition Fund; The Dietrich Foundation; The Edward W. and Grace C. Root Endowment Fund; The William G. Roehrick '34 Lecture Fund; and private contributions.

Published in conjunction with the exhibition
Pure Pulp: Contemporary Artists Working in Paper at Dieu Donné
Organized by the Ruth and Elmer Wellin Museum of Art at Hamilton College
198 College Hill Road
Clinton, New York 13323
www.hamilton.edu/wellin

Exhibition Itinerary:

Ruth and Elmer Wellin Museum of Art
Hamilton College, Clinton, NY
February 6–April 10, 2016

Robert C. Williams Museum of Papermaking
Georgia Tech, Atlanta, GA
June 9–August 5, 2016

The Dedalus Foundation
New York, NY
September 8–October 16, 2016

Graphic Design: Tim Laun and Natalie Wedeking
Editorial Production: SNAP Editions, New York, NY
Principal Photography: John Bentham, Andrew Kist, and Jason Mandella
Printed by GHP Media, West Haven, CT
Edition of 1,500

Published in 2016 by the Wellin Museum of Art and DelMonico Books • Prestel

DelMonico Books, an imprint of Prestel,
a member of Verlagsgruppe Random House GmbH

Prestel Verlag
Neumarkter Strasse 28
81673 Munich
Tel.: 49 89 4136 0
Fax: 49 89 4136 2335

Prestel Publishing Ltd.
14-17 Wells Street
London W1T 3PD
Tel.: 44 20 7323 5004
Fax: 44 20 7323 0271

Prestel Publishing
900 Broadway, Suite 603
New York, NY 10003
Tel.: 1 212 995 2720
Fax: 1 212 995 2733
E-mail: sales@prestel-usa.com

www.prestel.com

ISBN: 9783791355443
Library of Congress Control Number: 2015960209

Cover:
Richard Tuttle
The Triumph of Night (detail), 2009
Hand-cast cotton and wire in painted wooden box
14 × 32 ⅛ × 6 ¼ in. (35.6 × 81.4 × 15.9 cm)
Courtesy of the artist and Dieu Donné, New York

Pure Pulp

CONTEMPORARY ARTISTS WORKING IN PAPER AT DIEU DONNÉ

Curated by Bridget Donlon

DelMonico Books • Prestel
Munich London New York

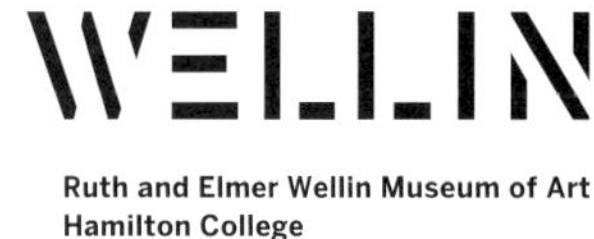

Ruth and Elmer Wellin Museum of Art
Hamilton College

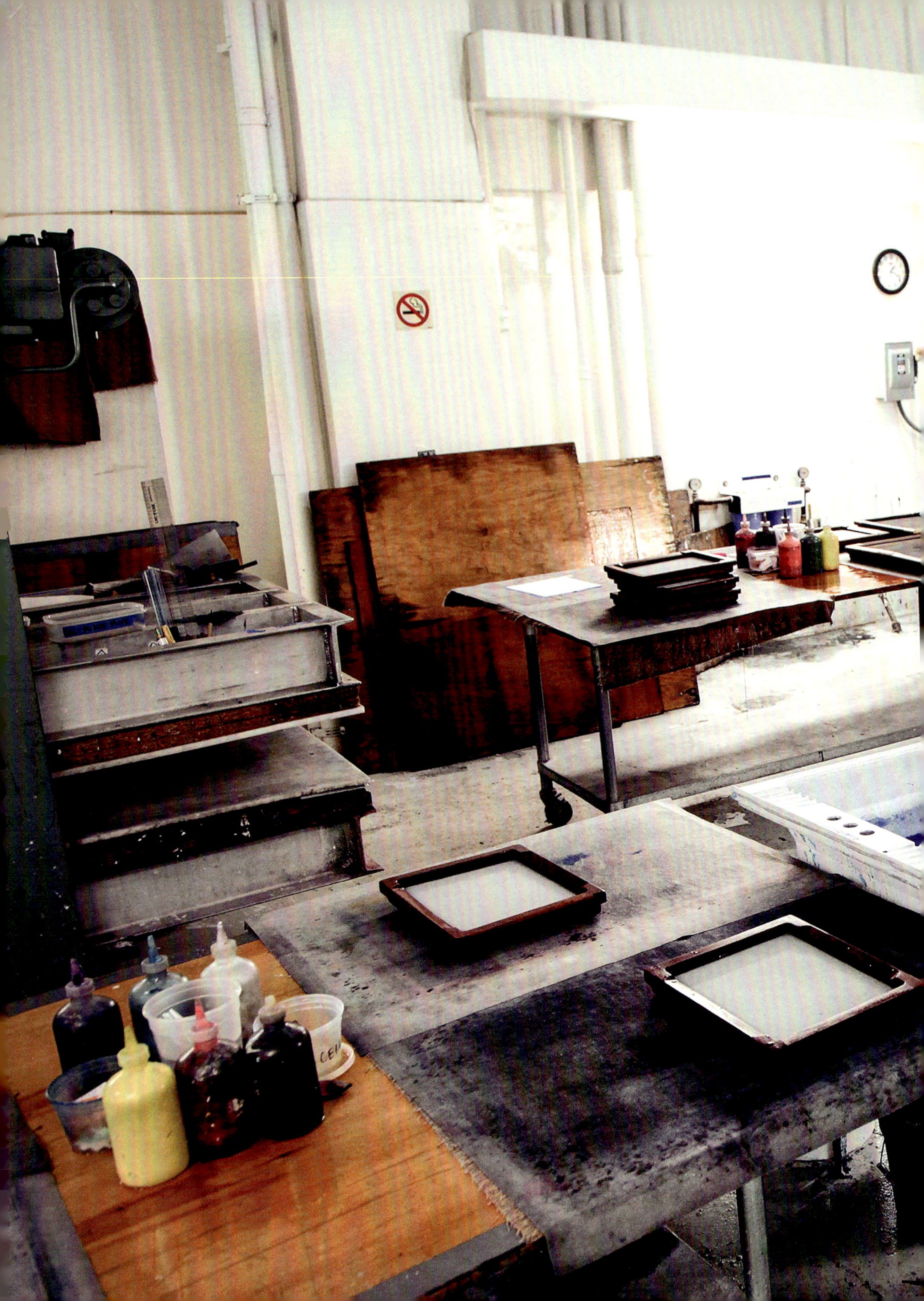

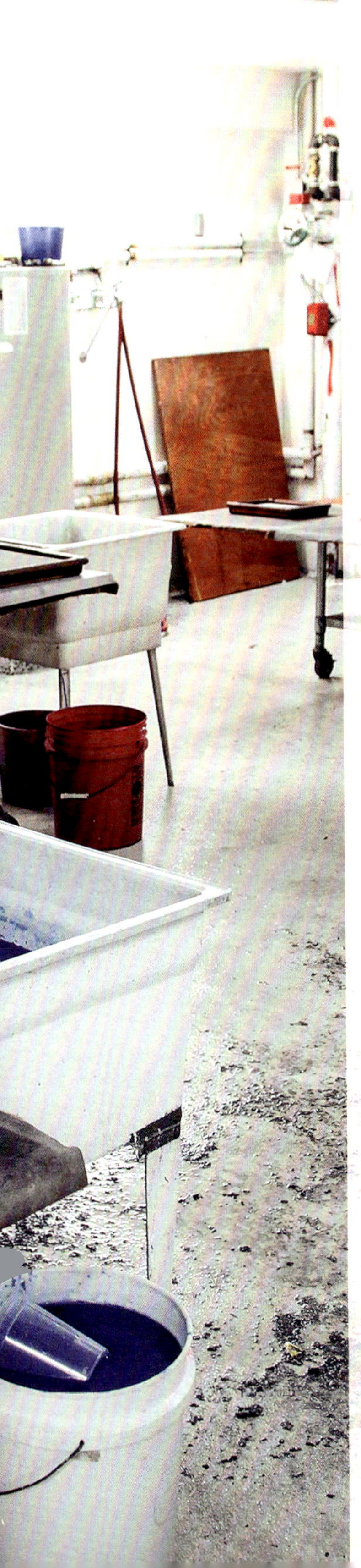

Director's Foreword

TRACY L. ADLER, DIRECTOR, RUTH AND ELMER WELLIN MUSEUM OF ART

Upon stepping into the Dieu Donné workshop, one immediately senses that this is a rarified place. Vats of soupy paper pulp made from cotton, abaca, and linen fibers; squeeze bottles of pigment in every color imaginable; screens for creating sheets of paper small and large; hand-crafted molds; and an array of collage materials framed by dozens of rain boots and full-length aprons that line the studio wall—all attest to the wet and highly immersive process of making artwork in the medium of paper. In the words of artist Jim Hodges, the papermill's workshop is a "perfect laboratory where ideas and materials mix in a sloshy slippery world of possibilities." Indeed, no experiment in paper is off limits at Dieu Donné.

For more than four decades, Dieu Donné has worked behind the scenes to guide emerging and established artists in the creation of remarkable works of art through its studio residency programs. As such, this current exhibition, aptly titled *Pure Pulp*, focuses on the past fifteen years of these programs, highlighting not only the striking range of output that can be achieved through working in, on, through, and with the medium of paper, but also underscoring Dieu Donné's reputation as one of the most valuable artistic resources in the New York City art world, and beyond.

The Wellin Museum of Art and Dieu Donné share similar ideals: we both are committed to collaborating with artists, promoting the exploration of new territory, and helping realize opportunities for experimentation. At the Wellin, we work closely with artists for years leading up to exhibitions, supporting original projects that push each artist's practice in new directions. In this spirit, the Wellin has initiated a residency at Dieu Donné for artist Yun-Fei Ji, whose exhibition *The Intimate Universe*—the largest survey of the artist's work in the U.S. to date—is on view concurrently with *Pure Pulp* at the museum.

First and foremost, we would like to thank the team at Dieu Donné: Bridget Donlon, former Program Manager at Dieu Donné and the curator of this exhibition; Kathleen Flynn, Executive Director; Paul Wong, Artistic Director; Amy Jacobs, Studio Collaborator and Education Manager; and Lisa Switalski, Studio Collaborator and Production Manager. Their passion for creating paper-based works of art is infectious and we are honored to have been able to work with them on *Pure Pulp.*

At Hamilton College, I am very grateful for the support of the administration: President Joan Hinde Stewart, Dean Patrick D. Reynolds, and the Offices of the President and Dean of Faculty. Many thanks to our colleagues in the Art Department, Art History Department, and Office of Communications and Development for their ongoing engagement with the museum. I am also grateful to our benefactors for their generosity, including: The John B. Root '44 Exhibition Fund; The Dietrich Foundation; The Edward W. and Grace C. Root Endowment Fund; The William G. Roehrick '34 Lecture Fund; as well as private contributors. In particular, I would like to extend a special thanks to Wendy and the late Keith S. Wellin '50, whose visionary patronage continues to inspire us. Much appreciation is also due to the Trustees of Hamilton College for their commitment to and continued support of the museum's programming.

This exhibition could not have been possible without the tireless dedication of my staff at the Wellin Museum of Art: Megan Austin, Manager of Educational Programming and Outreach; Katherine D. Alcauskas, Collections and Exhibitions Specialist; Christopher Harrison, Building Manager and Preparator; Amber Spadea, the Andrew W. Mellon Educator for School and Community Programs; Amy Sylvester, Office Assistant; Matt Makuch, Museum Security Administrator; and Alexander D'Acunto, Lead Security Officer. I wish to also extend my appreciation to our graphic designers Tim Laun and Natalie Wedeking; to the editorial team at SNAP Editions, led by Sarah S. King; to John Bentham, Andrew Kist, and Jason Mandella for their photography; to Sarah Windham for coordinating the loans and the shipment of artwork; to Jennifer Scanlan for assisting in coordinating the exhibition; and to Fred Hoxie and his team at GHP Media for the printing of this book. I would also like to thank Mary DelMonico at DelMonico Books • Prestel for working with us to distribute this publication.

We are grateful to the artists in this exhibition for sharing both the results of their experiences at Dieu Donné and their insights, which are chronicled in this publication. Their work stands as a testament to what can happen when age-old materials and artistic innovation are brought together in a place that embraces risk and the pursuit of new possibilities.

Introduction

KATHLEEN FLYNN, EXECUTIVE DIRECTOR, DIEU DONNÉ

Dieu Donné is a place where artists are encouraged to take risks. Our role is to provide a supportive environment to spur creative breakthroughs through skilled artistic collaboration and experimentation. One of the comments that I hear most frequently from our residency artists when they are reflecting on their initial exposure to our paper studio is: "I thought I'd be the first to fail." Taking a chance and exposing oneself to a situation that would allow for that possibility can encourage unforeseen opportunities as well as unexpected and often wholly rewarding results. Nonetheless, the confidence required to cede control to an unpredictable medium, and place oneself in a position of uncertainty is admirable.

The artists who engage at Dieu Donné inspire and challenge us daily in the studio, where they arrive with varied ideas about paper. For many artists, paper is an artistic medium utilized as a substrate for drawing or painting; or a place to sketch, or plan. But when one looks deeper—at fibers and pulp, at pigments and surface treatments—a process that is full of potential and free of seemingly endless boundaries is exposed.

In the studio, our artistic collaborators are required to continuously reinvent, develop, and adapt papermaking techniques to suit the goals of each new artist while also bringing their own working methods to the process. The initial phase of a residency or project is very experimental and replete with questions: "Can we? Will it? How would we...?" The common answer is: "Let's try!" No one has ever "failed" at Dieu Donné. As many of us at Dieu Donné have witnessed firsthand, the moment this world opens up to an artist you can sense a change in their creative thought process.

The Wellin Museum of Art takes a similar experimental attitude and approach to fostering learning and growth. Through partnering with artists to produce commissions and engaging with students in that process; sharing artworks in a less traditional "open storage" setting; as well as introducing the Hamilton College community and beyond to new contemporary artists and innovative art forms. We are extremely grateful for the opportunity the Wellin Museum has provided us to present an exhibition of works created at Dieu Donné's studio over the past fifteen years. Furthermore, it has been a distinct privilege to work with artist Yun-Fei Ji to create new work for his exhibition at the Wellin through a residency originated by the museum.

As *Pure Pulp's* exhibition curator, our former colleague Bridget Donlon has keenly selected works that upend the viewer's notion of works "in paper" and illustrate the wide array of approaches that artists have taken at Dieu Donné. In choosing works for this show, as well as for past exhibitions in the Dieu Donné gallery, she has shown clarity in her vision, dedication, and enthusiastic support for artistic discovery.

We are extraordinarily grateful to Director Tracy L. Adler, and her team at the Ruth and Elmer Wellin Museum of Art—Megan Austin, Katherine Alcauskas, Christopher Harrison, and Amber Spadea. We would like to thank them for their commitment and adventurous exploration of our work. We have enjoyed many visits with members of the Wellin's staff and community as they donned rubber boots and aprons, and reveled in the experience of papermaking firsthand. I would also like to extend our gratitude to *Pure Pulp*'s additional venues, the Dedalus Foundation—especially President and CEO Jack Flam and Programs Director Katy Rogers; and the Robert C. Williams Museum of Papermaking at Georgia Tech, Atlanta, in particular Director Teri Williams and Education Curator Virginia Howell.

In addition, I am privileged to lead a wonderful team at Dieu Donné and wish to first thank Bridget Donlon, who initiated and shaped this project from its inception. In selecting just thirty works from the last fifteen years of residency and studio projects Donlon's job was not an easy one. The making of these pieces would not have been possible without the inspiring, creative work of our studio collaborators led by our Artistic Director, Paul Wong, along with Amy Jacobs, Studio Collaborator and Education Manager; and Lisa Switalski, Studio Collaborator and Production Manager. I am also grateful to Desiree Adams, Registrarial Assistant, for her diligent documentation and care of the works of art on display in the exhibition.

At Dieu Donné, we are greatly indebted to our founder Susan Gosin who had the foresight and pioneering spirit to introduce handmade paper to artists when she established Dieu Donné in the SoHo district of New York City in 1976. In keeping, our Board of Directors is comprised of an extremely dedicated team, and we are fortunate that they have chosen to give their time, support, and passion to our organization. I am also thankful to our generous circle of funders and individual supporters who have played a vital role in supporting our ability to provide artists with this unique opportunity.

Finally, it is an honor to be able to share a vibrant and lyrical essay Richard Tuttle wrote about his journey in pulp and in our studio for this book. We are also grateful to Rachel Wolff for her thoughtful and provoking interview with our studio collaborators, which provides the reader with a dynamic picture of the unique role our staff ensures by working together with artists in the "wet studio" as the creative process unfolds. The artists represented in this exhibition have also each generously shared their thoughts about the residency and process, enabling us to bring this experience to you in their words. In addition, we would like to acknowledge Tim Laun and Natalie Wedeking for the striking design and the entire team at SNAP Editions, led by Sarah S. King, for its editorial work toward the realization of this exhibition catalogue; and DelMonico Books • Prestel whose distribution has made it possible for us to to share this book widely.

In both print and practice, this book has been a true collaboration and we are thrilled to share the incredible work of artists who have found the reward of working in a new visual language at Dieu Donné. With this exhibition, we hope to inspire creative thought and to indulge your eyes and mind in the outcomes of that transformative experience.

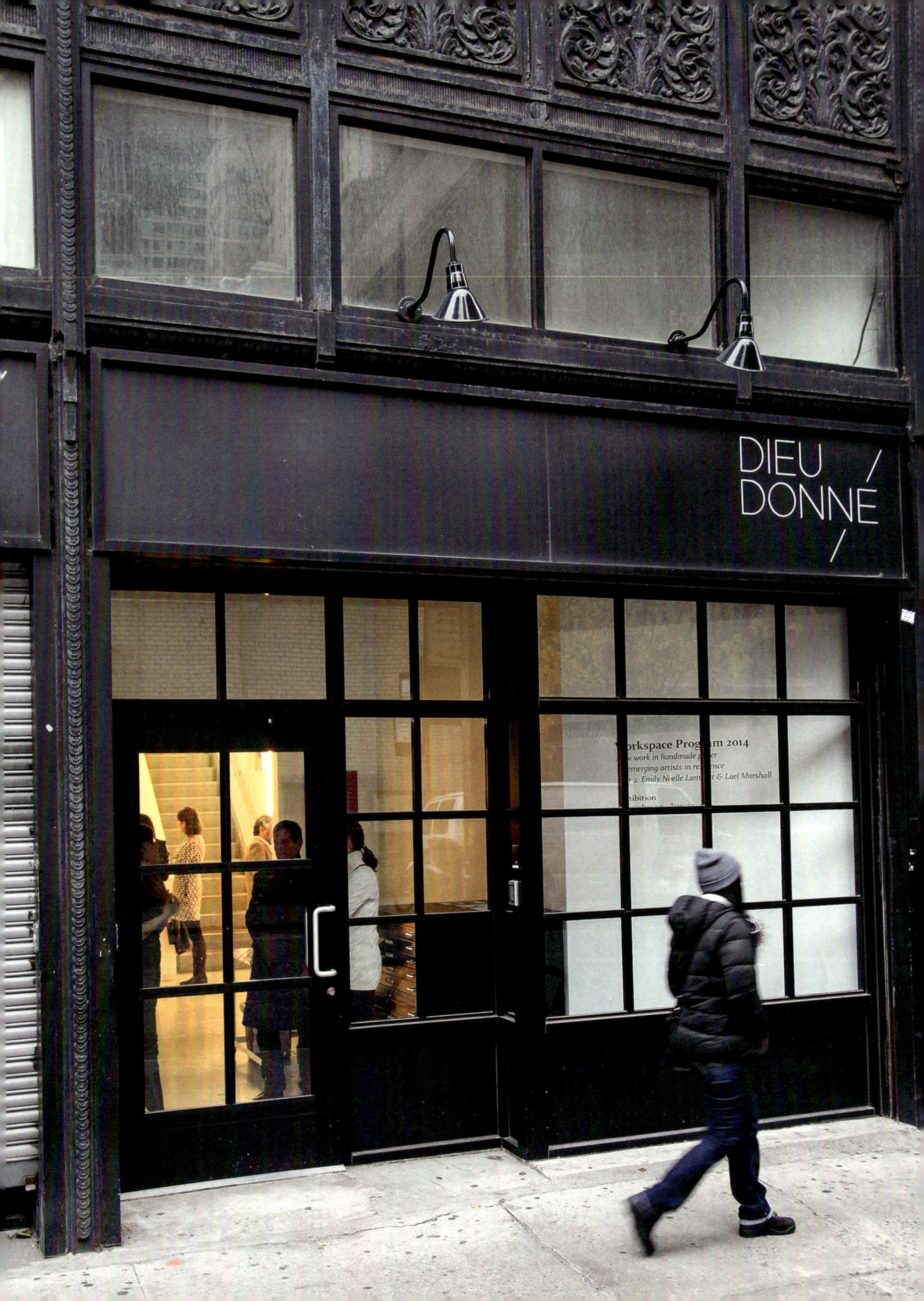
DIEU
DONNÉ

Material Synergy: Paper, Process, and Potential

BRIDGET DONLON

From the beginning, we were motivated to be a part of this hand-papermaking movement because we believed, and still believe, that papermaking offers an almost endless potential for creative expression. —SUSAN GOSIN, FOUNDER OF DIEU DONNÉ[1]

Pure Pulp: Contemporary Artists Working in Paper at Dieu Donné presents a diverse range of sculpture, books, and two-dimensional works created over the last fifteen years at Dieu Donné, the iconic New York City papermaking studio. The exhibition features works by twenty artists who have participated in the organization's Workspace and Lab Grant residency programs. These works represent a wide range of achievements in this practice that defy the expectations of paper's capacity as an artistic medium. At a time when new media technology such as 3-D printing, high-performance cameras, and digital equipment are increasingly pervasive and affordable, Dieu Donné offers a unique return to traditional materials through innovative methods that make handmade paper particularly relevant to contemporary artists working today.

This exhibition highlights the aesthetic experience at the Dieu Donné studio—an unparalleled site of creative exploration and experimentation. Collaborative residencies at Dieu Donné provide established and emerging artists alike with a unique opportunity to create new bodies of work through the medium of handmade paper pulp. Artists who are primarily known for working in sculpture, painting, and mixed media, as well as for their performative and conceptual practices, are paired with expert papermakers to provide technical guidance as they explore the seemingly infinite possibilities of paper. This supportive environment results in surprising and dynamic works of art that push the potential of paper and open new avenues for each artist-in-residence.

Dieu Donné was founded in 1976 by Susan Gosin and Bruce Wineberg in order to create a new form of fine art derived from an ancient craft. It was conceived when the two discovered papermaking while working collaboratively on an illustrated book of poems during their time as printmaking students.[2] Together, Gosin and Wineberg established the studio in an industrial loft in SoHo that operated as a workspace, research lab, and central point of community for a group of artists—roles that remain at the core of the organization. As the only working papermill in New York City specializing in handmade paper as an artistic medium, Dieu Donné has maintained that spirit of the times in which it was created. Founded at the same time and geographic location as many other alternative art spaces in downtown New York, these young organizations, spurred by their mutual unbridled creative ambition, also benefited from abundant and

Opposite: Entrance to Dieu Donné at 315 West 36th Street, New York City.

inexpensive real estate.[3] Within this fertile setting, the New York papermaking community was small but passionate about resuscitating a craft that had all but disappeared, and eager to forge new paths of creative production and dissemination. The achievements of Dieu Donné are as impressive as they are varied—yet, none are so important as the development of handmade paper as a vital artistic medium in its own right.

A work *on* paper is a known category—materials like charcoal, pastels, and watercolor are used on paper as a substrate. A work *in* paper is something entirely different. Creative papermaking shares common ground with printmaking, painting, and sculpture. It permeates these three forms, yet is its own entity, and this undefined position poses a challenge for the artists who work at Dieu Donné. The art begins with paper pulp, a slurry that resembles mushy oatmeal and can be used in a wide variety of artistic applications. It is also a material that can go awry if not properly controlled, which is why each artist is paired with an expert papermaker as a studio collaborator who provides a technical framework and creative sounding board. The artists are then let loose to experiment and fail, to make new work, and to push their own respective practices in new directions. Chuck Close (p. 30), the first artist brought into the Dieu Donné studio expressly to be introduced to the medium in the early 1980s, summed it up as a place where, "with team effort the finished art is greater than the sum of its parts—a product of the distinct mix of people, process, and creative interaction. In a sense, collaboration is chemistry."[4]

The chemistry of collaboration at Dieu Donné provides each artist with a unique experience, with some common threads throughout. There is the initial impulse to re-create an existing working practice in a new material, yet through diverse approaches artists come to embrace the unpredictable nature of pulp. During their time at Dieu Donné, they explore games of chance in creating their work; take on the one-of-a-kind ability of paper to create an image within the structure of itself (rather than on top of it); and are struck by its malleability and employ it to simulate other media and textural appearances, never before seen or achieved in paper.

INITIAL IMPULSES

Re-creating an existing artwork is a common starting point for many artists while they become accustomed to the peculiarities of paper pulp. In a medium with as many technical challenges as this one, an initial impulse is to use the material to make an image or to follow a familiar process. For example, Melvin Edwards originally planned to use objects from his sculptures of welded metal tools to create two-dimensional pieces as he had previously experimented in spray-paint on newsprint. Chains, work gloves, and other tools were used as stencils for three unique works—*Dakar Days*, *Sud foire*, and *in Gorée* (all 2006, pp. 50–53)—but rather than use paint to fill in negative space around them on top of dry paper, water was sprayed to wash away wet pulp exposed on the surface of a screen not covered by the objects. The remaining pulp was pressed onto a base sheet, still retaining a shadow of the image created through a reductive process where positive and negative spaces are reversed. Edwards's venture into the studio allowed both artist and papermaker to explore the technique, developing the use of an image-making process known as a "blowout," a trademark of artistic papermaking at Dieu Donné.

This same technique was used by Mary Temple, who works in many different mediums to explore perceptions of natural light and shadow. At Dieu Donné, her subtle installations of white paint on similarly toned walls were translated into unpigmented cotton pulp on natural abaca in the work *Spring Light* (2007, pp. 96–99).[5] Shadows of windowpanes and houseplants, together with a beam of light passing through a window, are suggested by forms in white cotton paper on top of exposed abaca. The two types of papers, although each neutral in color, become distinct in contrast to one another as they combine to form the image. The large paper pieces maintain the representative scale of the artist's wall paintings, but here, paper lends a new sense of translucency and fragility to Temple's work.

In a similar vein, Kate Shepherd, who has also translated an existing process into a new medium, first wanted to re-create the thin, tight lines she typically paints in acrylic on panel. The slippage of pulp under Mylar stencils coupled with the bleeding of wet pigment prevented the intended effect, and this occurrence prompted the artist to turn her focus to color and form instead of the drawn line. Adapting her practice to these constraints led to a physical, tactile effect not characteristic of her paintings. In her works *Great Cousin Mary* and *Dark Orange White Stacks, Notched (4, 5),* both 2011 (pp. 86–87), each square is made of pulp and then placed on the base sheet in individual physical layers, like the stacks of boxes the forms represent. Instead of reaching a dead end, the challenges of pulp led Shepherd to a fresh artistic approach.

In other cases, pulp naturally dovetails with an artist's existing practice. Arlene Shechet is known primarily as a sculptor, but has incorporated paper into her methodology. She uses sheets of paper and pulp paints, in a similar way to her application of glazes on ceramic sculpture, with unexpected color combinations and improvisational marks.[6] Rubber molds from her ceramics studio, for instance, are used in the artist's series "Parallel Play" (2012, pp. 82–85). Integrating the processes of paper and ceramics, and creating depth for what could otherwise be perceived as a two-dimensional work, Shechet captures the qualities of the wet states of glaze and clay or pigment and pulp in the finished work.

Painter Natalie Frank uses pulp as deftly as oil paint and pastel, translating her palette and compositional style seamlessly into paper. Her psychologically loaded imagery is present in *Portrait (Woman I)* and *Portrait (Woman II)*, both from 2015 (pp. 54–57)—each a baroque work exuding vitality. Her applications of pulp through layers and washes look convincingly like paint, though are in fact little more than pigmented linen and cotton paper. The tactile nature of the material allowed Frank to experiment with marbling colors, embedding, abstracting, and moving the image beyond the paper's natural edges.

GAMES OF CHANCE

Paper pulp is a fickle medium, and its control is elusive to even the most technically skilled papermaker. Some artists are apprehensive about this inherent quality of paper, while others are delighted by its unpredictability. At Dieu Donné, a hydraulic press, originally intended for industrial use, aids in the process of removing water from pulp fibers. Its effects can be controlled to an extent with speed and padding, but it can also create "happy accidents" that could never have been intentionally produced, and that enthrall some artists. Molly Smith, for instance, used conventional papermaking techniques, but ultimately let nature take its course during the drying processes. *Swamp* (2012, p. 88) was created by layering sheets of green and brown paper culled from leftover pulps found by Smith in the studio refrigerator. The press caused rivulets and breakages in the layers that suggest the topographical map of an imaginary landscape. *Dust* (2012, p. 89–91) was made by layering unregistered sheets and pushing them together while wet, leaving the paper ripples to dry. The work hangs from brackets, and the gradation of grey tones implies gravity and weight that belie the weightlessness of paper. Both works were accomplished by a simultaneous understanding of material and an openness to the unexpected.

For Ursula von Rydingsvard, renowned for her massive cedar wood sculptures, the hydraulic press also became an essential tool in the creative process of her intimate two-dimensional works from the Dieu Donné studio. She embedded textiles into thin sheets of linen paper using white pulp, and extended the bottom edges of the paper with delicate looking tendrils of paper and thread. The artist added dry pigment onto the surface of wet paper pulp, in parallel to the way she works graphite into the surface of cedar. Both of her untitled sculptures from 2010 (pp. 104–107) were made following the same processes, but each work is ultimately subject to the effects of the hydraulic press, resulting in atmospheric diffusions that would not, nor could, be achieved intentionally.

Since the 1960s, conceptual artist Richard Tuttle has iconoclastically used a diversity of materials such as cut canvas pinned directly to the wall, segments of sailing rope, and soldered metal. Furthermore, he was a champion and innovative adapter of printmaking and textiles at a time when industrial materials were de rigueur for many of his colleagues. Through several decades of experience working at Dieu Donné, Tuttle has become familiar with pulp in its many forms and possibilities. For his earlier projects, he made traditional use of paper such as artist books and editions; more recently he has become engaged with the sculptural qualities of pulp itself, especially when flung or otherwise left to entropy. Each of the four individual components of *The Triumph of Night* (2009, pp. 101–103)—an homage to the fourteenth-century poet Petrarch—was created following a series of instructions devised by the artists. Steps listed include layering colors, poking them with tools, tossing pulp, and smashing piles of pulp by hand. The choreography in creating each piece of the suite allowed the work to be published as an edition of ten, humorously reproducing something that seems spontaneous.

Pulp lends itself equally well to abstract painter Suzanne McClelland's style of working quickly and gesturally. The work the artist made during her residency at Dieu Donné grew out of personal research about domestic terrorists on the FBI's "Most Wanted" list. One series, "Internal Affairs," culminates with *Seven* (2015, pp. 79–81), depicting seven individuals along with collaged text. McClelland worked on the surface of a fresh sheet of paper with pigmented pulp in the same fashion as oil or acrylic paint. She dropped clippings of xeroxed images and text directly into the pulp, allowing gravity to dictate the placement. The drying process binds all of the elements together as a hybrid of painting and collage.

Sculptor Jon Kessler also approached pulp as a catalyst, allowing the process to unfold in the studio. He describes the beater (the machine where pulp is made) as an instrument of torture, one that he used to manipulate large-format inkjet printouts of faces—his own, and those of well known figures including Angelina Jolie and Barack Obama. Fibers from money and hair were mixed in with any pulp available (rather than pulp custom-produced for his time in the studio), along with other elements, like plastic bags, and then everything was collaged into the surface, and the resulting pieces were put through the press. A few working methods provided the framework that led to Kessler's surreal, cartoonish, and disturbing abstract portraits *Me Hate* (2008, p. 70) and *Suicide Bomber #1* (2008, p. 71), but the driving force unequivocally behind them is Kessler's embrace of chaos.

Firelei Báez was similarly open to allowing her work to unfold through the artistic papermaking process, albeit with a less anarchic mentality than Kessler. A technical as well as aesthetic achievement, her piece *Amidst the future and present there is a memory table* (2013, pp. 40–43) combines techniques traditionally used with dry papers, such as collage and marbling, that she translated into wet pulp. The ingredients used were adjusted to slow down the drainage process, allowing the artist to draw freehand and to marble with wet pulp. Báez and her Dieu Donné studio collaborator improvised with techniques and materials to create a mural-sized work that features silhouettes and figures related to female and racial identities in a dreamlike setting of fantastical color and pattern. The artist arrived at Dieu Donné with a plan to use her residency to work with entirely different techniques, but ended up creating her own unique methodology through experimentation.

IMAGE WITHIN

Paper is a vessel on which to convey a narrative or image. Working with paper in its wet, pulpy stages allows artists to contain the subject of the work within, rather than on, its surface. South African artist William Kentridge, for example, explored watermarks to create imagery within the structure of paper. His artist book, *Sheets of Evidence* (2009, pp. 66–69), appears at first to be a sheath of blank pages. When held up to light, however, intimate portraits and still-life subject matter such as bowls of fruit and memento mori skulls are revealed, along with the text of his own poetry. At first look, the work celebrates the seductive qualities of paper, and then its intricate possibilities when the watermark is discovered.

The watermark is best known for its use as an anti-counterfeit measure in currency, created by raising the surface of a paper mold so that the pulp will be thinner in certain areas and revealed when held up to the light as with the sheets from Kentridge's book. To use this technique in a more graphic, painterly way, B. Wurtz created a watermark using laser-cut, adhesive-backed rubber applied to the top of a papermaking mold. The watermark is of an emblematic logo that has appeared throughout his practice exploring themes of basic human need, comprising the letters of the word "life" arranged in the form of a face. Using this watermark, Wurtz pulled a sheet of pigmented abaca paper, which he then pressed onto a white cotton base sheet. The opaque backing paper allows for the watermark image to be visible. The paper contains the image both within its integral form and on the surface, as well as Wurtz's hand-drawn, pulp-painted logos in the bottom third of the work.

Wurtz's *Untitled (7864)* from 2013 (pp. 108–109) juxtaposes an image that is hand drawn with one that is mechanically reproduced, a relationship likewise evident in the series of "thread drawings" by Korean-born artist Do Ho Suh (pp. 92–95). Imagery familiar in his interdisciplinary work, such as bodies (self-portraits, in particular) and architectural structures (large-scale textile installations based on the homes he has lived in throughout his life) were replicated in vibrant embroidery thread and backed with gelatin. Sheets of white cotton paper were formed with wet pulp, and the thread drawing was laid on top. As the gelatin dissolved in water, the threads bonded with the fibers of the paper, indelibly fixing image and surface. Unlike a collage, where glue holds two different entities together, the thread imagery and supporting paper are interconnected.

Taking a different approach, E.V. Day embossed textile onto paper, leaving traces of the fabric's texture rather than fusing the two elements together. She stretched cheap fishnet body stockings—the kind that are sold wholesale in the Garment District of Manhattan—over wooden frames, creating forms that resemble spiderwebs, bodily orifices, and landscapes. Painted with pigment, the manipulated fishnet stockings were pressed into wet sheets of paper, leaving behind bleeding colors and intricate patterns. The large-scale abstract works such as *Shazam (Black and Phosphorescence)*, from 2009, were achieved through testing many types of pigment to achieve a definition of line as well as flowing color (pp. 48–49). The low relief produced by the textile's impression on the paper surface is described by the artist as "compressed sculpture." Day's terminology describes the capacity of Dieu Donné paper artwork to exist between two and three dimensions, where dimensional form is present in artwork that could also be interpreted as a painting, print, or drawing.

The multifaceted nature of paper is also evident in the form of an artist book, which can be a container of artwork but also an art object in and of itself. *Be Zany, Poised Harpists/Be Blue, Little Sparrows* (2002, pp. 58–61) by Jane Hammond is an artist book published by Dieu Donné that unites form and process. Comprised of four distinct sections, each based on poetry by Raphael Rubinstein, it is a work of art from cover to cover, each book hand-bound with an individually illustrated binding, handmade paper pages and letterpress printing. The third section, which illustrates a poem called "Day's Path," collages silhouettes of animals, insects, and humans between translucent paper. A string is also embedded between the folded pages to reveal the image when pulled, thereby allowing the viewer to unfurl the narrative.

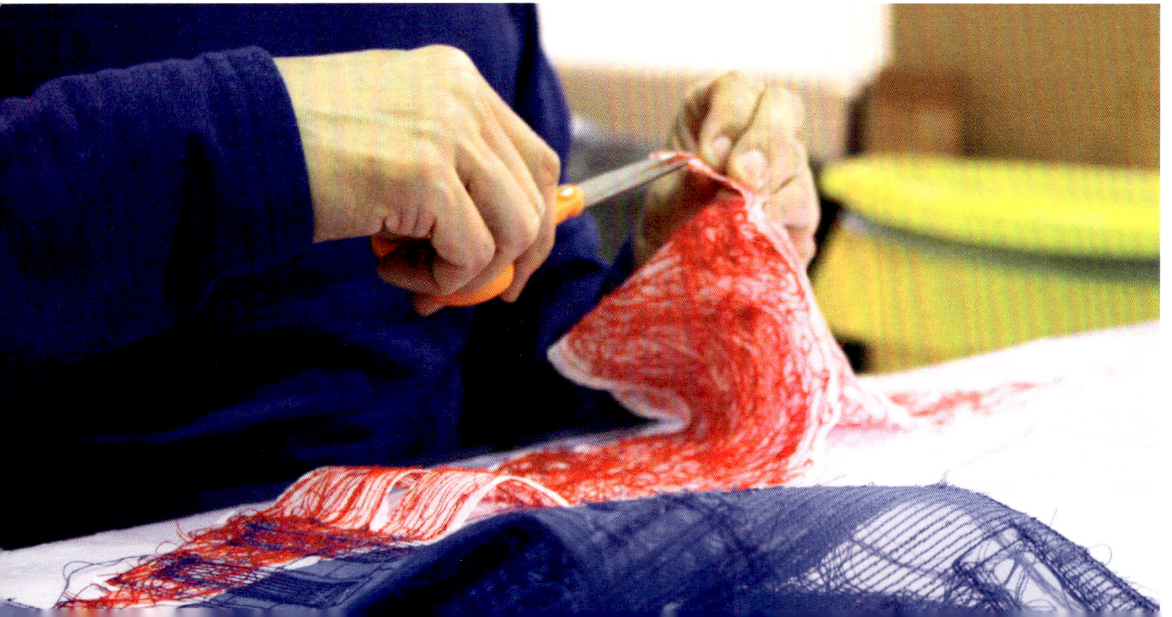

CHAMELEON MATERIAL

The studio is also a place of learning, not only for the artists-in-residence, but also for the papermakers who staff the organization. The collaborative relationship is truly symbiotic, as the papermakers' skills continue to be built upon by working with each artist. A typical response from a studio papermaker to an artist's question of whether or not an idea will work is: "Let's try it and see what happens," and the result is usually a mutual artistic breakthrough. Through collaboration, Dieu Donné's papermakers have built up an arsenal of techniques to meet an artist's vision.

Paper can be pigmented to any custom color, and it takes on the texture of whatever surface it is dried on, so these qualities mean it can also be used like paint or as a sculptural material. All of these possible variations make paper a chameleon-like medium that can simulate metal, wood, and plastic, or mimic industrially produced items. For example, consider two pieces by Glenn Ligon—an artist who makes complex work that deals with issues of identity, history, race, and sexuality—whose investigations in pulp were a natural extension of his practice that includes many different media. *End of Year Reports* (2003, pp. 76–77) is a portfolio edition of handmade paper screen-printed with grade school report cards from Ligon's own childhood. The mass-produced carbon-copy typewriter paper and cardboard folio were painstakingly simulated by hand. Based on the cover art for the Stevie Wonder compilation album *Looking Back*, *Self-Portrait at Eleven Years Old* (2004, pp. 73–75) was created with several registrations of stencils and a blowout technique. The image has the look of the Ben-Day dots used in the commercial printing of newspapers, but with pigmented pulp instead of printer's ink.

Similarly, Ian Cooper's *Chalice* (2010, pp. 44–45) also takes advantage of paper's ability to mimic a range of materials, but in this instance the handmade version of mass-produced objects adds a level of uncanny representation that is unsettling. *Chalice* is a three-dimensional piece based on a tabloid image of a bizarre disguise worn in public by Michael Jackson's youngest son Blanket. It consists of fake hair attached to a baseball cap and is positioned upside down on a pedestal, appearing as a vessel spilling over. The entire piece—down to the Puffy Paint-like rainbow spelling "love" on the brim of the hat—is entirely made of paper pulp mixed with denim for the hat, and plastic trash bags for the fake dreadlocks. This work is disorienting—not only in its larger-than-life-size scale, but also in its highly specific imagery and mysterious construction, solely from paper.

Likewise, Jim Hodges's series "In Wet" employs the duplicitous ability of paper to represent flesh. He embraces the skin-like quality of paper, especially in its still-wet stages when it still has a vibrant sheen, in his seamless moves between media to make work about the delicate balance of life and nature. The pulp used by Hodges was pigmented with cosmetic foundation to give it a color approximating the artist's own flesh tone. In its initial display at the Dieu Donné gallery, fresh sheets of this paper were laid over chain links crafted from black paper every day. The pulp forms were covered up each evening to remain moist, giving visitors a glimpse of what the artist works with, before the alchemy that occurs when paper dries. *In Wet III* (2010, pp. 62–65) is a document of the original piece, finally dry and laid to rest.

Artists have equal wonderment at the strange ability of pulp to metamorphose, becoming a completely unidentifiable medium. At Dieu Donné, David Kennedy Cutler combined materials

Opposite: Do Ho Suh working in the Dieu Donné studio, 2013.

and techniques not conventionally used in papermaking, such as scratching the metal-embedded data from the bottom of compact discs into cotton pulp. He applied the mixture to a wire armature, creating a six-foot-tall paper sculpture titled *Mount* (2011, pp. 46–47) that evokes something organic, like a gigantic geode, made of an unrecognizable material. It could be perceived as a textile, like felt, or a form welded from metal or carved from rock, something that is heavy and dense. Eschewing the typical appearance of its material composition, the sculpture is suggestive of anything but paper.

PURE PULP

Recent years have seen a resurgence in the popularity of experiencing materials—things made with craftsmanship that take time, and have a soul. A possible explanation is the desire for an authentic connection with tangible entities in a world inundated with visible but superficial digital media. Handmade paper connects the maker to the physical, a millennia-old lineage that is still adaptable to unfamiliar ways of working. Paper remains relevant as Dieu Donné inspires new sets of eyes and new perspectives to reinterpret and reimagine the medium, continuously adding to its unique legacy.

Bridget Donlon is the exhibition curator of Pure Pulp: Contemporary Artists Working in Paper at Dieu Donné *and former Program Manager at Dieu Donné.*

NOTES

1 Susan Gosin, "Dieu Donné Papermill, 25 Years: The Sacred in the Commonplace," *Rags to Riches: 25 Years of Paper Art from Dieu Donné Papermill* (New York: Dieu Donné Papermill, Inc., 2001), p. 23.

2 Dieu Donné's founding and development have been outlined in depth in the 25th anniversary publication, *Rags to Riches: 25 Years of Paper Art from Dieu Donné Papermill* (New York: Dieu Donné Papermill, Inc., 2001), a valuable resource for anyone researching on how to start an artist workspace; to learn about the downtown New York arts culture; or the lineage of handmade paper. Though the name has a poetic French meaning, "God Given," it is not a literal translation, but rather is named for Gosin's father, Dieu Donné François Gosin.

3 As industrial shipping and manufacturing left downtown New York City in the 1970s, former warehouses were taken over by artists and converted into live/work studios, or the founding sites of newly formed organizations like Artists Space, White Columns, ABC No Rio, amongst others.

4 Chuck Close. "Foreword," in *Rags to Riches*, p. 8.

5 Abaca is a fiber derived from the bast of a banana plant found in the Philippines. Along with cotton and linen, it is one of the commonly used fibers in papermaking at Dieu Donné. It is strong—the same fiber used in tea bags, which can be soaked in water without tearing. It can also be wrapped around an object and take its form as a sculptural material; and if left to dry naturally will cockle in unpredictable wrinkles.

6 "Pulp paint" is paper pulp mixed with pigment and used like acrylic paint or ink. It can be thinned to create washes or built up in layers. When the work is pressed and dried, it creates a single sheet of paper with the image created within the structure of the artwork.

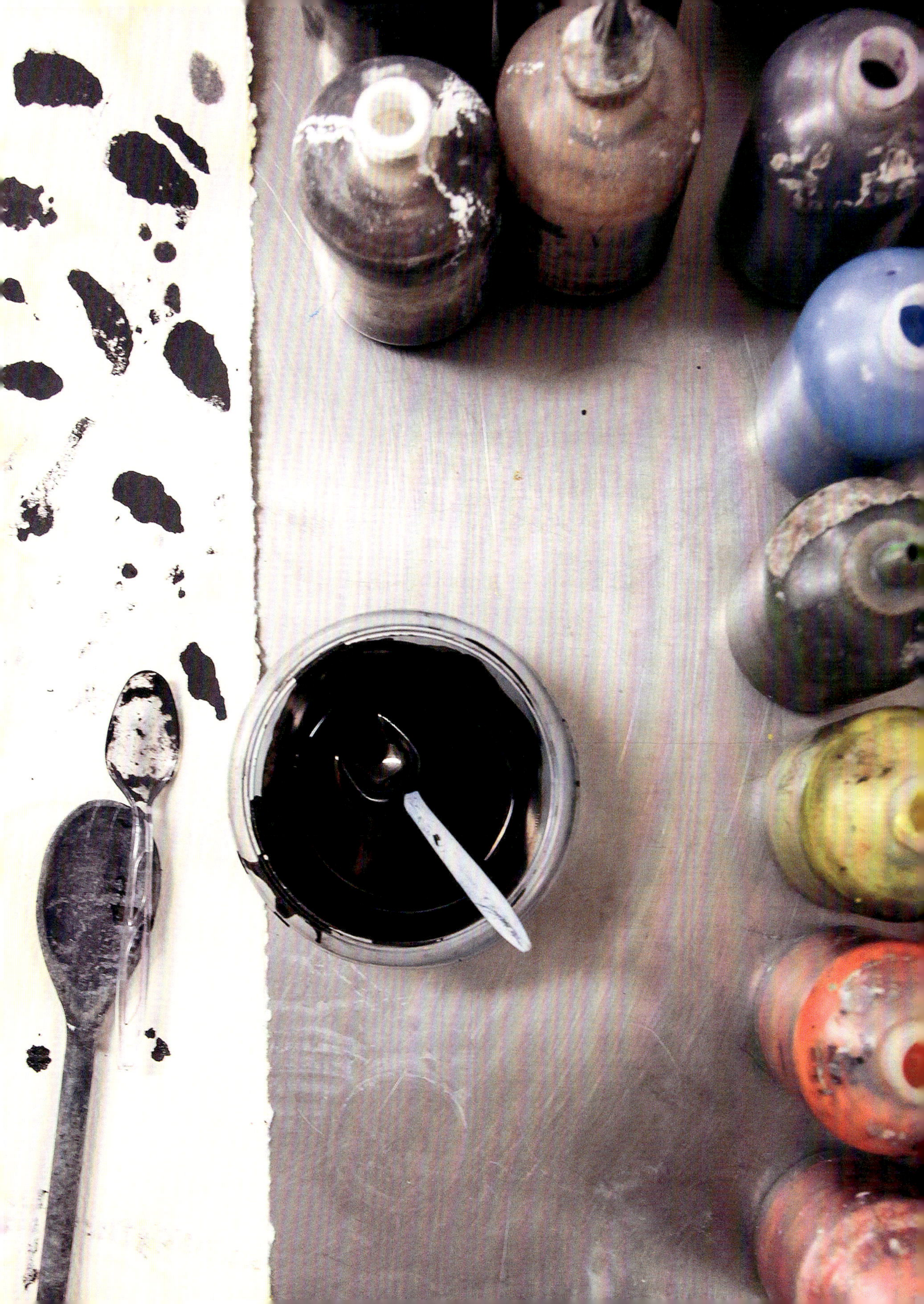

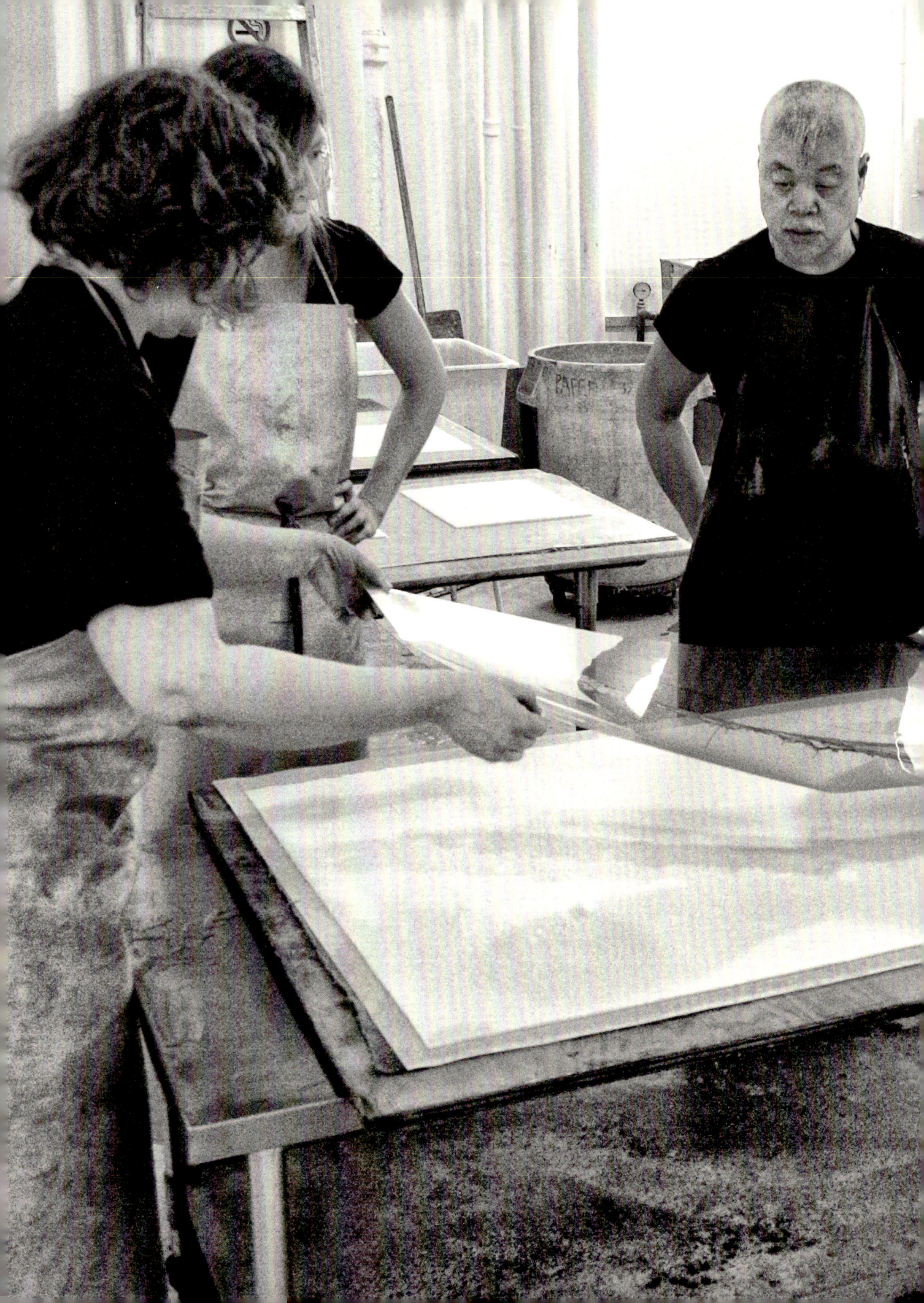

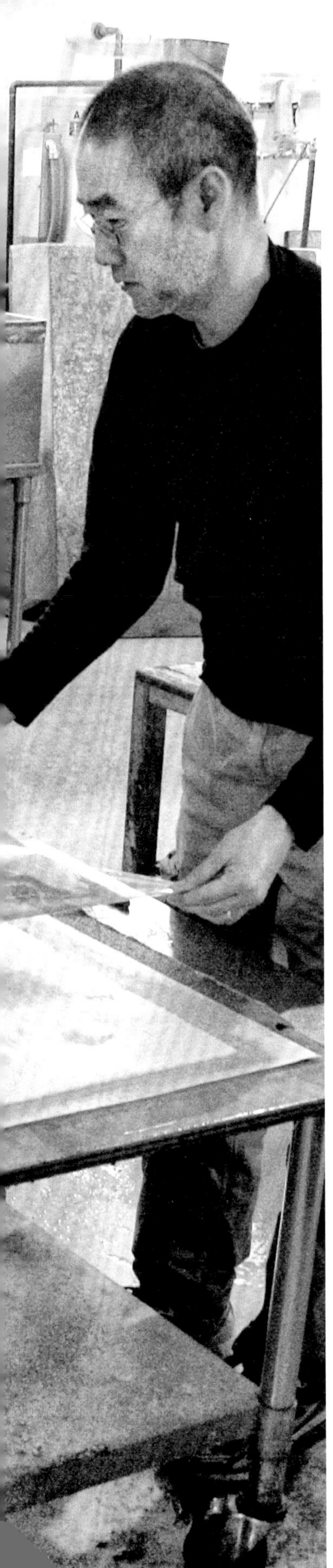

In the Studio

A Conversation with Dieu Donné Studio Collaborators Amy Jacobs and Lisa Switalski and Artistic Director Paul Wong

RACHEL WOLFF

Though they are all artists in their own right, Amy Jacobs, Lisa Switalski, and Paul Wong step into a different role at Dieu Donné: they are partners, educators, and facilitators for artists working in the studio, primarily through several different types of residency programs. All three share a love of the material, a passion for the method, and a talent for helping artists navigate the papermaking process in a way that remains true to the artists' wider interests and oeuvres. As Studio Collaborators, Jacobs, Switalski, and Wong provoke dialogues. They encourage experimentation; troubleshoot; create; advise; reassure; and they learn from these experiences as well. Their collective reflections on their time at Dieu Donné follow.

Studio Collaborators (from left to right) Amy Jacobs, Lisa Switalski, and Paul Wong working with artist Do Ho Suh (far right) in the Dieu Donné studio, April 2013.

THE MEDIUM

What is it about paper and the papermaking process that continues to hold your interest?

LISA SWITALSKI (LS): I'm attracted to tactile mediums and malleable surfaces. After having explored many disciplines, I felt the closest to papermaking—I was seduced by the material. Everything clicked when I learned about embedding things in handmade paper and pulp painting. I started going to the studio and making paper for ten hours daily, coming home, going to sleep, getting up, and doing it all over again.

AMY JACOBS (AJ): I grew up in a family of makers. I love textiles and fibers and weaving. I like working with my hands; I like working wet. There's a lot of process involved in papermaking and I enjoy all of it. There are these happy accidents that naturally occur in the papermaking process, which I really like to embrace.

PAUL WONG (PW): I started out in printmaking. I got interested in papermaking in graduate school at the University of Wisconsin, at Madison, where I met Sue Gosin. I was interested in exploring sculpture but to cast something in bronze seemed too foreign, too outside of my comfort zone. Paper was more of a constant for me. It could be sculptural, but it also had these affinities that had significance for me. My initial attraction to paper was what it meant as an extension of possibilities.

MEL BOCHNER *Language Is Not Transparent*, 1999. Watermarked abaca on cotton, 40 × 30 in. (101.6 × 76.2 cm). Edition of 16. Courtesy of the artist and Dieu Donné, New York.

LS: We describe it to people as being a "chameleon medium," which is why it's possible to work with so many different artists. Nothing has the same look coming out of here. It's not a fixed material, and you can change your approach depending on what you're interested in exploring.

PW: Papermaking is intrinsically chaotic. It's wet and watery. And it's not like printmaking where you can repeat an impression precisely. But that's the beauty of it too. And in a way, that brings something to the work; it gives it a certain kind of character.

LS: Working with pulp, there is this constant awareness of both yourself in space and the material you're working with. People ask, "How do you know exactly how much pulp to add for this? Tell me the measurements and the math..." And you can explain that to a certain extent, but once you get it, once you practice it enough, a lot of that becomes second nature. Recently, I was pulling large cotton sheets with an artist, and with cotton, you can stand it vertically very soon after you've made the sheet. Every time I did that, he would gasp because he would imagine all of the pulp falling down. But after you've made them enough you just have a sense of when you can tilt it and drain it. So I'm listening to music, dancing a little, holding the sheet, and he's standing there with bated breath.

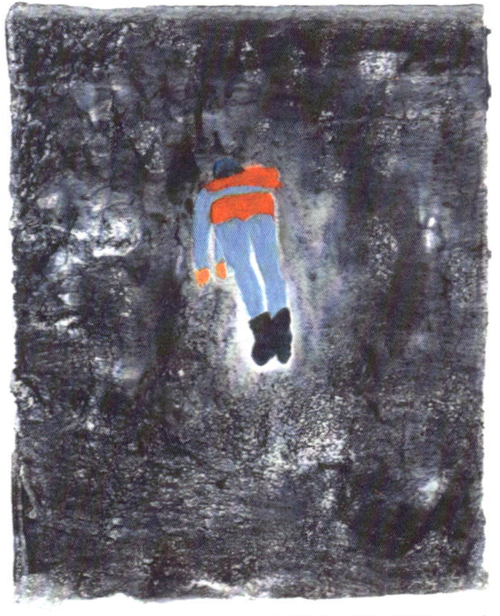

KATHERINE BRADFORD *Superheroes & Divers*, 2014. Pigmented linen on cotton base sheet and colored pencil, 14 × 11 in. (35.6 × 27.9 cm). 25 unique variants; proof 1/2. Courtesy of the artist and Dieu Donné, New York.

THE STUDIO

How did your interest in papermaking lead you to Dieu Donné?

PW: After college, Sue moved to New York and started Dieu Donné as Dieu Donné Press and Paper on Crosby Street, in 1976. When I joined her shortly thereafter, we refocused the business toward trying to bring in artists and working more creatively. This was totally new to us. Each artist who we worked with brought a very particular vision and set of challenges that we had to solve in the papermaking process.

LS: I came to New York and visited the mill when it was still in SoHo. I remember seeing pieces by William Kentridge and Glenn Ligon and being so blown away by the craftsmanship and refinement. I saw Paul working in the back and I thought, "I want to work here and I want to be him."

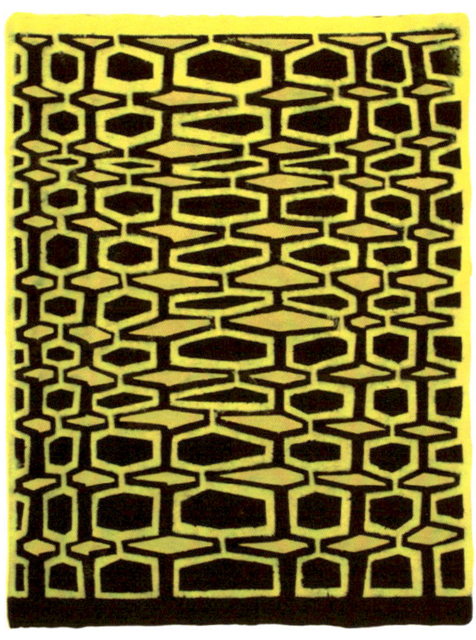

JAMES SIENA *Two Perforated Combs*, 2006. Stenciled pigmented linen on pigmented cotton base, 10 × 8 in. (25.4 × 20.3 cm). Edition of 50. Courtesy of the artist and Dieu Donné, New York.

AJ: Whenever I shut the gate here when I leave, I still go, "Oh my god, I can't believe I work here." I remember visiting Dieu Donné when I was in grad school and asking for a tour. A lot of master printmakers work with other people, but I never really thought about collaborating with artists in paper. It was so unique what Paul did. I thought how interesting it must be to work with all these artists and to make work that was so varied.

LS: One thing that makes Dieu Donné so different is that it's always been dedicated to papermaking and I think that's a really important distinction from other studios. We're constantly asking for more from the material. We're taking it as far as it can go and then sometimes beyond that. We're pushing the parameters all the time, which is important.

PW: Over the years, we developed a lot of the techniques that we use now. We have a repertoire of ways of working that we can apply to whatever artist or imagery comes our way.

THE ROLE

How would you characterize the role of "Studio Collaborator"?

LS: Something that we always communicate to people applying to our residencies, and even to artists who are interested in a studio rental is that this is not a place where you have access to a studio and we're very hands-off. We are engaged with the artist the entire time in the process. We help realize their vision.

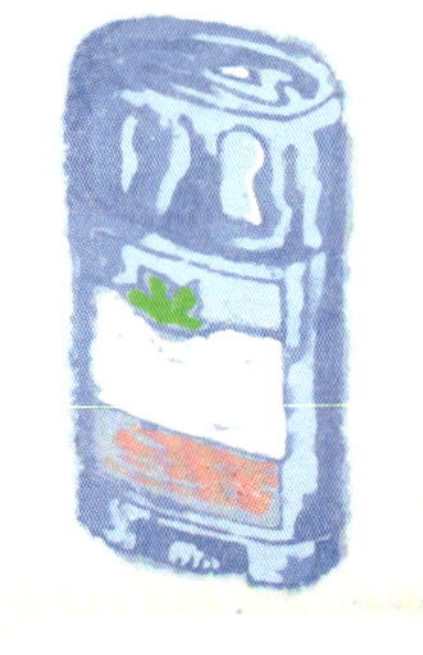

PW: There is give-and-take. We'll suggest things; we figure things out. There is also this sense of both instructing and being a facilitator. Oftentimes in collaboration, it's not only our inherent knowledge of the process and the techniques, but it's also our skill that is involved in producing the work—we'll often pull the sheets of paper ourselves because we can form sheets professionally. And to get the artists up to par, technique-wise, is not necessarily efficient given the brief time that they're here.

AJ: Many of the artists with whom we collaborate have never worked with handmade paper and many know nothing about it. It's our job to help facilitate the making of their work by handling the technicalities of the material; to help them translate all of those things that they work through in their own artwork into papermaking. It's working side-by-side with someone to help guide them in the papermaking process—whether that is physically making the sheets, or working together to come up with the piece, and then taking it from there. I also feel like I'm there to make sure everything's okay because people have a very hard time with failing at something, especially when they're at a certain point in their career. They're embarrassed; they don't want anyone watching them. I always tell them not to worry and I try to create a nice studio environment that people will feel comfortable working in.

BETH CAMPBELL Top: *Untitled (Deodorant)*, 2003. Pulp paint on watermarked translucent abaca, 14 × 11 in. (35.6 × 27.9 cm). Courtesy of the artist and Dieu Donné, New York. Above: *Untitled (One Day)*, 2003. Pulp paint on watermarked translucent abaca, 14 × 11 in. (35.6 × 27.9 cm). Courtesy of the artist and Dieu Donné, New York.

PW: Every artist brings their own personality and their own set of challenges with the imagery that they do. With every artist, you have to strategize and figure out how you're going to relate to them; you have to really understand their work.

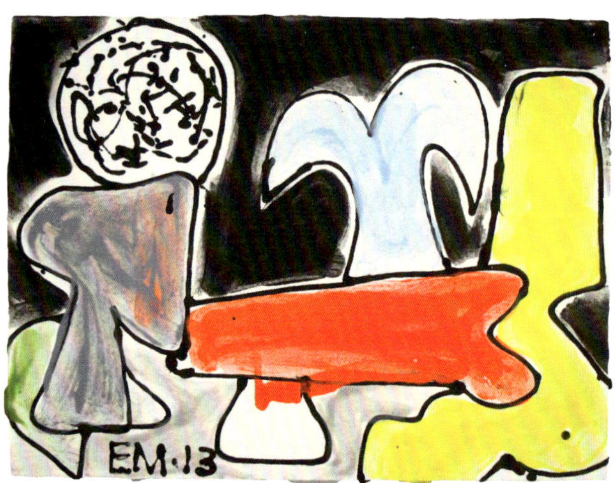

EDDIE MARTINEZ *Untitled*: from "Untitled" series, 2013. Pigmented linen paper pulp on cotton base sheet, 18 × 24 in. (45.7 × 61 cm). 25 unique variants; proof 2/2. Courtesy of the artist and Dieu Donné, New York.

IN PREPARATION

How do you embark on an artist collaboration?

PW: Most artists know nothing about handmade paper so in the beginning it's sort of like show-and-tell. You have to draw them in by showing them the process and the potential of the materials so they can start thinking about how it relates to their work.

MATT KEEGAN *Picture Perfect (Monoprint #3)*, 2010. Stenciled pigmented linen pulp on cotton handmade paper, 26 × 22 ½ in. (66 × 57.1 cm). Courtesy of the artist and Dieu Donné, New York.

LS: We look at the fibers, we show them the beater, we give them a tour of the studio, and we look at artwork. With the Workspace residents, we do a three-hour orientation and conduct a small private class so that they can start with as much information as possible. They have a chance to ask questions and then we decide who we will be working with.

Amy, Paul, and I are similar in that we've all worked with a lot of different techniques. And we have a similar approach in that we all like the first day to be somewhat experimental—to be a day of testing out ideas, and then to refine that into a direction for the other days that the artist is in the space.

AJ: Before I start a collaboration with an artist, I try to do a studio visit and I try to see how they work. You can tell if someone works in a more controlled way or if they're looser and like to experiment.

LS: Some artists will send you color swatches and they'll start to map it out. Other artists want to walk into the studio and react to pulps left over from other artists' projects. It's kind of like how people go shopping. Sometimes they need to see it to know what they want to work with.

AJ: Once they're here, I try to see what they're drawn to—what fibers, what techniques, and so on. Sometimes it's quite surprising.

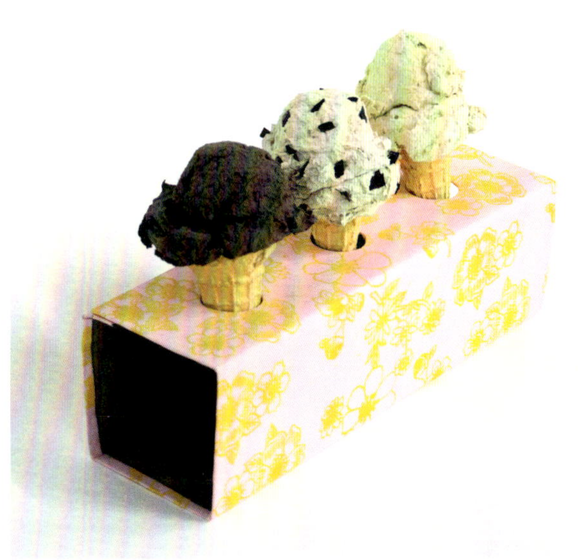

JONATHAN SELIGER *Three Scoops: Chocolate, Chocolate Chip, Vanilla*, 2004. Pigmented Celluclay (ice cream) on pigmented cast cotton (cones) on cotton base sheet with pigmented abaca/cotton stripes (base), 7 × 10 ½ × 3 in. (17.8 × 26.7 × 7.6 cm). Courtesy of the artist and Dieu Donné, New York.

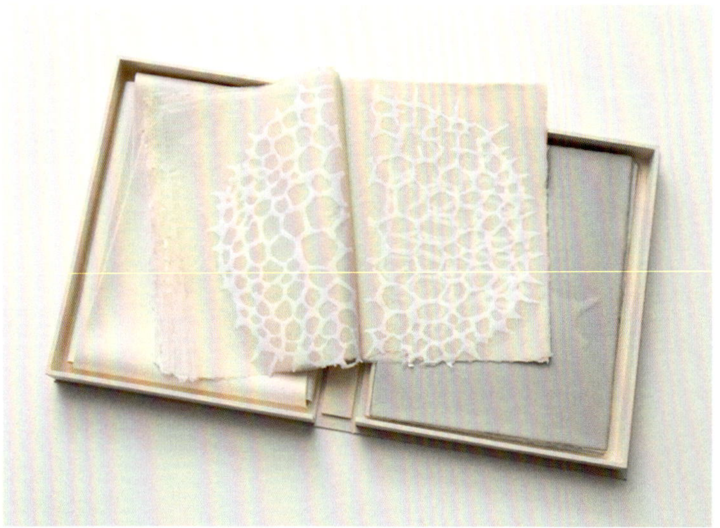

MICHELE OKA DONER *What is White*, 2010. Hand-bound artist book with abaca and cotton, letterpress and archival wax cover. Book, closed: 19 ½ × 16 × 1 ½ in. (49.5 × 40.6 × 3.8 cm). Edition of 30. Courtesy of the artist, Dieu Donné, New York, and Dieu Donné Press, New York.

LS: One of the things that makes Dieu Donné unique is its long, in-depth history. And included in that is our archive, which allows us to pull out physical examples of past work, which is really an exciting thing to do. It allows you to show the range of work that's been done and gives us a place to start talking.

AJ: For a Mylar stencil, we'll pull out a Glenn Ligon, a Barbara Takenaga, or a James Siena. For free-hand pulp painting, I pull out Beth Campbell, or sometimes, newer works by Eddie Martinez, Natalie Frank, or Katherine Bradford. For collage, I'll pull works by Jessica Stockholder and Matt Keegan. For blowouts, I might pull pieces by Kate Shepherd and Michele Oka Doner. For watermarks, we'll bring out the Chuck Close and works by Mel Bochner. And then there's casting, so we'll show the Do Ho Suh pieces, the rubber mold from Lesley Dill's *Head*, as well as Jonathan Seliger, who did cotton-casting. I also pull out the Mylar stencil itself, the vinyl letters for the watermark, plaster molds, rubber molds...

LS: We try to make it clear that what we want out of a residency is for artists to be open to the process; not to come in and say that this is exactly what I want to make—rather, to go into the studio and take advantage of what Dieu Donné is, which is an artist workspace more than a fabrication facility.

AJ: I don't try to push them in one direction and I try to avoid saying "No" right away to anything. I'll look at their work and I can sometimes see what would be really cool on paper. But I don't want to suggest it at first. I want to see what they want to try to do. And if an artist *does* come in saying this is exactly what I want to do, it almost never turns out like that. They always go off in another direction.

IN PRACTICE

How does the collaborative process unfold?

LS: My approach is to start off by being very open-minded, to listen a lot to what they're interested in talking about, like what brings them to want to work with paper. At some point, you have to start making things, so you have to pick a place to start. Part of what we do is take these exploratory big-picture-kind-of ideas and then pin them down to what fiber we have to make, and how I am going to set up the studio.

AJ: The first studio day is always experimental.

LS: I like to think of it as a testing ground for the other days and try to take the pressure off immediately making art, because it is a very labor-intensive process—it's also a way to give them a sense of how long the processes typically take.

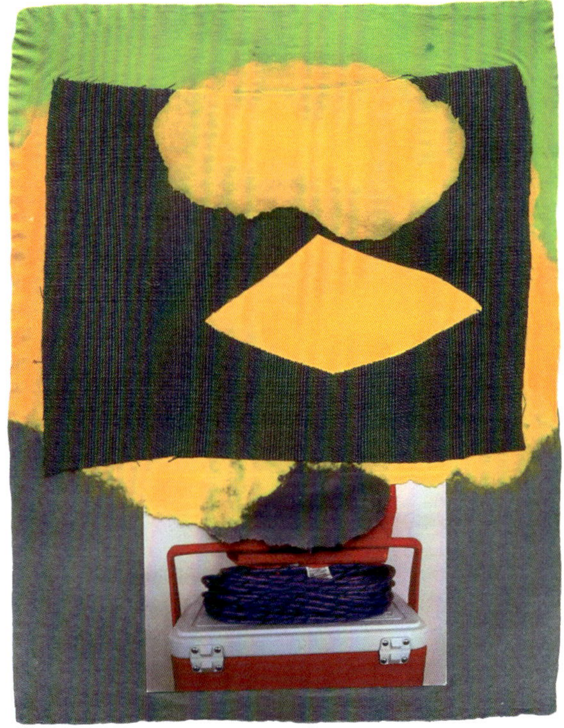

JESSICA STOCKHOLDER *Men's Suit*, 2006. Pigmented tricolor base sheet with wool fabric, pulp paint, and archival ink-jet print, 13 × 11 in. (33 × 27.9 cm). Edition of 15. Courtesy of the artist and Dieu Donné, New York.

PW: Before an artist comes in, everything has to be adjusted for them in a specific way. We try to give them as many avenues of working with the material as we can. For example, you have to mix the pulp paint in a very specific way to be able to use it with a brush. And if an artist is pulp painting, Amy will mix up to twenty different colors before they come in.

LS: After the first day, we usually like to do two days back-to-back, then another two days back-to-back. I think an important part of the process is giving yourself a little distance between the days, both physically and, once the work has dried, stepping back from it and taking it in and thinking about your steps forward. I think that's why we can be so productive—it's because there is that downtime in between. You get immersed in it, you get lost in the process, but you give yourself enough time to reflect and prepare for the next time too.

PW: There are some basic methodologies that we use, but it depends on the artist and what they're doing. Sometimes things get combined and you discover something new. Or sometimes you figure out a better, innovative way of doing something.

AJ: There are so many variables in paper, from how you pigment the fiber, to how long you beat the fiber, to what method you use to dry the work.

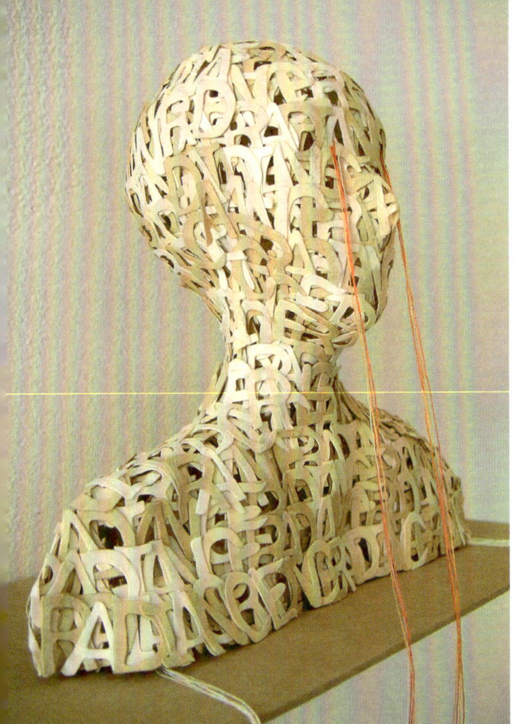

LESLEY DILL *Head*, 2003. Cast, die-cut pigmented abaca paper, thread, stainless-steel shelf covered in tea-stained muslin cloth, 6 × 7 × 3 ½ in. (15.2 × 17.8 × 8.9 cm). Edition of 25. Courtesy of the artist and Dieu Donné, New York.

LS: You're constantly making little micro-decisions along the way. And I think it can be fun if someone has the mindset that some of these are going to be failures, but they're going for it nevertheless.

AJ: If an artist wants to do something, I can tell them the best materials and techniques for what they want to try, and reasons why I think it may or may not work. But ultimately, I allow them to try it out.

LS: Our approach here is that if it won't negatively affect the equipment, we'll pretty much try anything. If the artist is looking for a certain effect and we know that this material isn't going to produce it, we'll try to redirect him or her a little bit. But if there's something that an artist just needs to see done, we just do it. That's part of the process too.

PW: There are things that are inherent with the medium but it's also about pushing the logistics of the material. And how far you can push it. The most exciting part of collaboration is when you discover something that you might not have done before; working with that artist brought it out of you. Something that you wouldn't have figured out yourself because there wasn't the opportunity, but then, when it comes out in collaboration, you jump up and down (a little bit).

THE YIELD

What do you, as a collaborator, learn along the way? What excites you about the work you help produce?

AJ: I feel like we invent little things all the time. I was working with Firelei Báez and she wanted to marble. We dumped way too much formation aid into the pulp and it ended up doing this really cool thing.[1] So we worked with that. We would pour the pulp in and then she would move it around with the end of a paintbrush. And then we started tearing things up. We tore when the paper was wet, glued it, and then we pressed it. In the end, you couldn't really tell how the piece was made. I think one of the best compliments that I got was when Paul said, "How did you do this? I can't figure it out."

PW: The blowout is a technique that no one else was doing in the beginning. All of Melvin Edwards's works were done that way. He's a sculptor and he uses found objects like chains and antique tools and he welds these materials together. He brought these materials to the studio and said he was going to lay them on sheets of paper and spray-paint around them to create images or silhouettes. Then we thought we could use the same objects and lay them on pulp and spray away the background with water. And that's how the blowout technique was born: because he brought the idea of using these real objects to create the imagery.

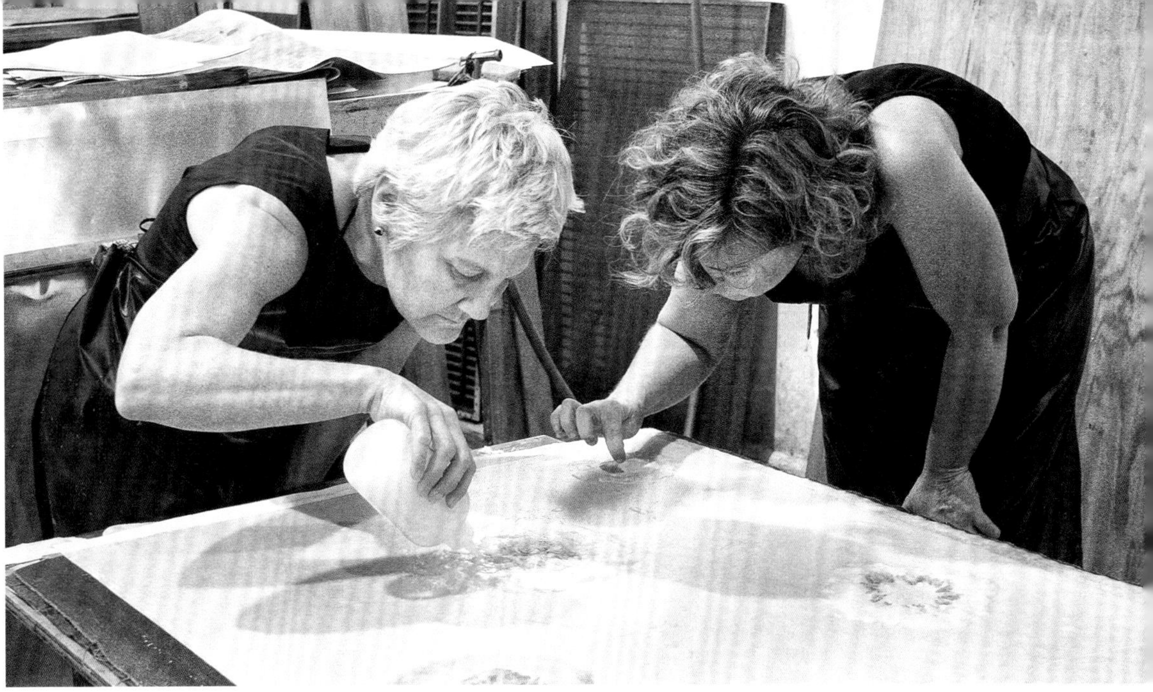

Artist Ann Hamilton and Studio Collaborator Amy Jacobs working in the Dieu Donné studio, August 2, 2011.

E.V. Day's work was an instance where we learned something technical about dry pigments that are ground up and emulsified and how they disperse with wet pulp. We were able to control where she did and did not want the pigment to bleed. That was something that we ended up applying to other situations too, like with Mel Kendrick— he wanted a certain amount of control in the bleeding of the pigment.

LS: Richard Tuttle was really fun to watch in the studio because his art is also a record of the process. A lot of people working in sculpture work from molds but his are actually all hand-formed pieces. One of his sculptures, *The Triumph of Night* from 2009, I believe, was created by throwing a rubber glove full of pulp. He had a series of actions that he performed for each of the four parts the edition. Each piece is different, but the way that he performed to create the piece remained the same.

PW: Jim Hodges created a wet piece—a chain embedded in a wet sheet. We made three of them and I kept spraying them every day but eventually they would start rotting so I would have to dry one out and then he would make another one for the next couple weeks of his show. The pieces looked so strange because they had been sitting wet for two weeks and picked up whatever weird things were in the air; it became part of the work.

AJ: You learn a lot from the artists you work with. The first day Ann Hamilton came into the studio, she knew she wanted to work with abaca.[2] She also brought silk from India and a lot of raw sheep's wool. That very first day we were embedding those things in abaca. Paul and I worked together on it. We would pull a sheet of abaca out and she would lay stuff down and then we would pull another one. And we discovered that she liked it when there were big air bubbles in the sheets because it would create this veiny pattern, so we had to figure out how to make huge air bubbles. It was truly experimental. To see how her mind works, and how she throws ideas around was really educational.

I've loved working with Arlene Shechet too because she works in the way that I myself like to work. She would bring twenty-five stencils, fifteen different molds, and we would just create a palette of all these different colors for pulp paint, and a palette for all of the base sheets—she would pick and choose as she went. Molly Smith was a little different. She knew she wanted to experiment but she also wanted to learn as much about paper as she could. She didn't want me to make pulps for her. She wanted to use things that were leftover in the walk-in.

LS: What you see in Molly's work is this moment in the process where so much pressure was put on this paper that it burst. If we were making production orders, someone would say that we pressed it too fast and the machine blew out. But these marks were actually what she was after.

AJ: We've also been working with Do Ho Suh continuously and it's been great being around him and seeing how his mind works. He has said that his "thread drawings" would look dramatically different if they were just drawings. They almost take on a tapestry-like quality in paper.

PW: For some of the artists who are painters, working with paper extended what they did in painting in a different way. Like Bart Wasserman, who was doing very minimal paintings on canvas with really subtle gradations of tone. His work was all about how light is reflected. Then when he started working in paper with us, the phenomenon of being able to see light *through* the paper brought new ideas to his work, and in the same minimal kind of way. Conceptually, it brought his work into another realm.

Ursula von Rydingsvard came to love working with paper so much that it's an integral part of her practice now. It was a breakthrough for her, I think. Because she's physically working with material, it has an affinity to her work in sculpture. And that's what excites her. It's wonderful to see how significant this has become to somebody of her stature and her focus. It is so satisfying to be able to offer that to someone else.

CHUCK CLOSE *Watermark Self Portrait*, 2007. Light and shade watermark, abaca and cotton fiber pigmented with carbon black, 11 ¾ × 9 ¼ in. (29.8 × 23.5 cm). Edition of 35. Courtesy of the artist and Dieu Donné, New York.

LS: The quality of the work that comes out of Dieu Donné is something that's very consistent and I think there's an unrelenting dedication to that. It's this combination of being open and being experimental but allowing space for research and having that commitment to making, to keeping the standard high on everything too. That's something all of us share, Amy, Paul, and I. It's sort of an obsession.

Rachel Wolff is an independent art writer, editor, and filmmaker.

NOTES

1 Formation aid is a viscous, plant-derived substance used in papermaking that thickens water so that it slows down drainage and allows time to manipulate the pulp.

2 Abaca is a fiber used in papermaking that is derived from the bast of a banana plant grown in the Philippines.

Molly Smith in the process of making *Dust* (2012) in the Dieu Donné studio.

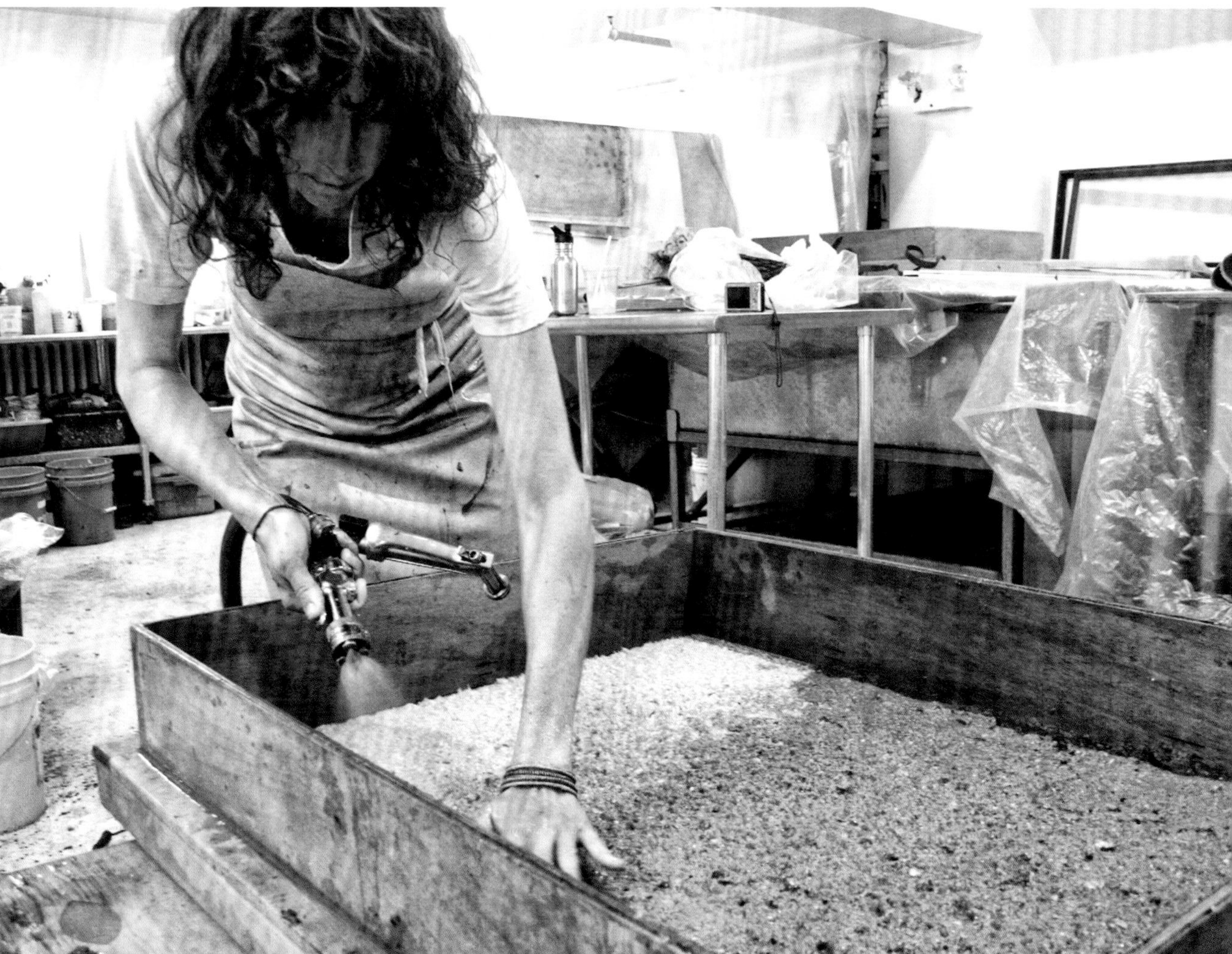

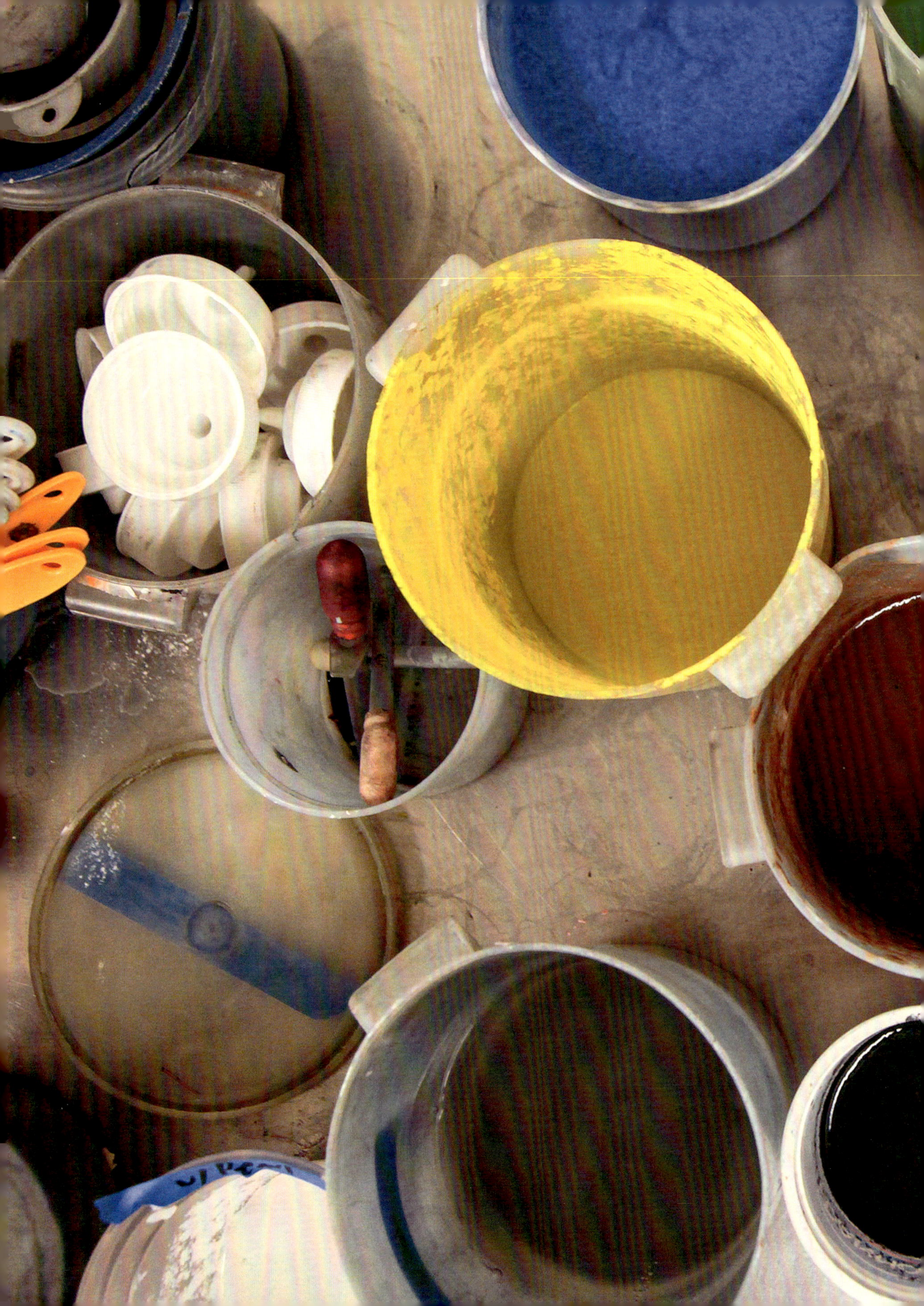

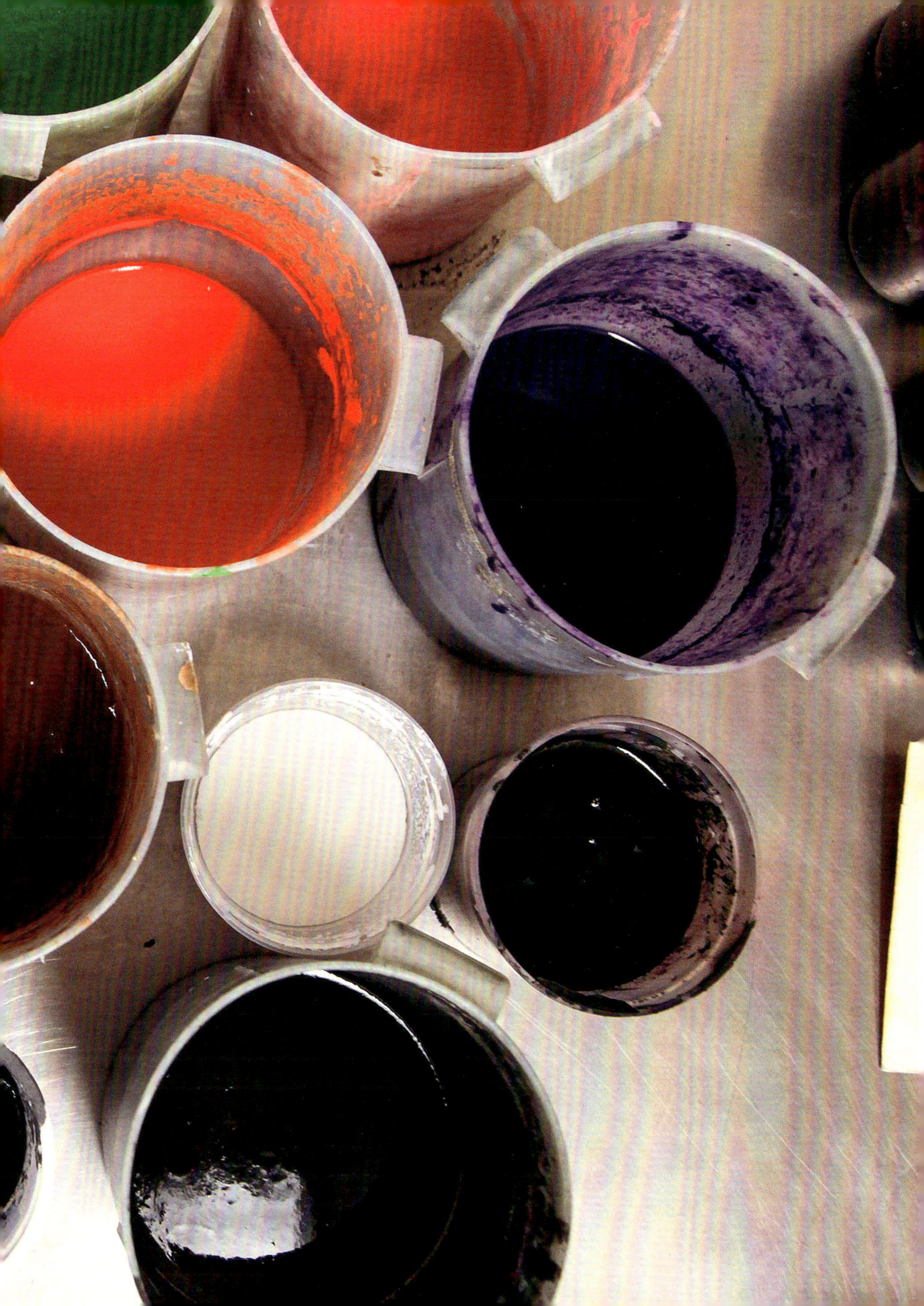

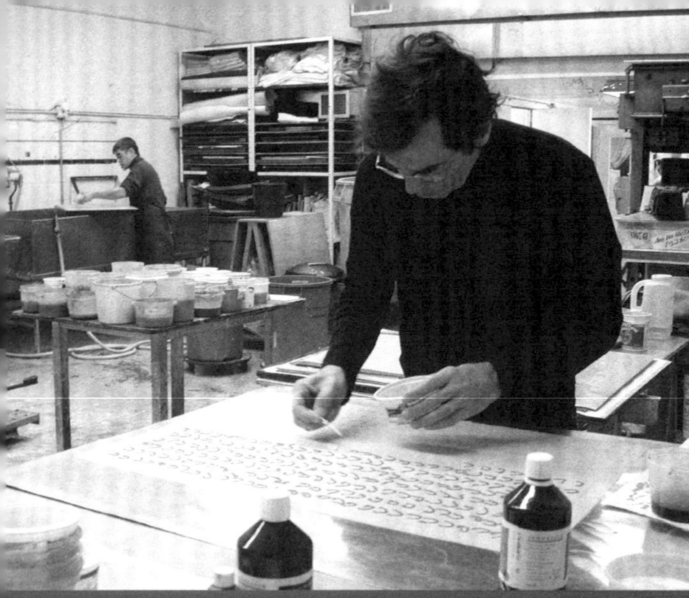

Richard Tuttle working on the series "Dawn, Noon, Dusk"
in the Dieu Donné studio, 2002.

When, Ever, and If

RICHARD TUTTLE

I used to know those guys out
There before we came back here.
You probably don't think of me
As wild enough to be out there
In the end of time, but we were
The same. Nature spirits are not
Far away, but far away is close
With these guys when they want
To masquerade—for nature spirits,
They are not. You can tell this
By their organs: hard as wood,
Deep as grain, soft as wool,
Practiced as cats. I was on an
Ordinary mission 'round the
Clock; they were probably look-
Ing for me, though I thought I
Saw them first. In fact, they
Seemed to be running away.
But there are so many mirror
Effects out there you respond
To them before knowing them,
And then they seemed to think,
I looked like them! Well, anyway,
No chance of that.

I would not want to tell you
About them except that they are
So changed... And you can see I
Am not—someone has to answer
To these strange beginnings...
Your comfort must feel secure,
Knowing what I tell you, and
Not having to go out there.
Things seem settled now. Well,
I, myself, can't stand these trans-
Formations, temporary silences,
Static poses, just to make you think
Everything is OK. They could go
Back to their old state any time,
I guess. Once you experience
Something, you can imagine it
In the future, again and again.
There is nothing real, except
Where we put real to be—or
Someone else can be real.
Of course, they have to decide
That, and then they can take
Any form they want. This is
What you see here, but you
Have to know it to see it,
For you to go out there!

Triumph of Night is a 4-part
Work made of pigmented pulp
Very consciously trying to mix
Natural and artificial pigments.
I would walk down the street
To visit Kremer Pigments
On 29th St., a world class purveyor,
Loving to bring together the two
Manhattan anomalies of Dieu Donné
And Kremer. Each member of
Triumph is built like a sandcastle
On the beach, which is then de-
Stroyed as if hit by a wave or
Disgruntled swimmer or the child
Who made it. 100% cotton fiber
Insures a uniformity and when air
Dried, retains appropriate color,
Usually lost when things dry out.
I believe I was in New Mexico when
I began thinking of an armature to
Hold the then smooth-backed images
Off the wall surface, their particular
Realism in art requiring an off-mount.
The vertical member, common to each
Mount in this system, refers to one-
Ment and singularity, I assume,
Without their being seen, of course,
In the finished piece.

About this time (which was in years)
Of making, Triumph, I was preparing
The exhibition, Triumphs, at the Hugh
Lane Gallery in Dublin. Artists of the
Renaissance, like Mantegna, had been
Called upon to make larger prints, a
Problem they solved by gluing more
Sheets of paper together, a physical
Gesture, combining the image of the
Triumph, a victory parade, and the
Triumphs written by the great 14th
Century poet, Petrarch, whom they
Loved. Petrarch could celebrate
Virtually anything by writing a tri-
Umph poem, the least attractive, the
More striking. Night is a great hero.
In a box, like mine, it is always on
Parade.

Every project with Dieu Donné takes
Longer and longer, as if celebrating
The genius of paper, itself. The particles
Of the beaten fiber are held in a matrix
Of time in such a way, anyone who is
Interested in the nature of time would
Be transfixed. Paul Wong of Dieu Donné
And some of us caught on in the early 60s
That paper held a great secret, the secret
Of the nature of time. Only in time do
Projects like my Dawn, Noon and Night
And Kathleen get closer to the nature
Of time by taking longer and longer—
It's almost as if this projection is enough,
At least for me, for nature and its esta-
Blishment are clear in time. The boxed
Group of Triumph of Night also dissolves
The knowability of the wall upon which
It is held, all the more provocative,
Because the mounts are stuck deep
Within, yet, simultaneously, and because
Of the nature of time, it can make a new
Wall of color facing outward in time.

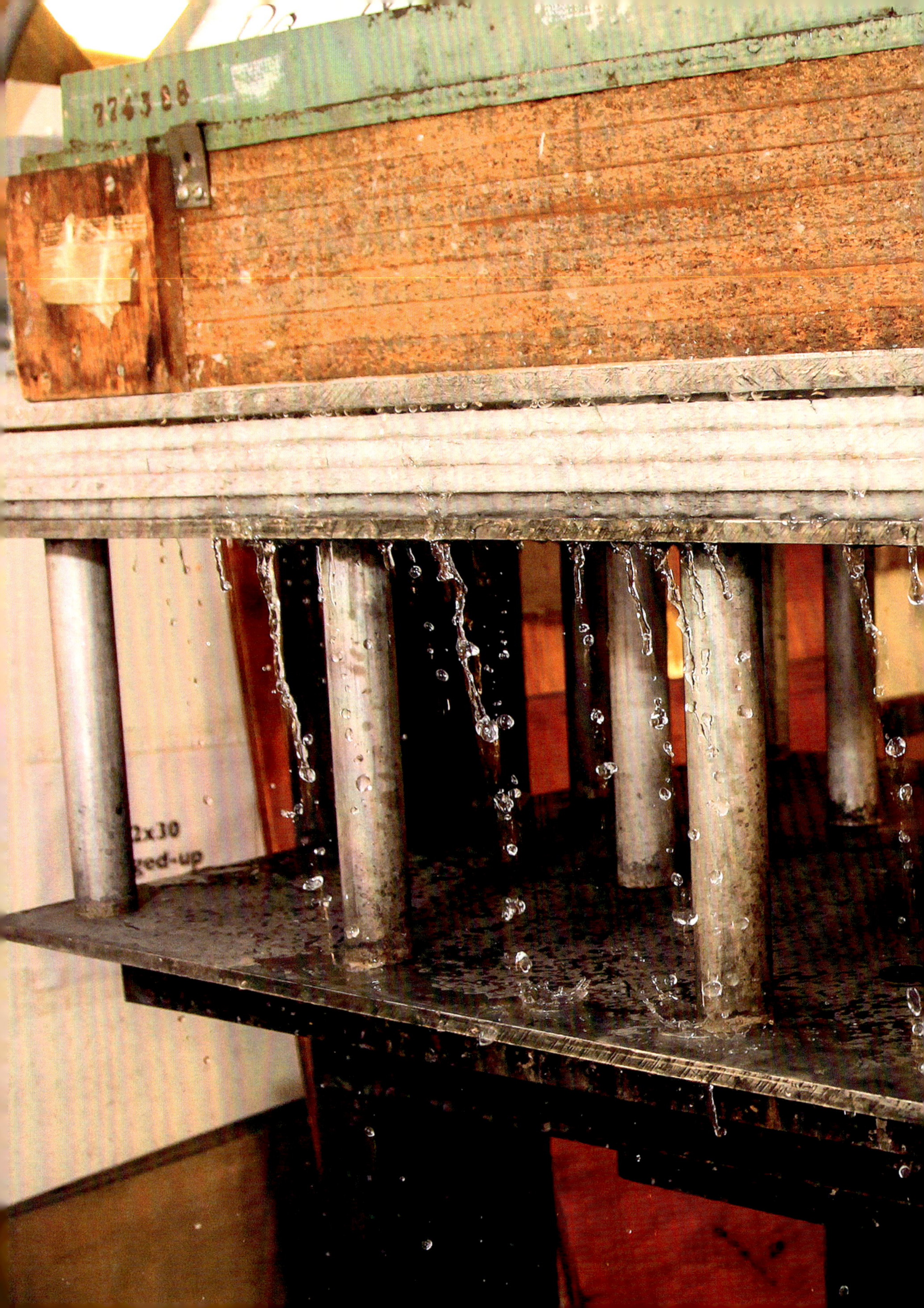
2x30
ged-up

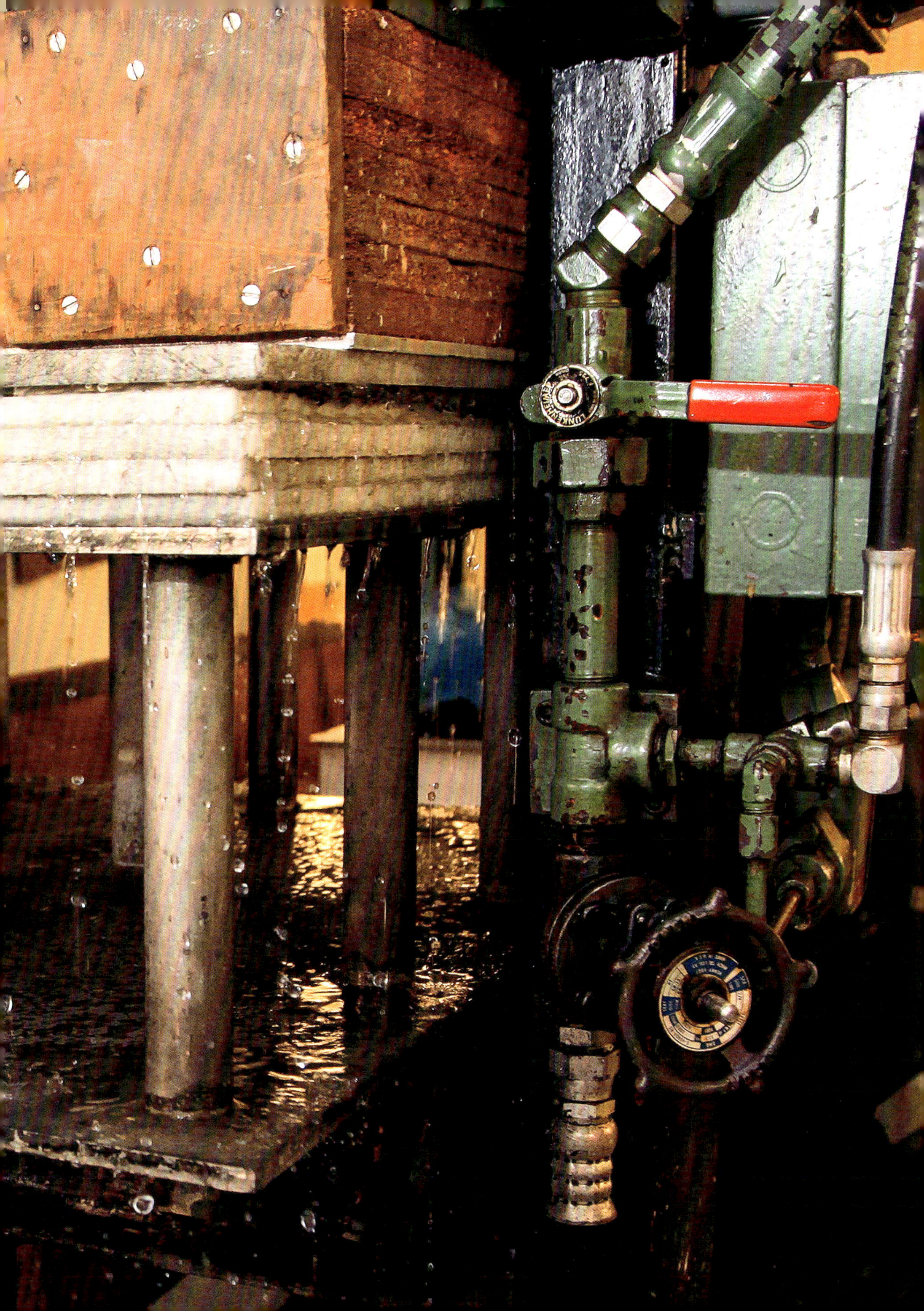

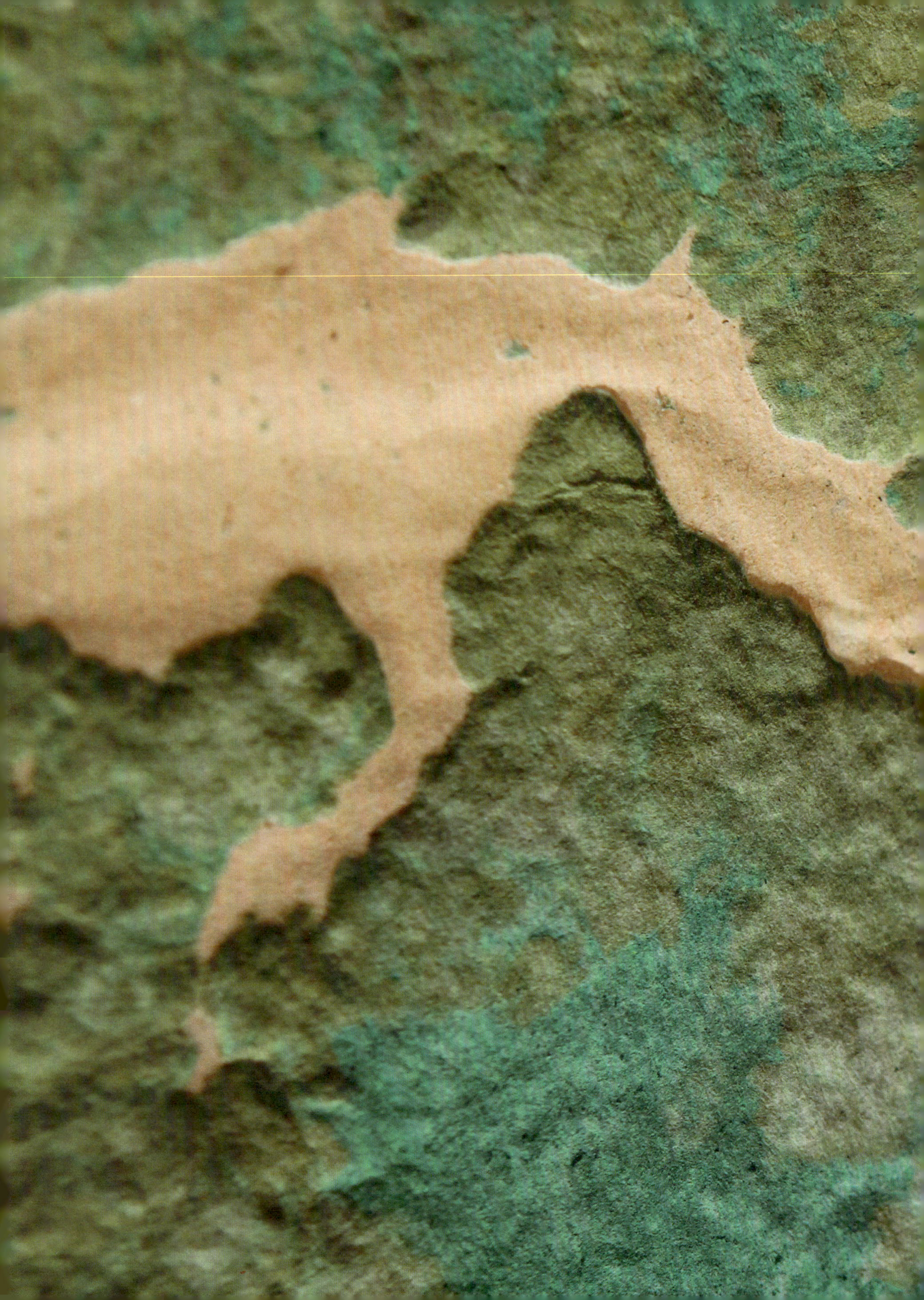

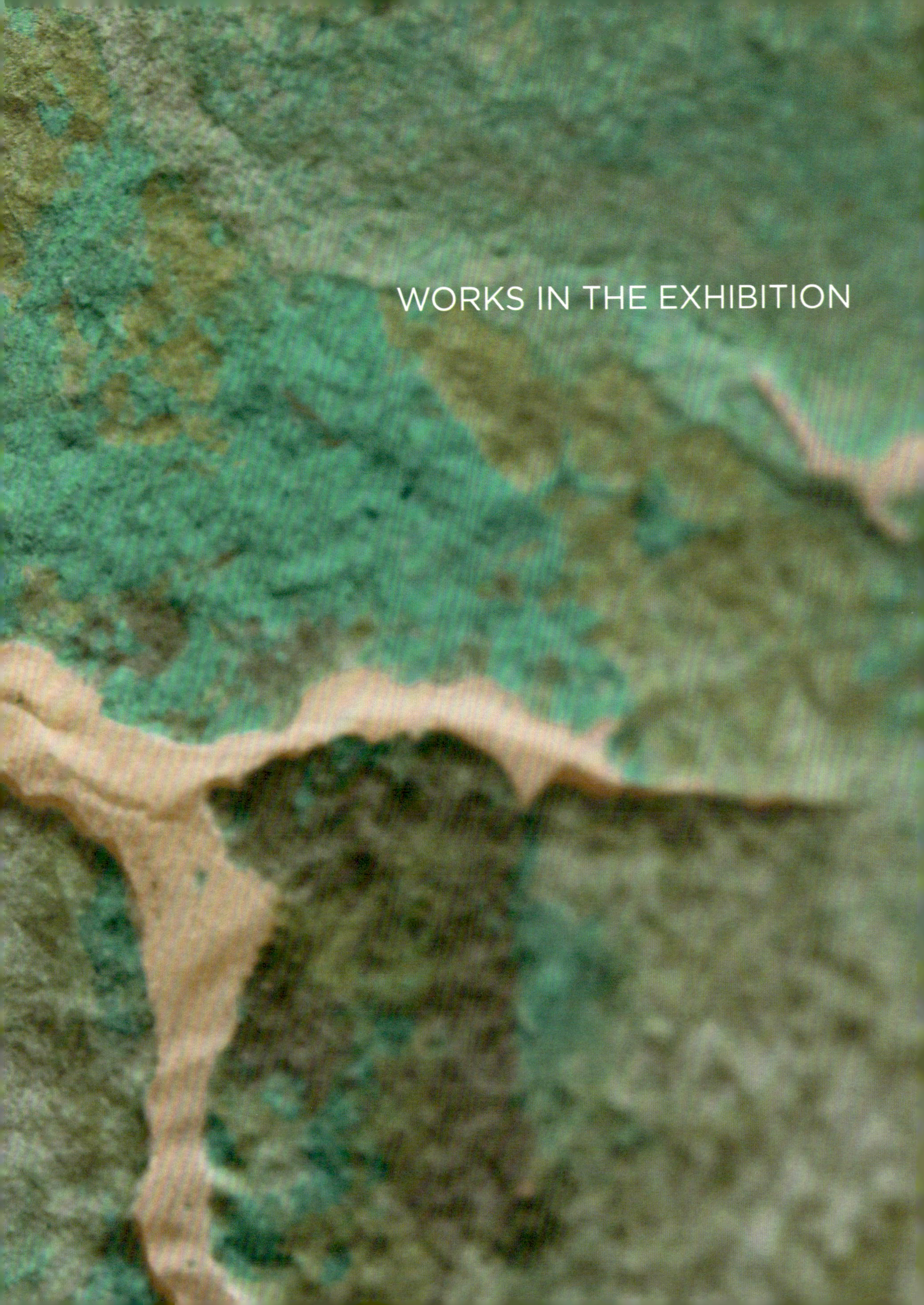

WORKS IN THE EXHIBITION

Firelei Báez

Amidst the future and present there is a memory table, 2013 (detail on following spread)
Pigmented abaca, cotton, and linen on abaca base sheet with radiograph opaque ink
39 ¾ × 60 ⅜ in. (101 × 153.4 cm)
Courtesy of the artist and Gallery Wendi Norris, San Francisco

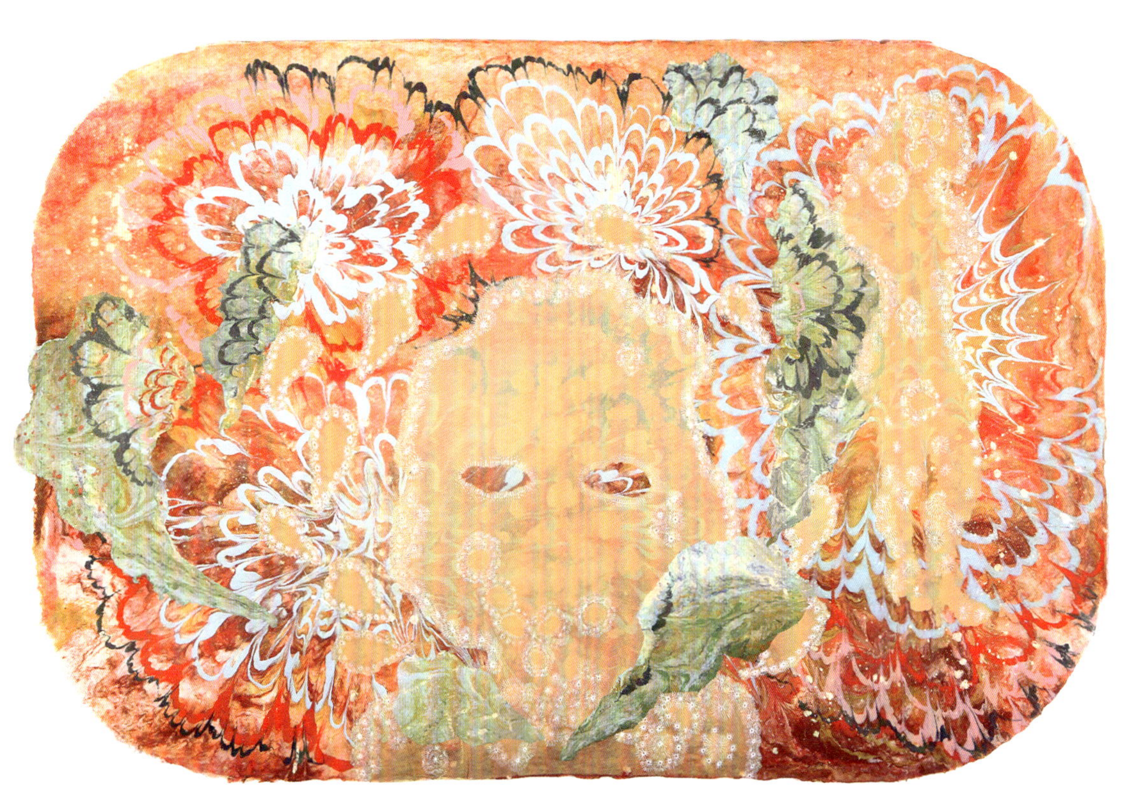

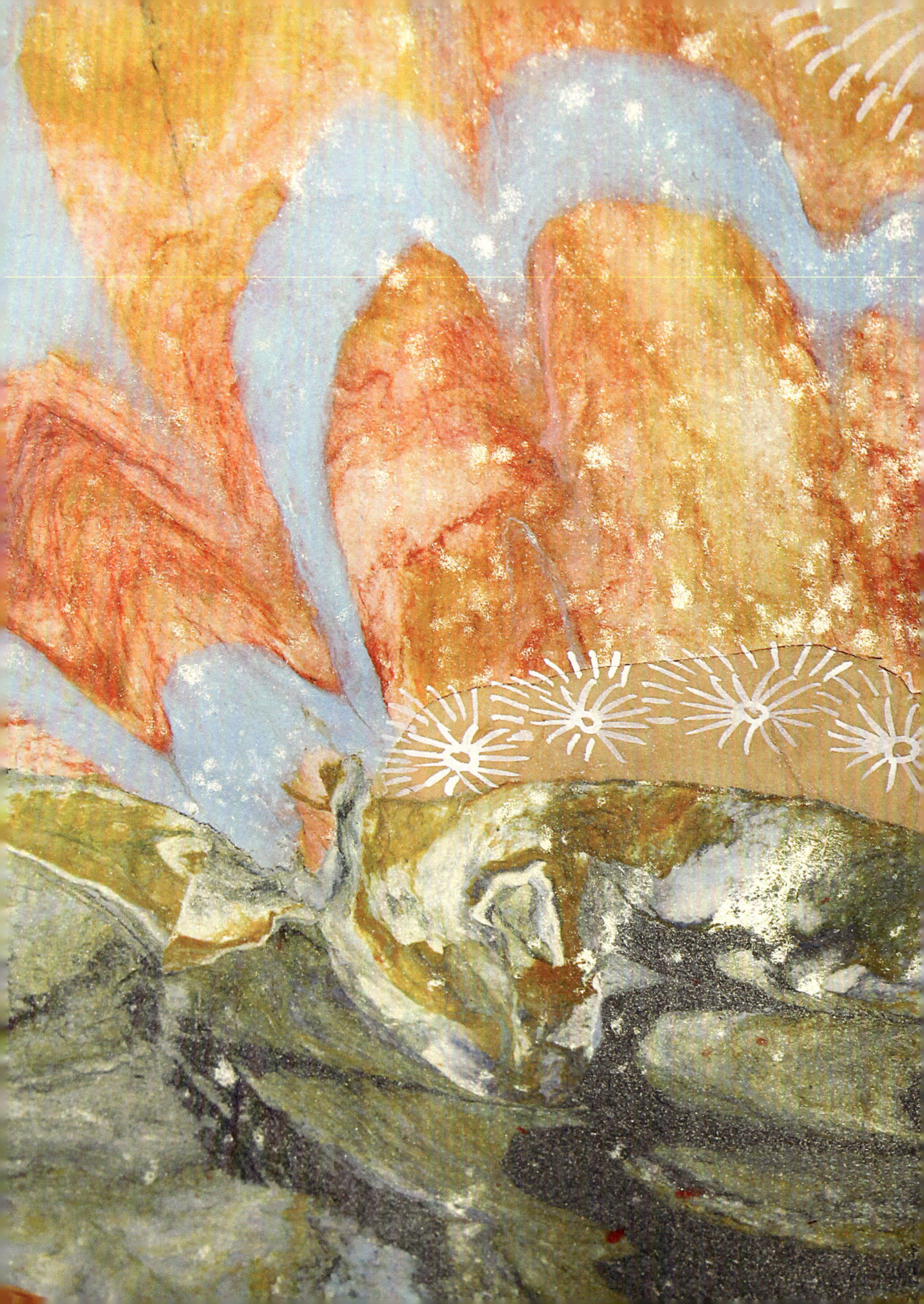

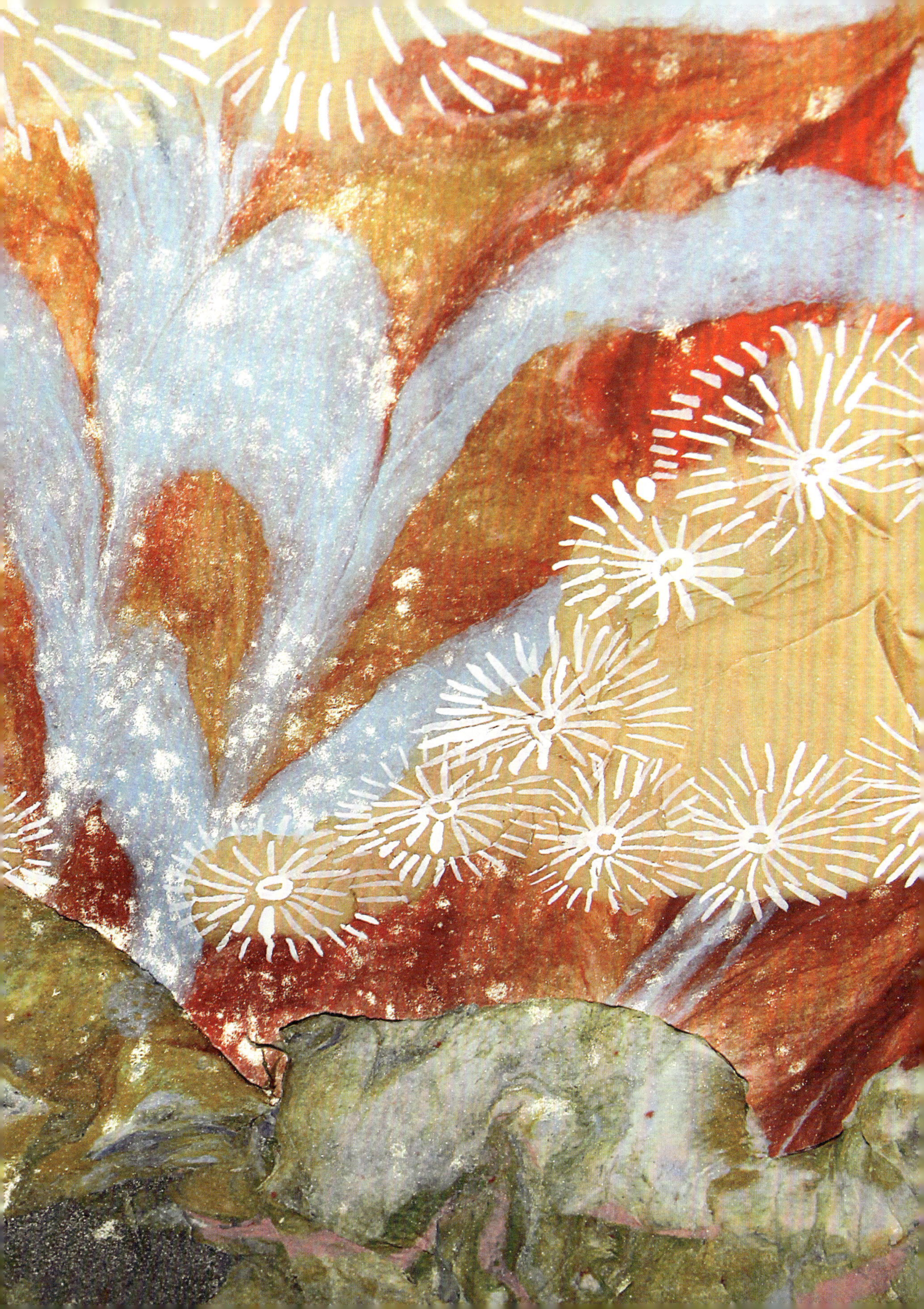

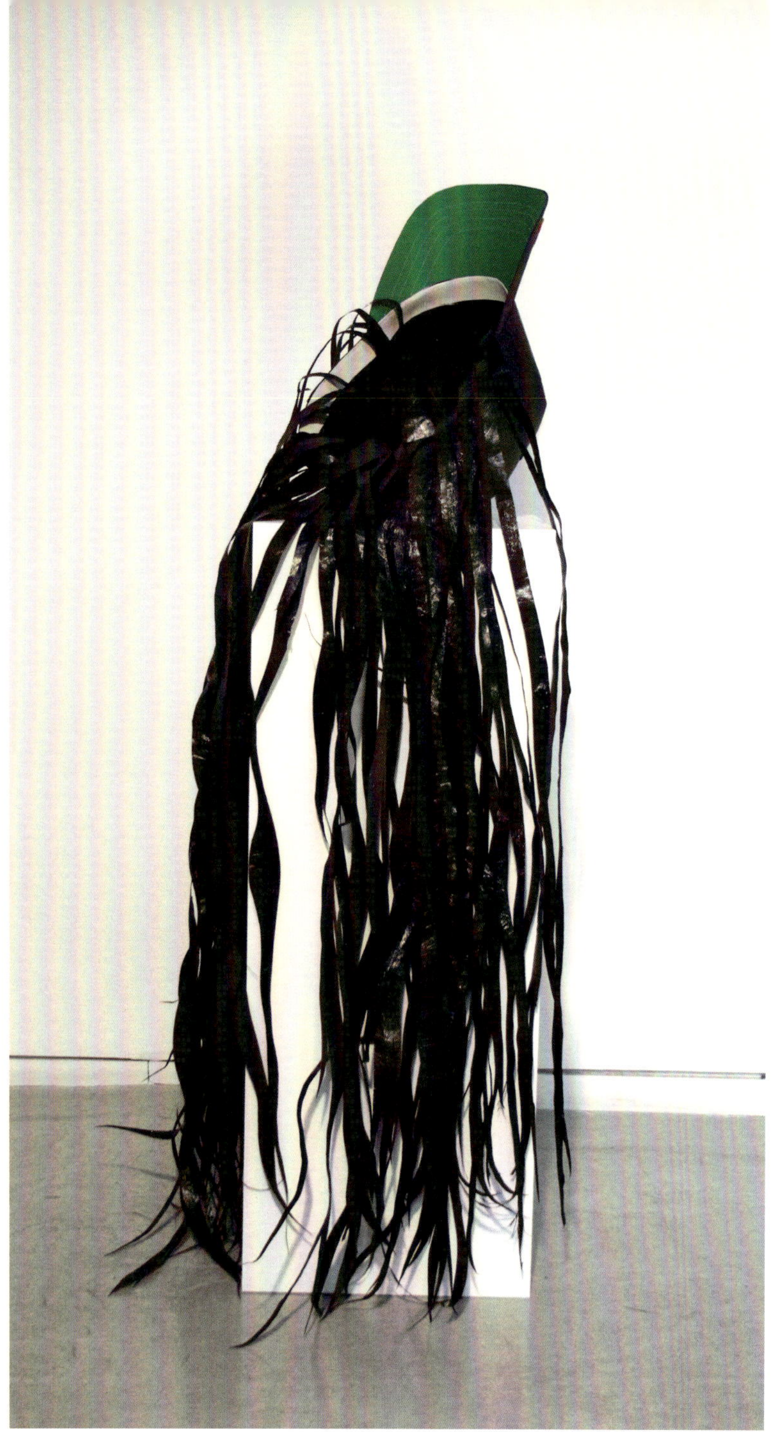

Ian Cooper

Chalice, 2010
Handmade denim and cotton papers, commercial papers, fabric,
cast paper pulp, trash bags, brush bristles, gloss medium, and jade adhesive
57 × 11 × 16 in. (144.8 × 27.9 × 40.6 cm)
Courtesy of the artist

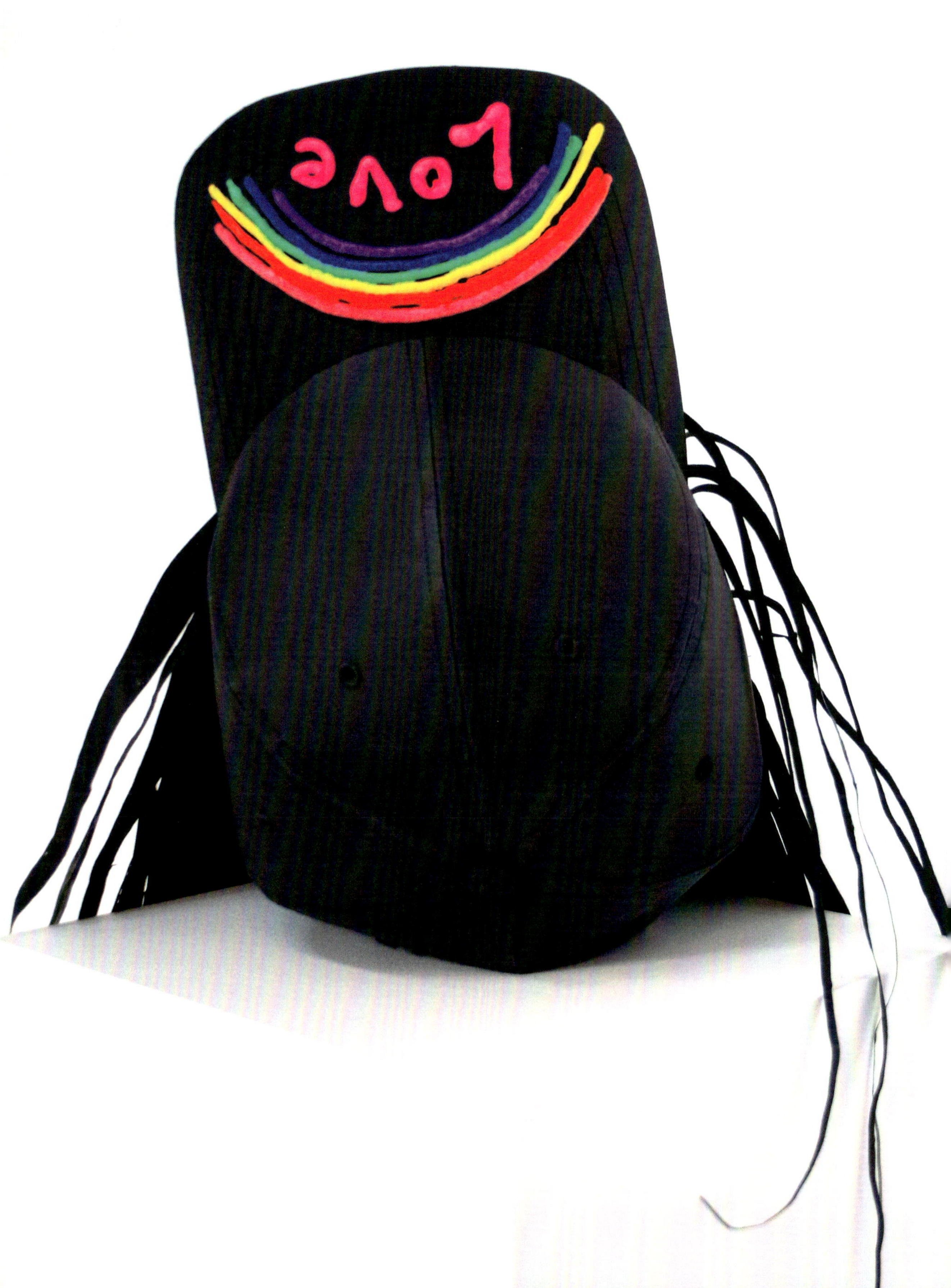
Love

David Kennedy Cutler

Mount, 2011
Archival inkjet on Japanese paper, metal-embedded data from compact discs, and pigmented cotton
81 × 18 × 17 in. (205.7 × 45.7 × 43.2 cm)
Courtesy of the artist and Derek Eller Gallery, New York

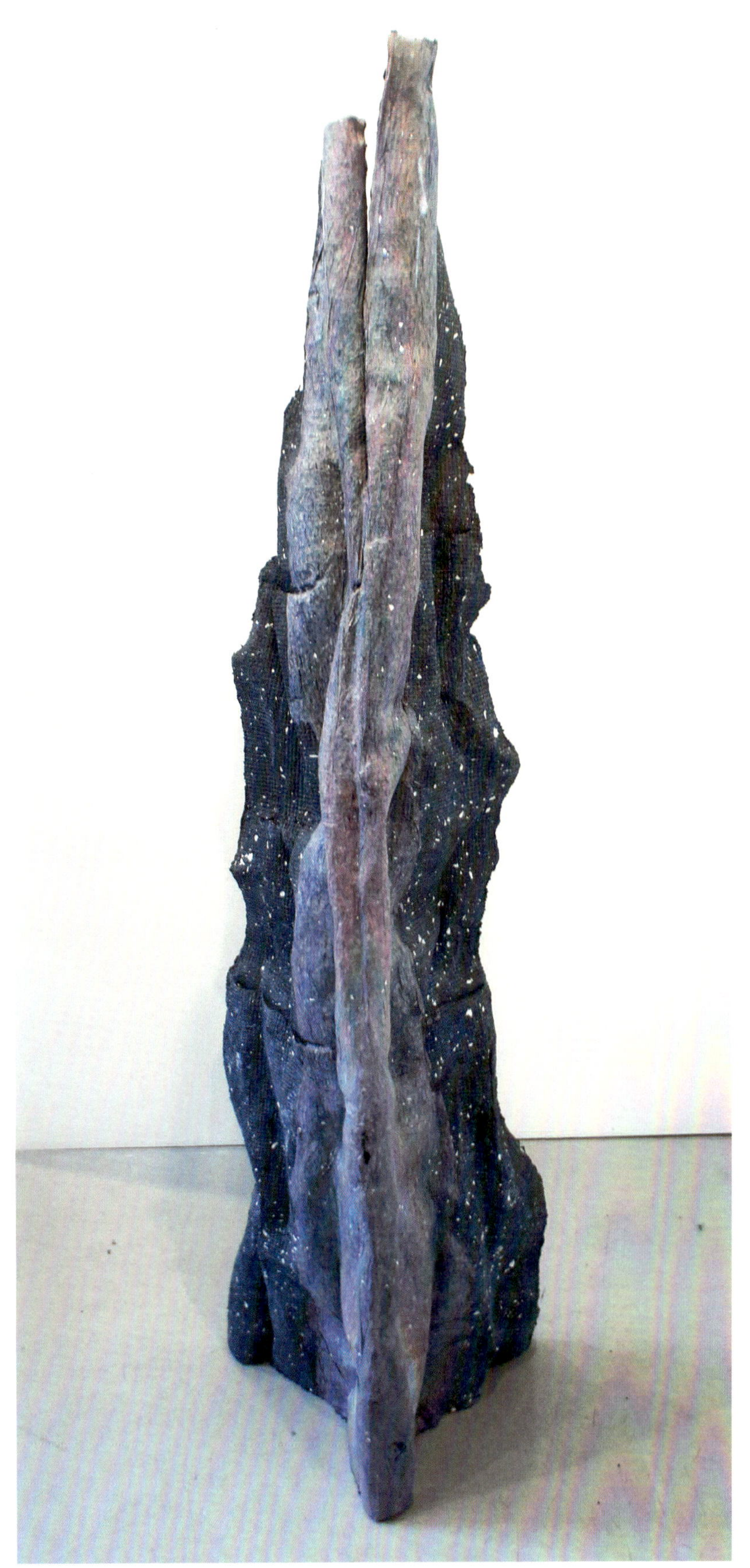

E.V. Day

Shazam (Black and Phosphorescence), 2009
Fishnet bodysuit pigment embossing on cotton base sheet
60 × 40 in. (152.4 × 101.6 cm)
Courtesy of the artist

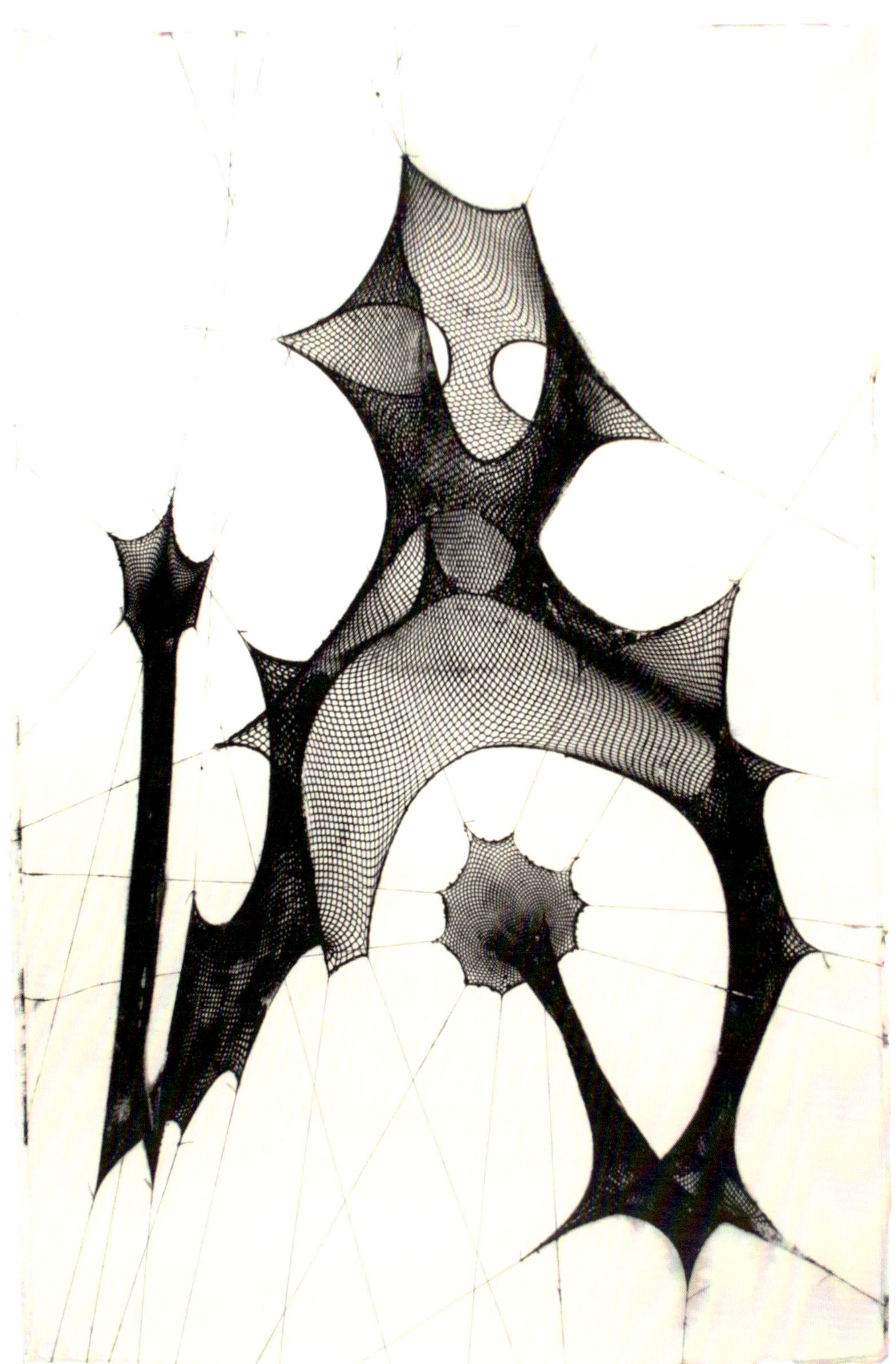

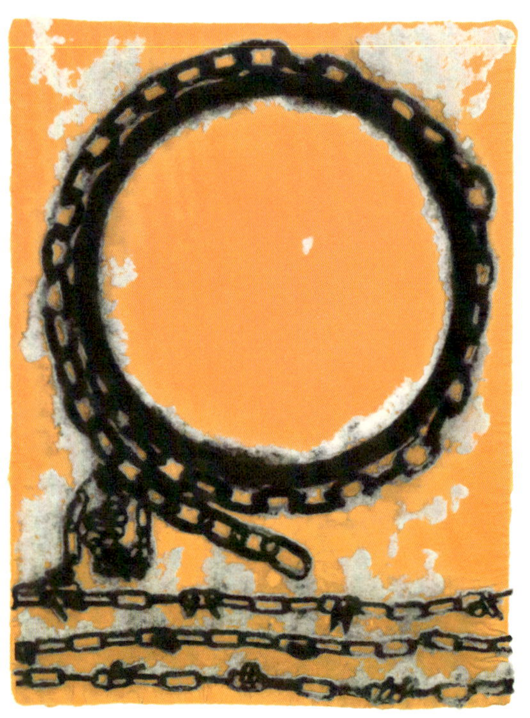

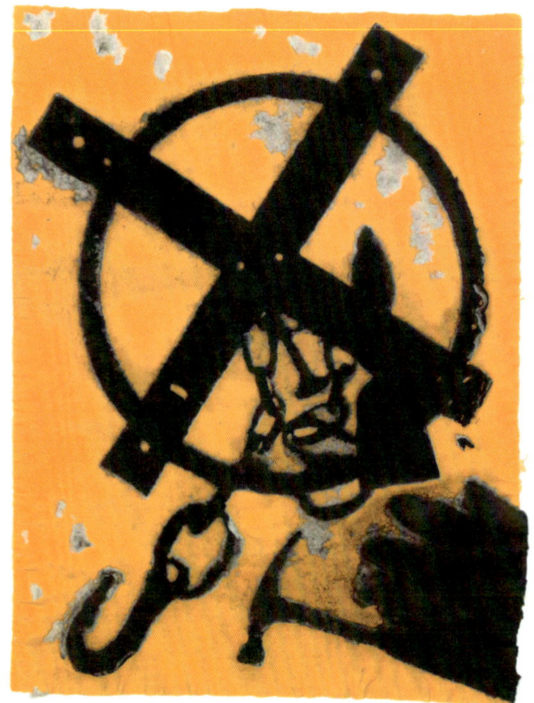

Melvin Edwards

Left: *Dakar Days*, 2006
Cotton blowout on pigmented abaca base sheet
21 ⅞ × 16 ⅞ in. (55.6 × 42.9 cm)
Courtesy of the artist and Dieu Donné, New York

Right: *in Gorée*, 2006 (detail on following spread)
Cotton blowout on pigmented abaca base sheet
22 ⅜ × 17 ⅛ in. (56.8 × 43.5 cm)
Courtesy of the artist and Dieu Donné, New York

Opposite: *Sud foire*, 2006
Cotton blowout on pigmented abaca base sheet
21 ¾ × 16 in. (55.2 × 40.6 cm)
Courtesy of the artist and Dieu Donné, New York

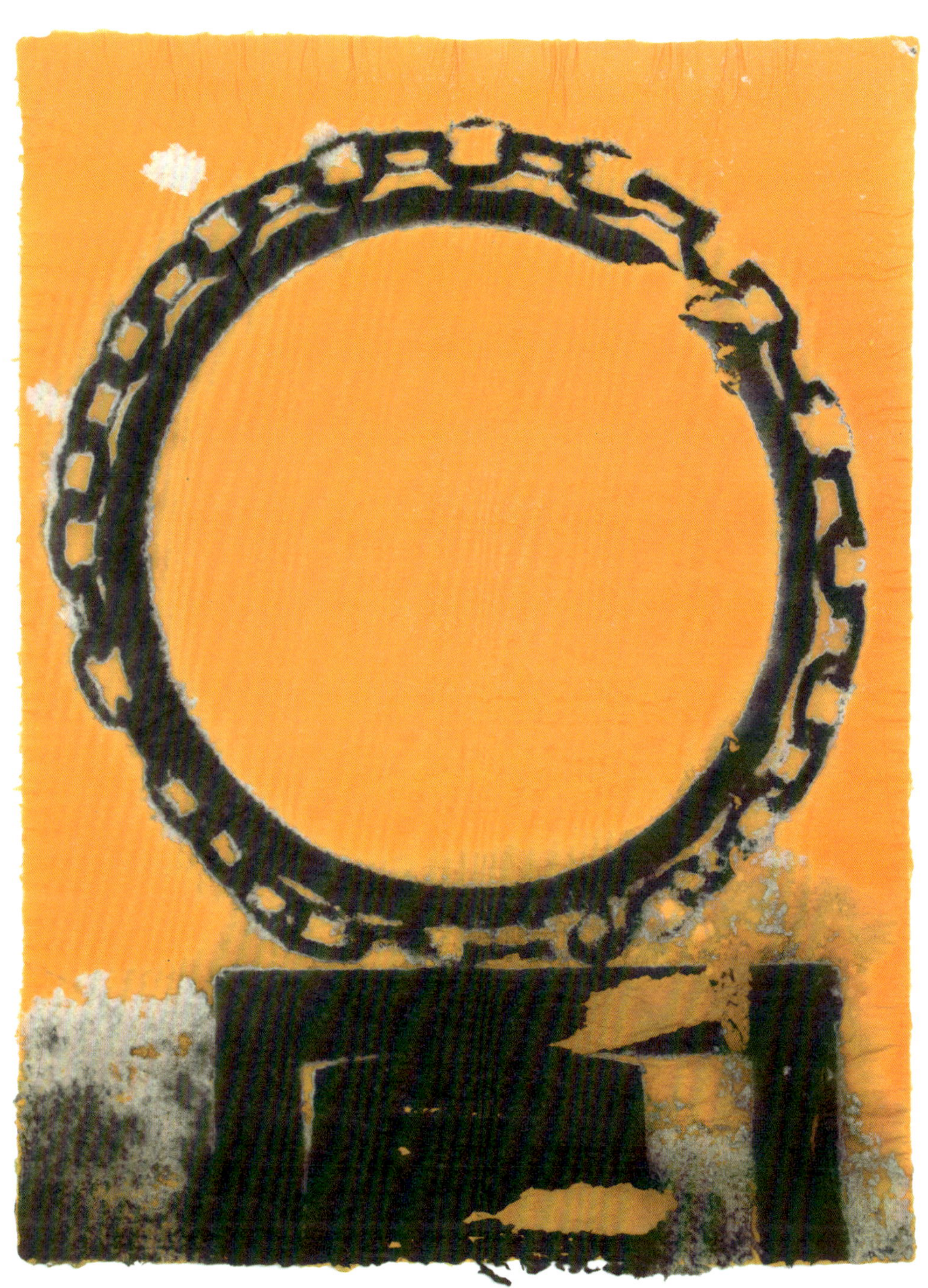

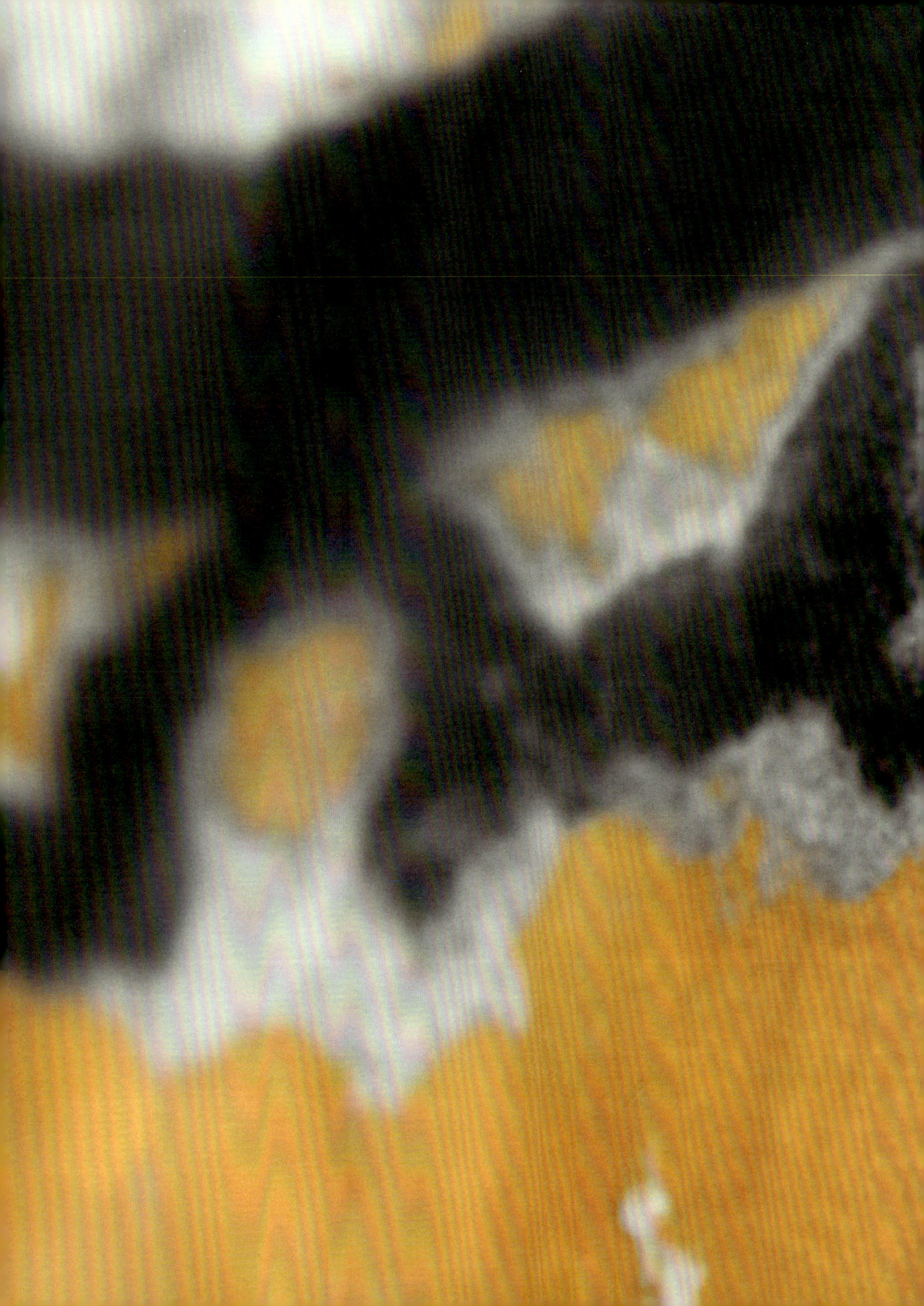

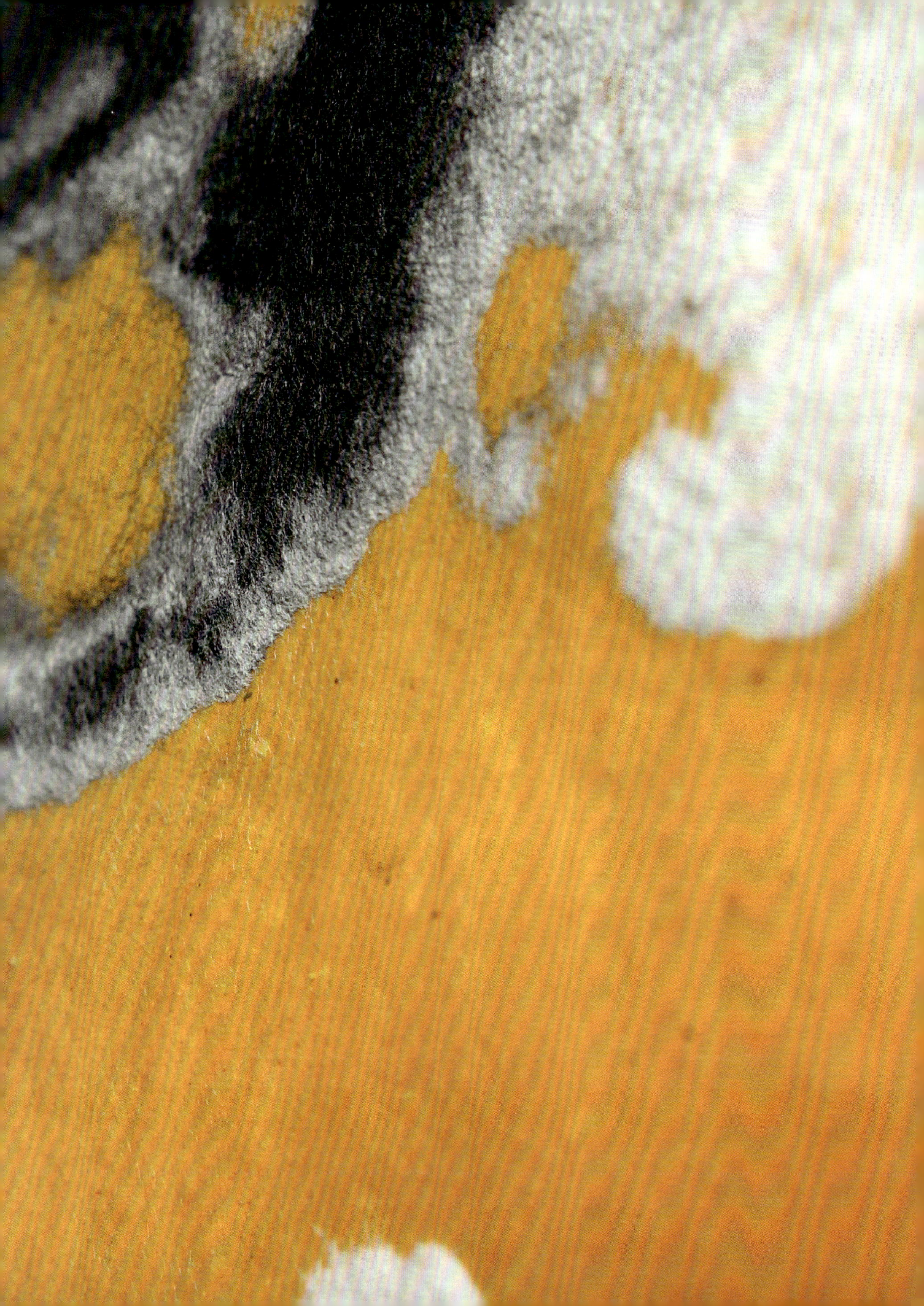

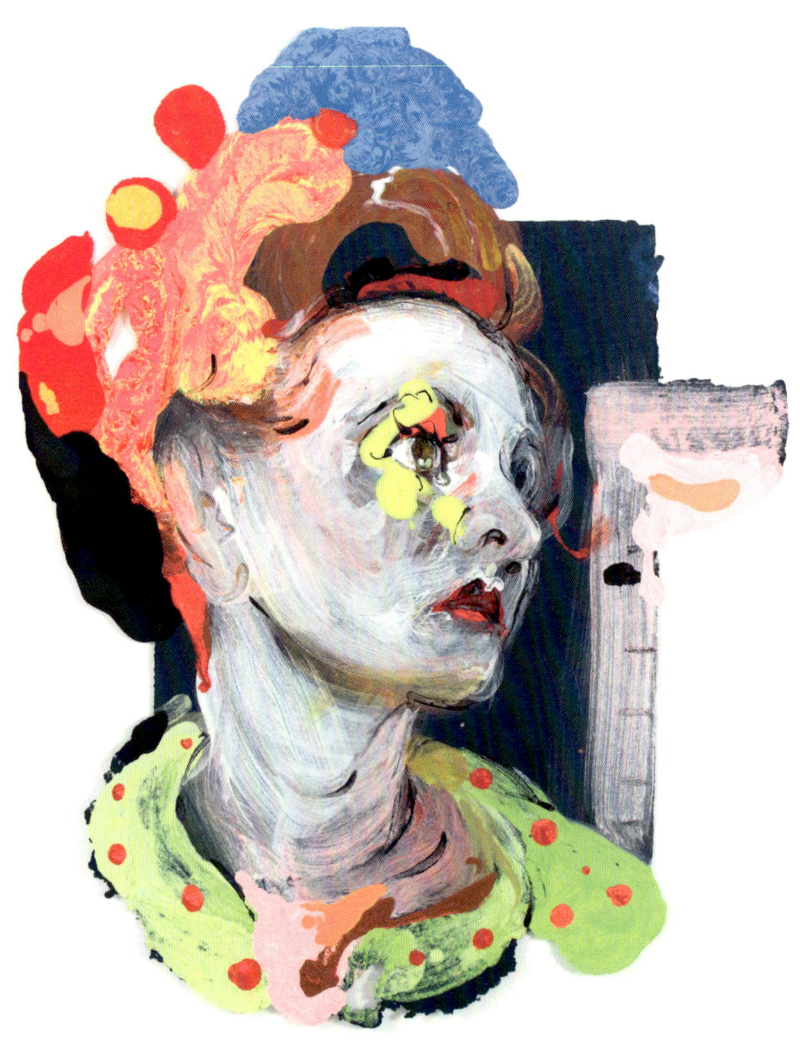

Natalie Frank

Portrait (Woman I), 2015
Pigmented linen pulp on cotton base sheet
35 ⅜ × 28 in. (89.9 × 71.1 cm)
Collection of Sylvia Shepard. Courtesy of Dieu Donné, New York

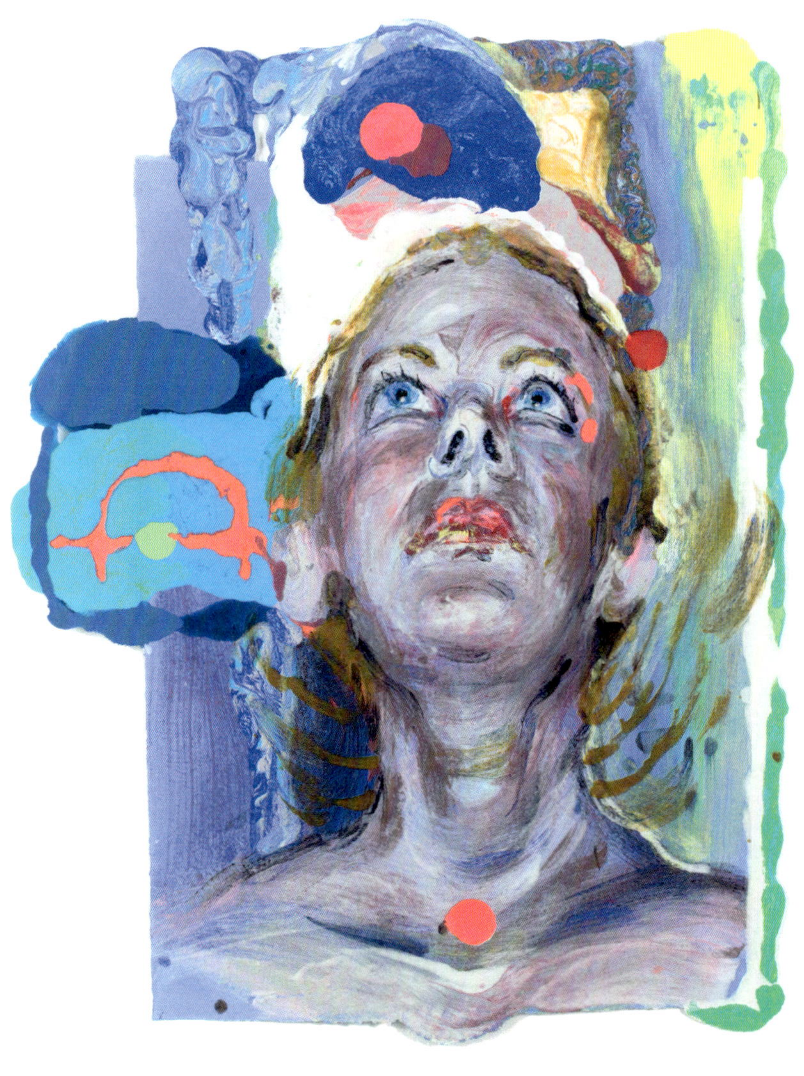

Portrait (Woman II), 2015 (detail on following spread)
Pigmented linen pulp on cotton base sheet
35 ½ × 27 ¾ in. (90.2 x 70.5 cm)
Courtesy of the artist and Dieu Donné, New York

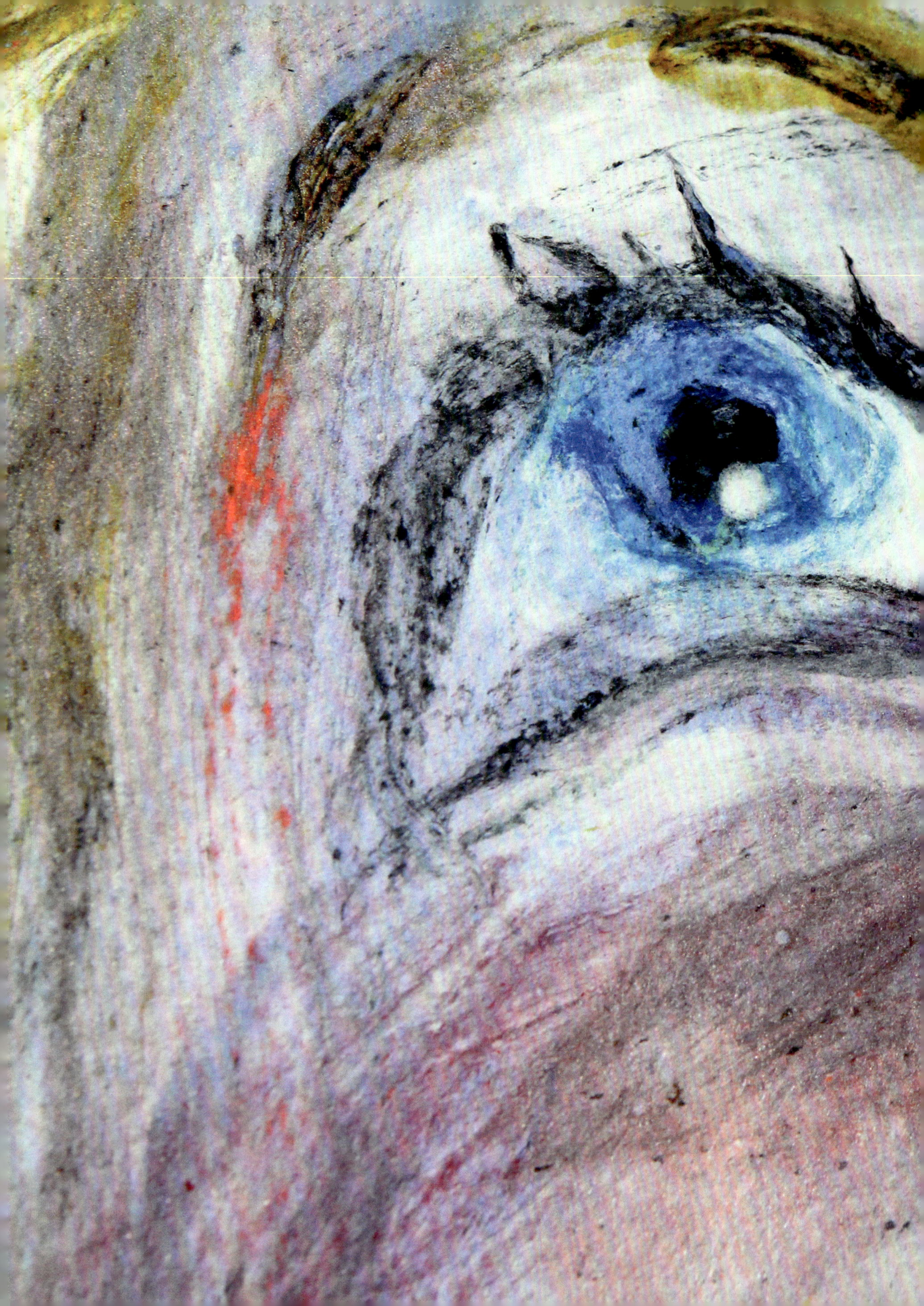

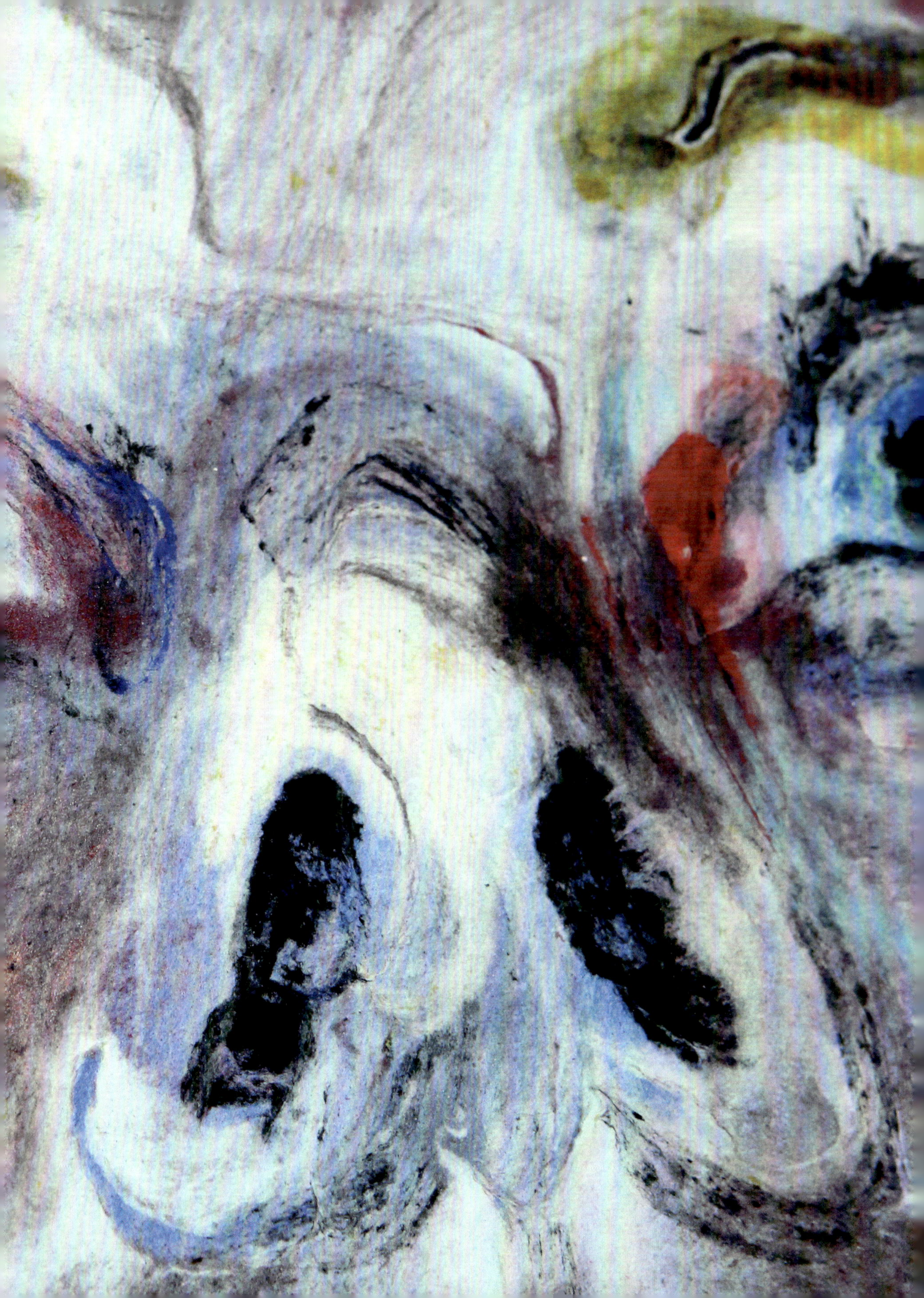

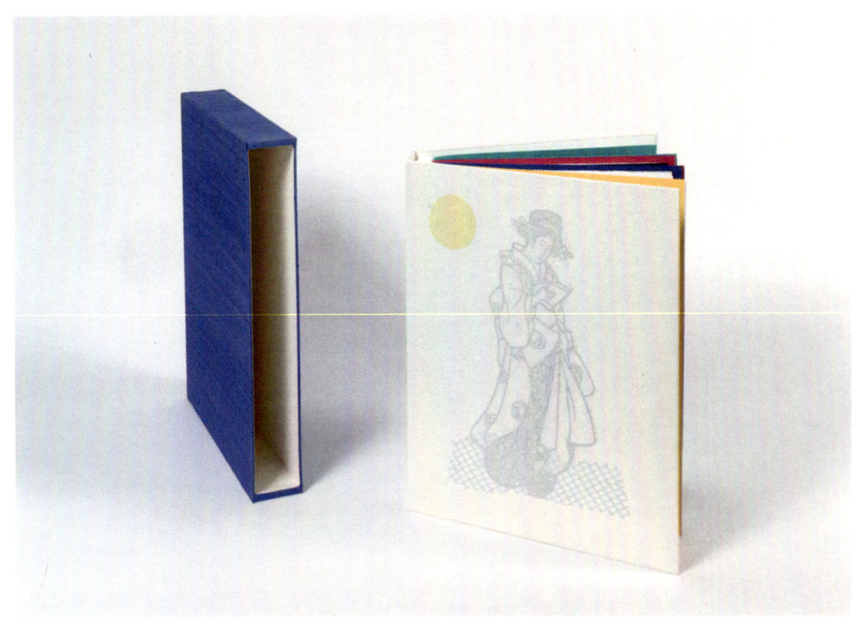

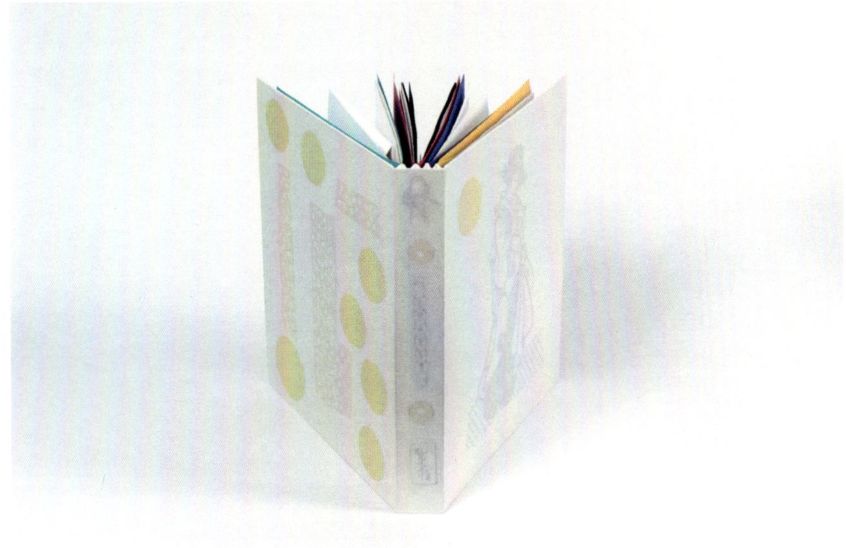

Jane Hammond

Be Zany, Poised Harpists/Be Blue, Little Sparrows, 2002 (detail on following spread)
Artist book with poems by Raphael Rubinstein
Raw Indian silk, letterpress, digital prints, photocopies, vintage postage stamps, hand-coloring, rubber stamping, and collage on a variety of archival materials in a slipcase of raw Indian silk
13 ¼ × 10 ½ × 2 in. (33.7 × 26.7 × 5.1 cm)
Copublished by Dieu Donné Press, New York and Dieu Donné, New York
Courtesy of the artist and Dieu Donné, New York

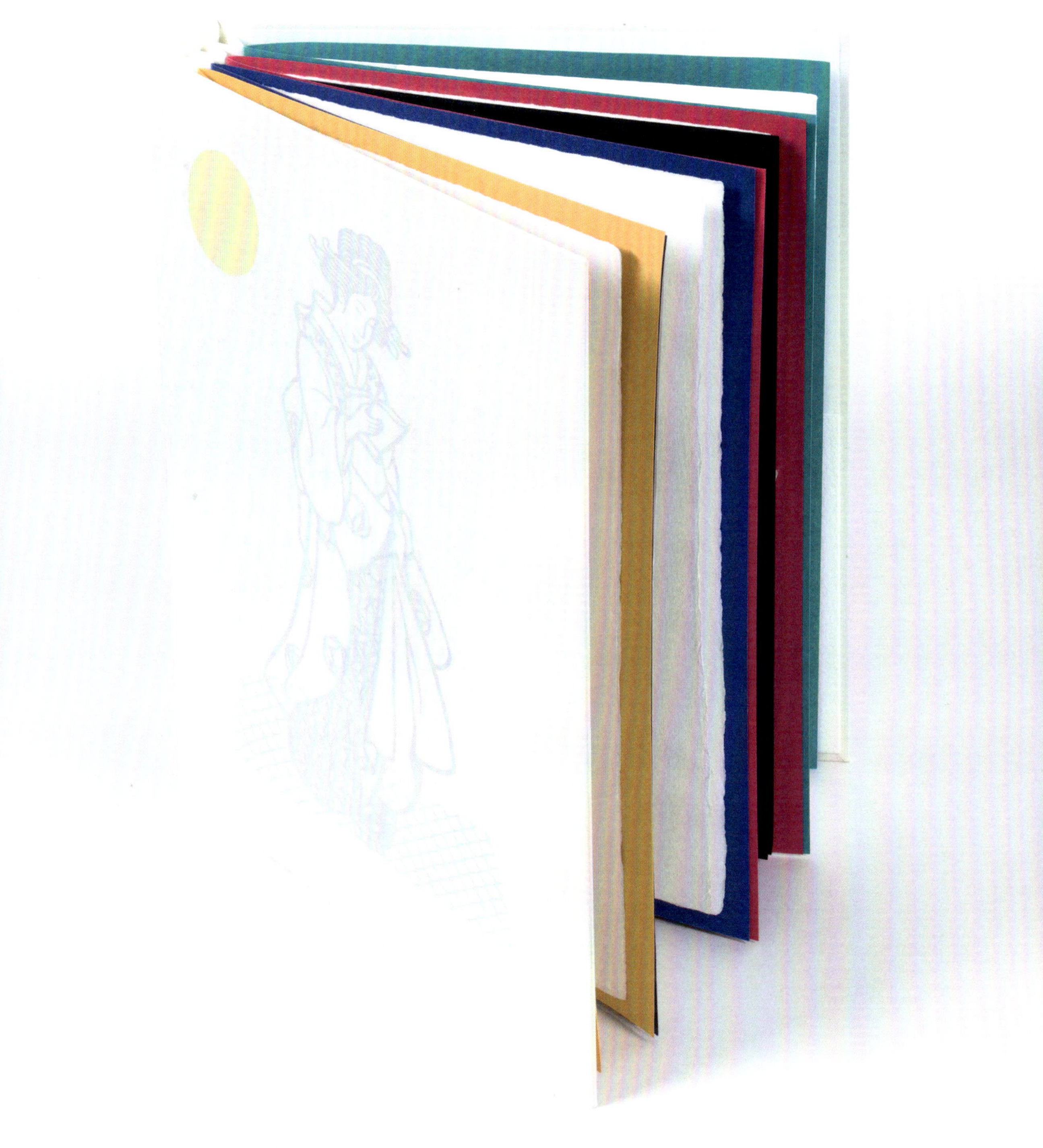

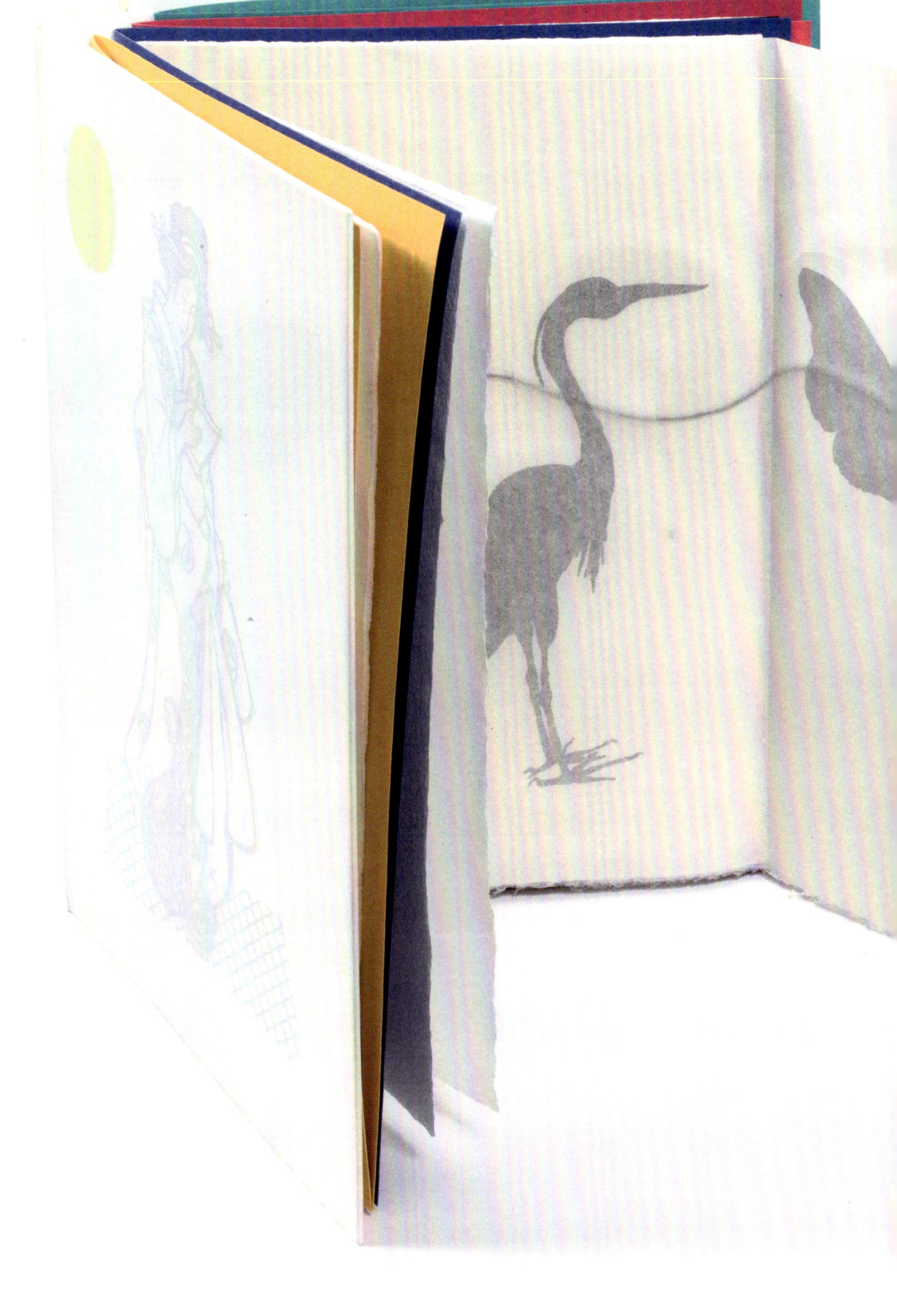

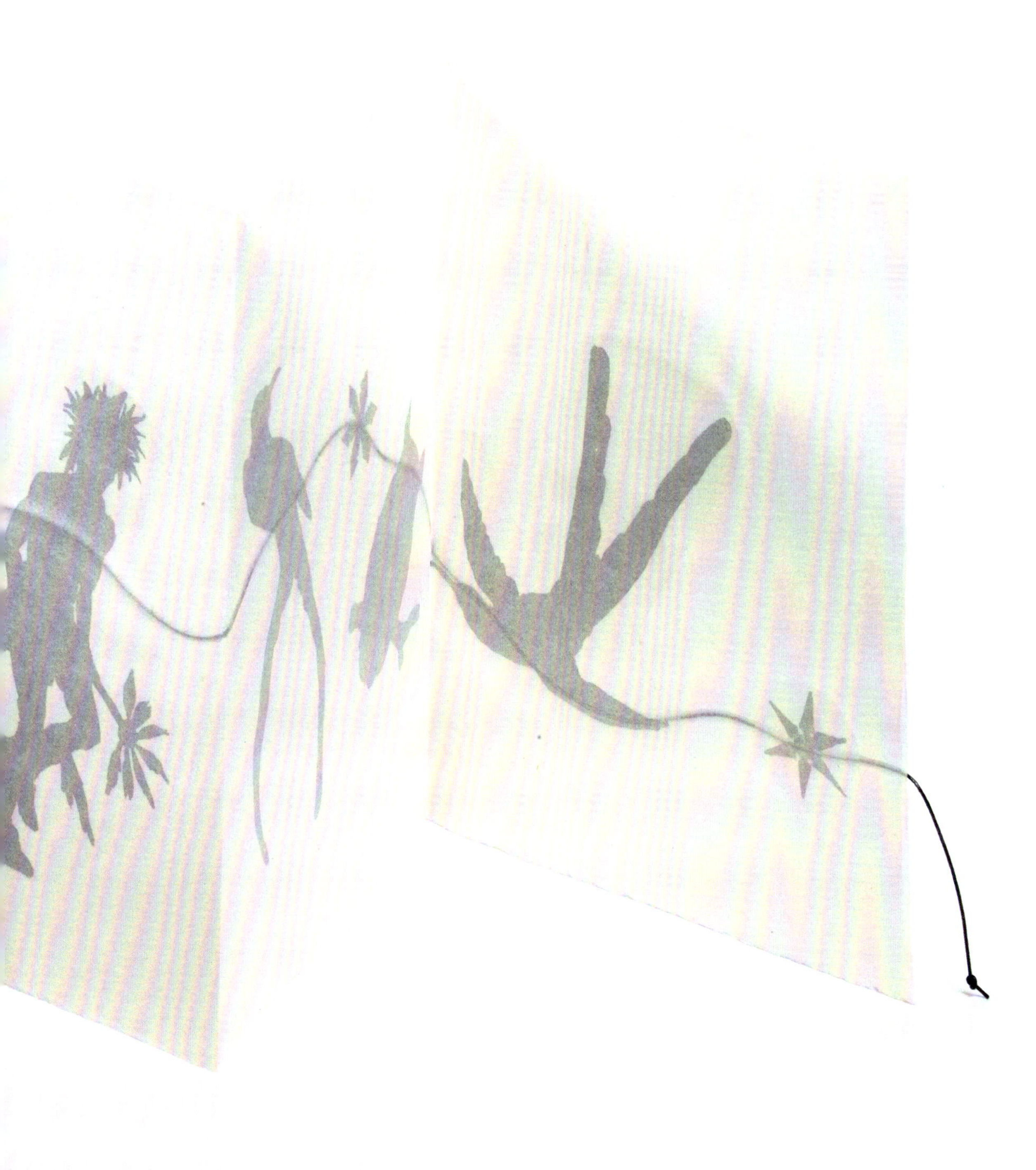

Jim Hodges

In Wet III, 2010 (detail on following spread)
Pigmented and cast cotton
41 ⅜ × 19 ¾ × 1 in. (105.1 × 50.2 × 2.5 cm)
Courtesy of the artist and Dieu Donné, New York

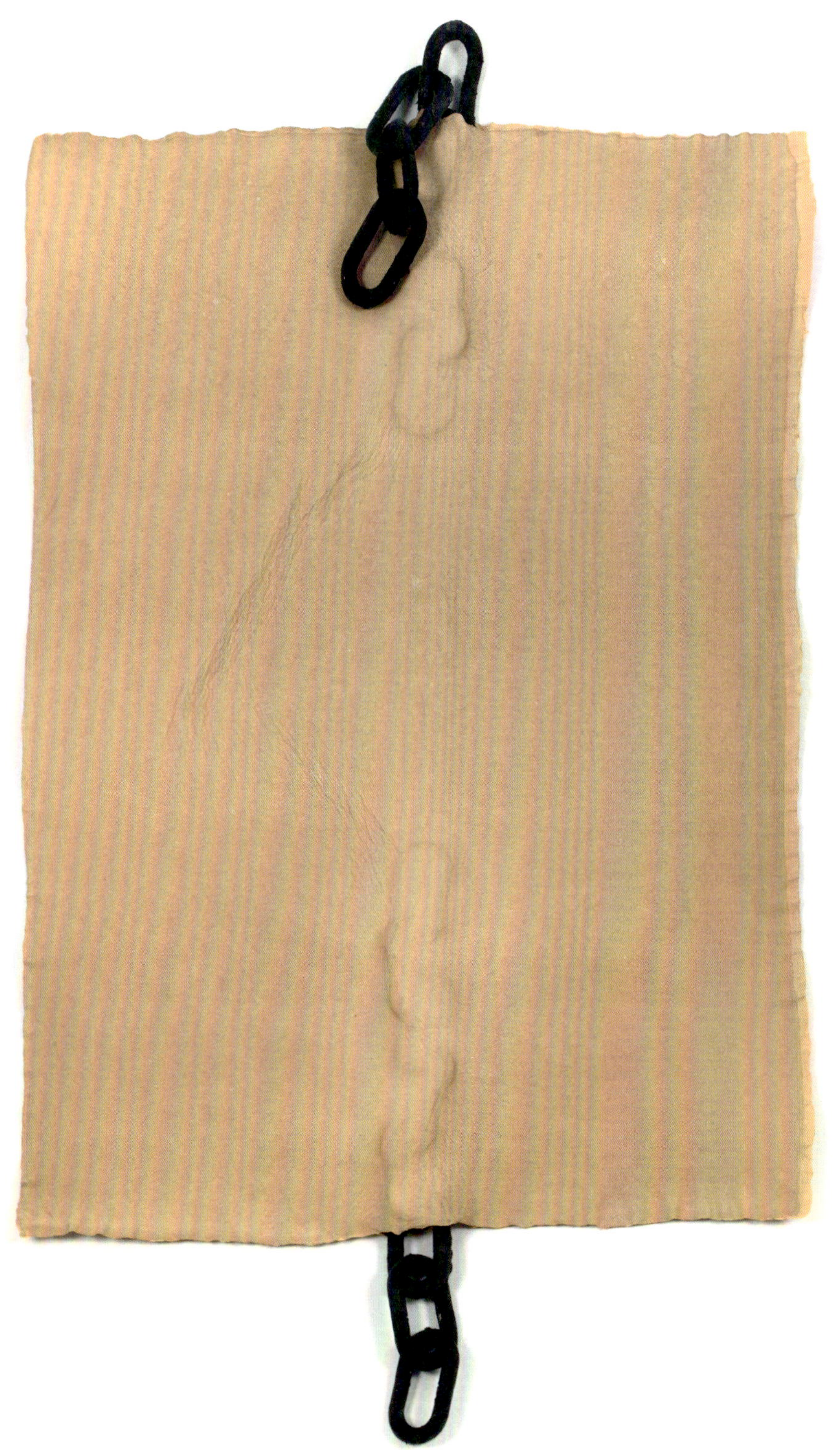

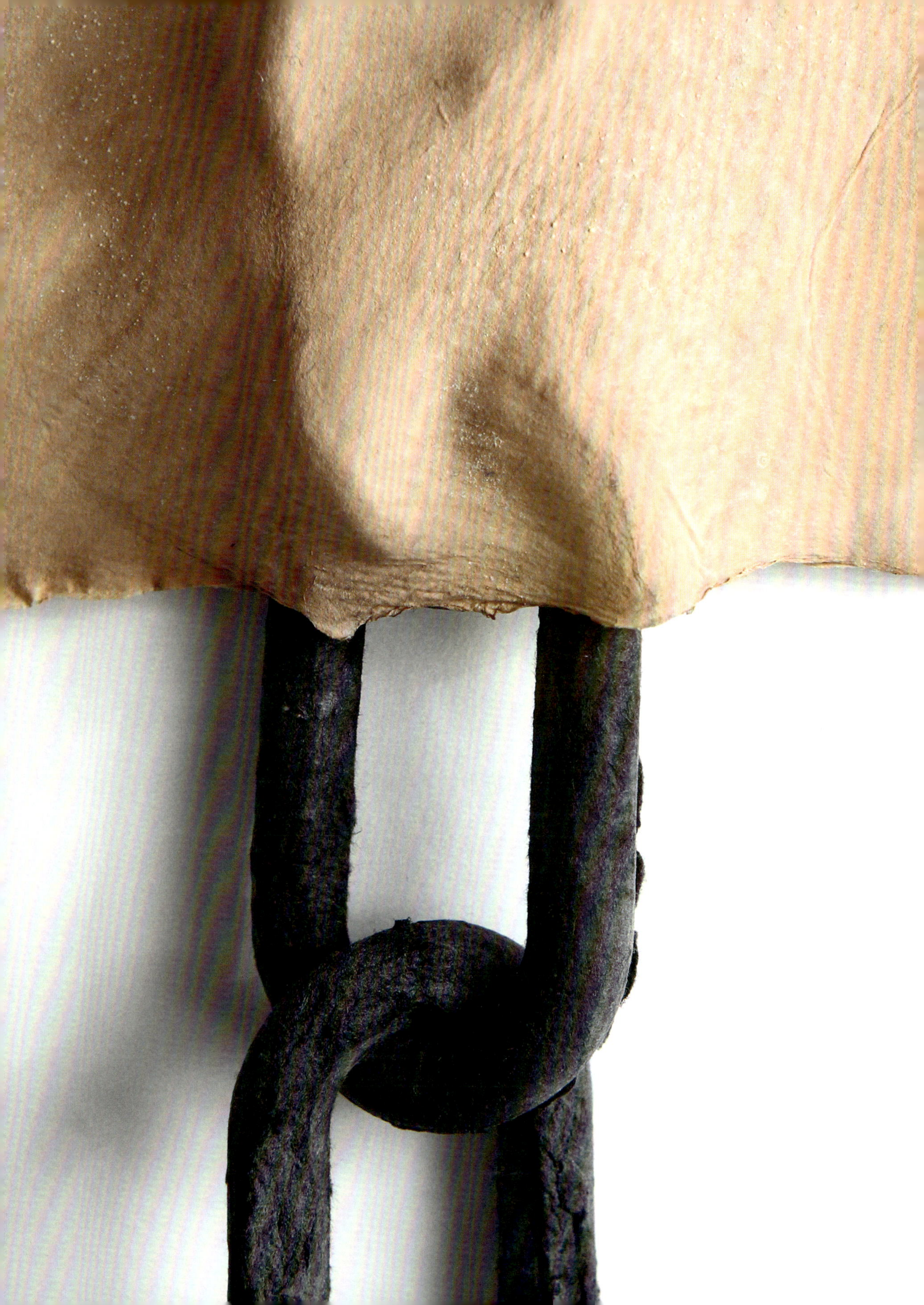

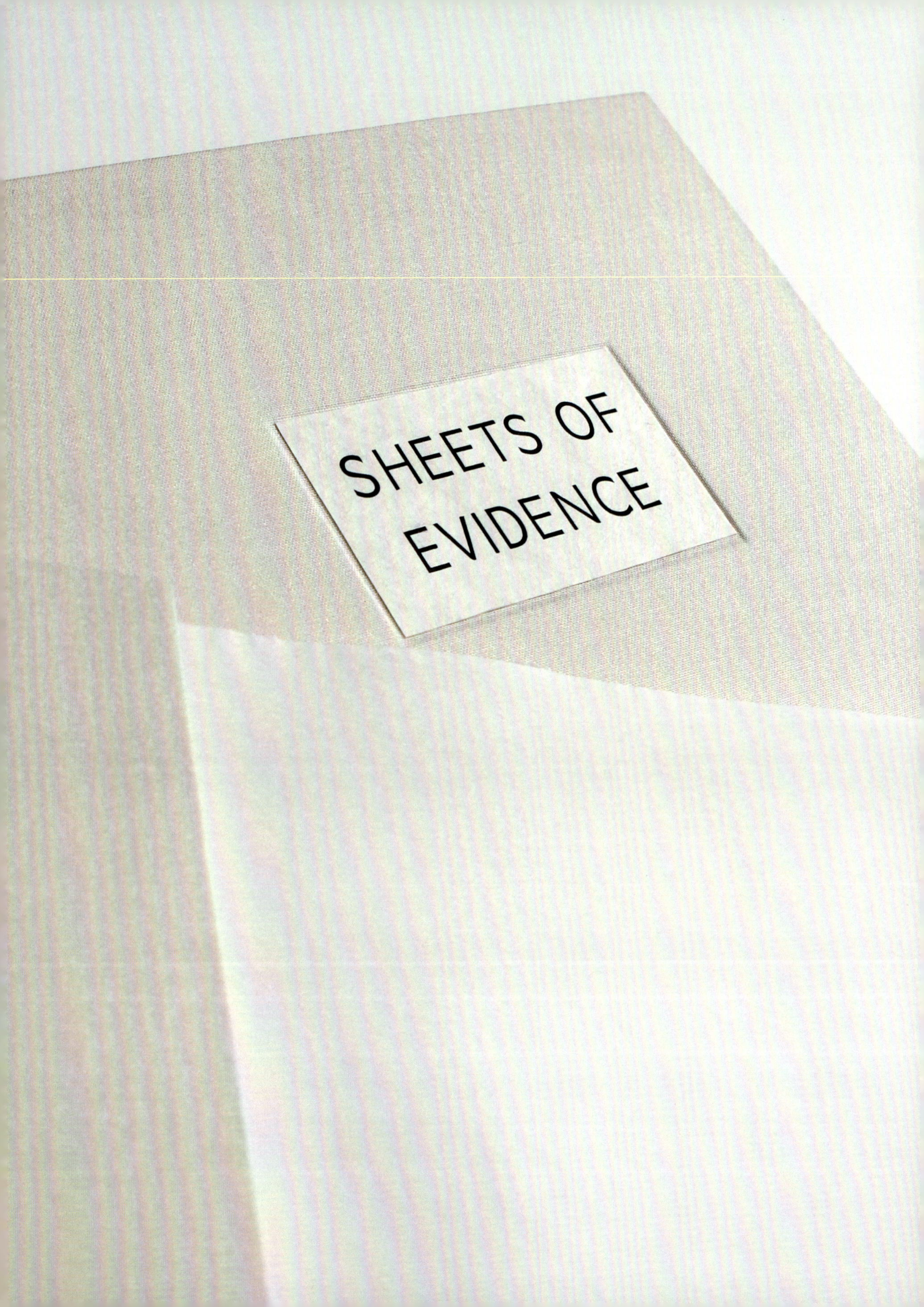

SHEETS OF
EVIDENCE

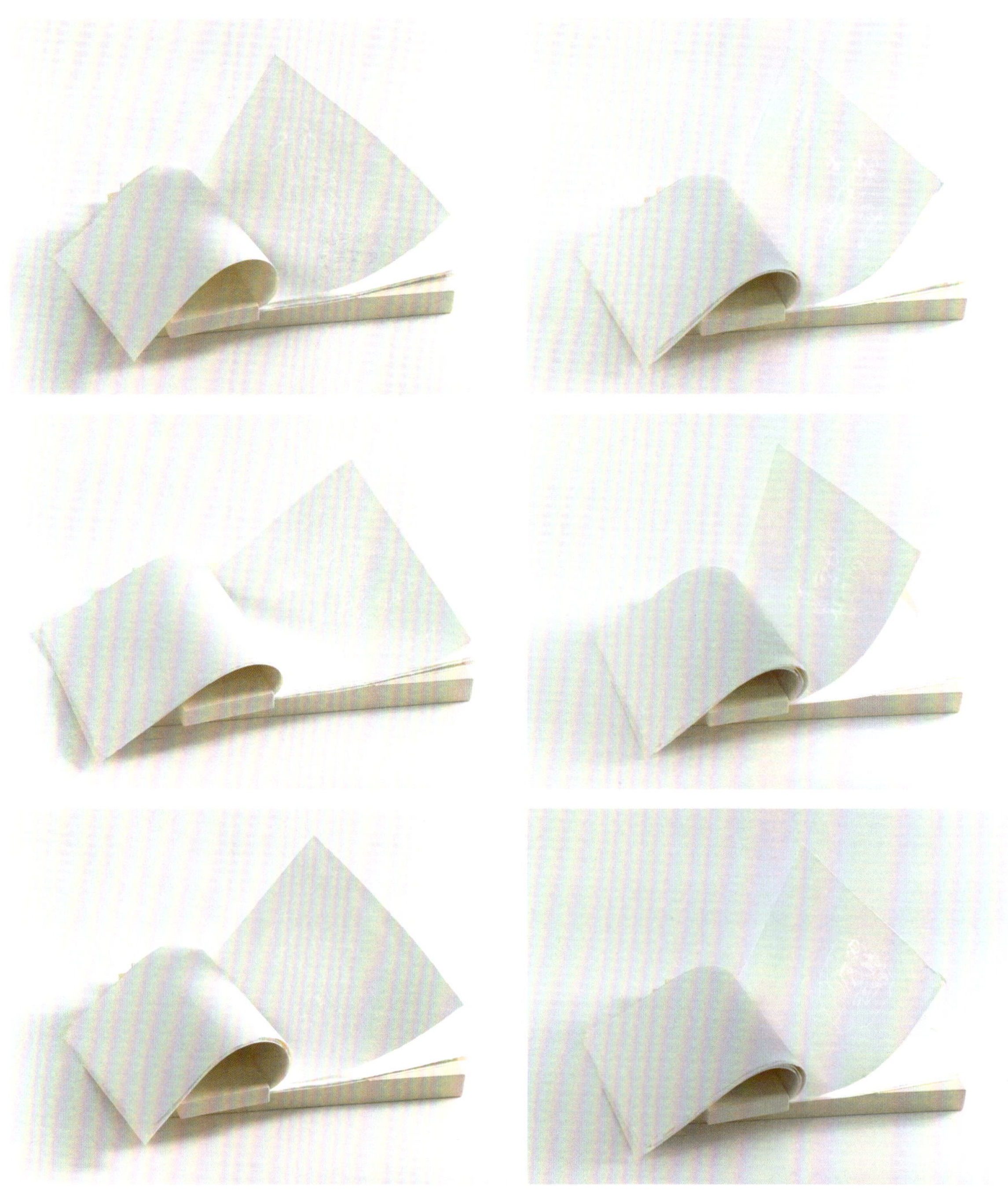

William Kentridge

Sheets of Evidence, 2009 (details on following spread)
Artist book of eighteen watermarked drawings
12 ⅝ × 15 × 1 ¼ in. (32.1 × 38.1 × 3.2 cm)
Copublished by Dieu Donné Press, New York and Dieu Donné, New York
Courtesy of the artist and Dieu Donné, New York

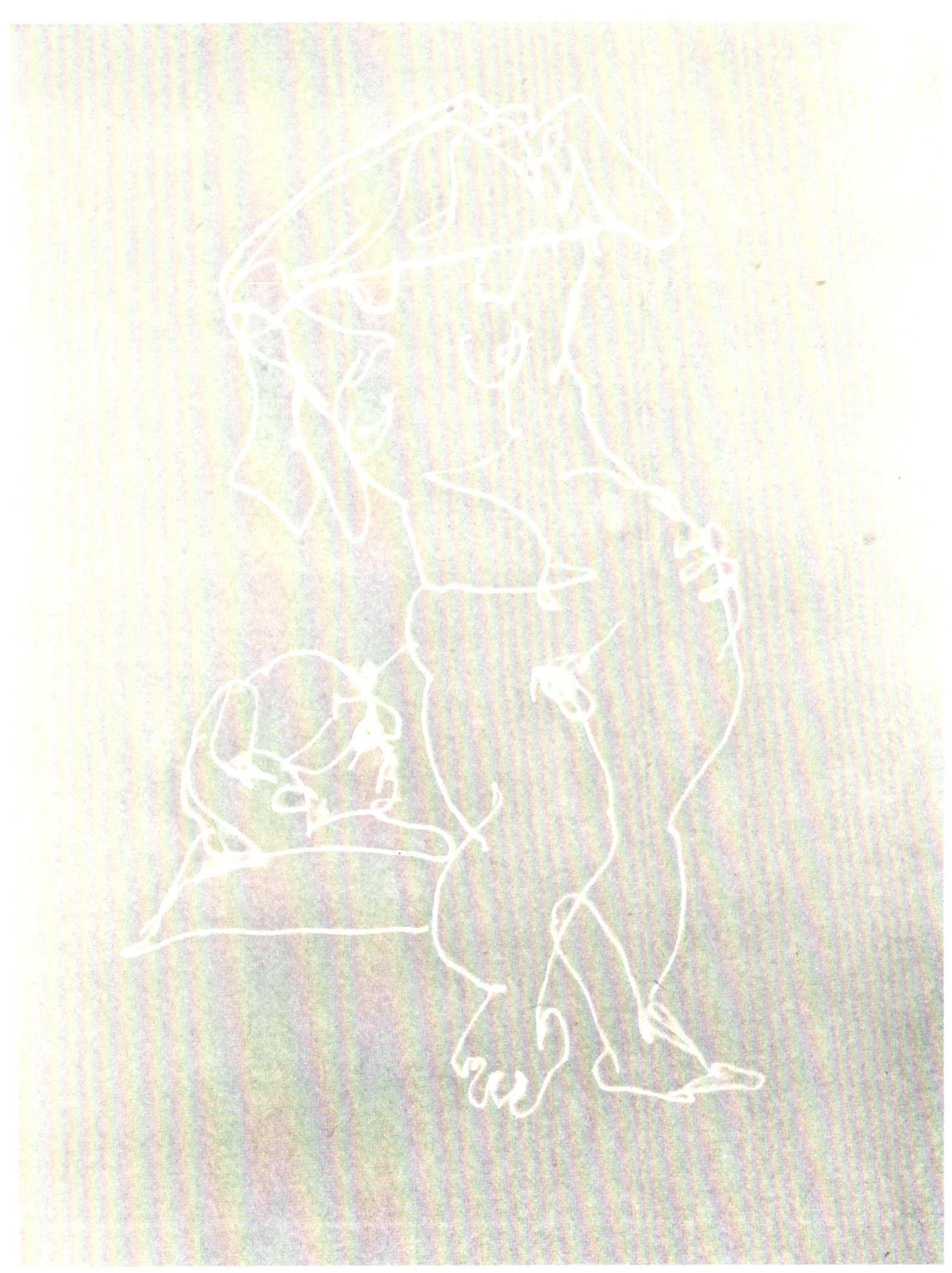

DINNERS FOR

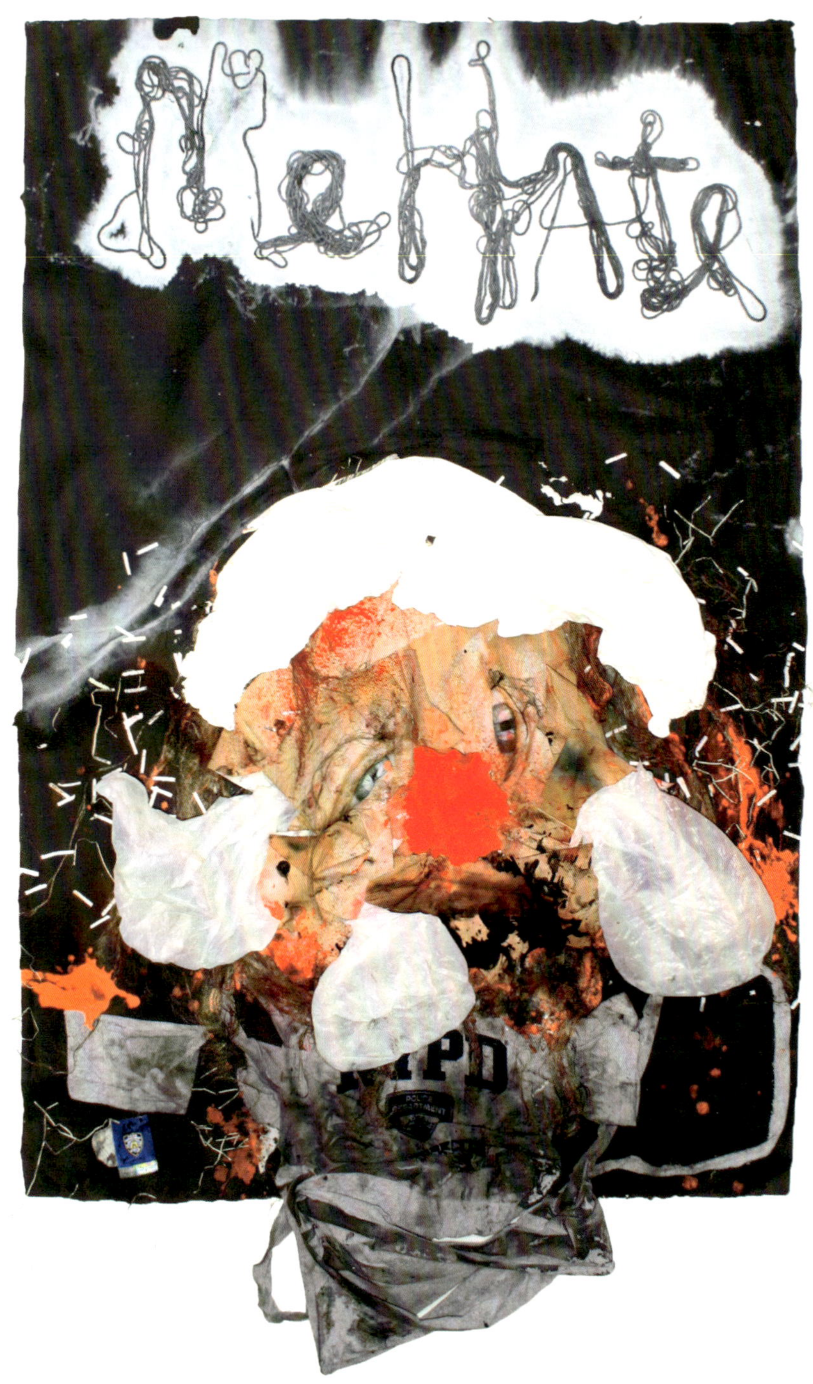

Jon Kessler

Me Hate, 2008
Pigment, paper pulp, mirror, yarn, horsehair, cotton, plastic bags, U.S. currency, and digital print on handmade paper
60 × 38 × 1 in. (152.4 × 96.5 × 2.5 cm)
Courtesy of the artist and Salon 94, New York

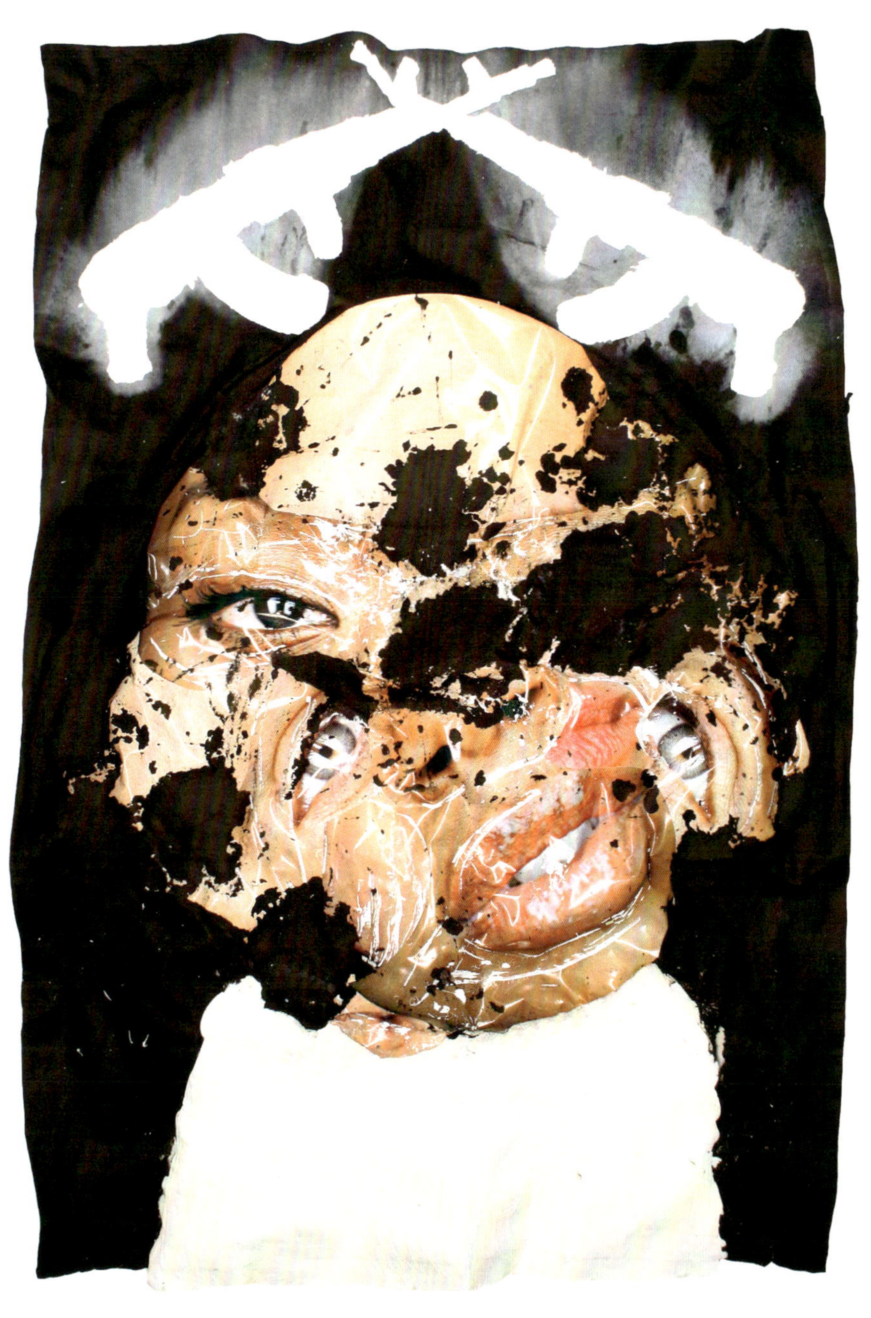

Suicide Bomber #1, 2008
Pigment, paper pulp, and digital print on handmade paper
55 × 36 × 1 in. (139.7 × 91.4 × 2.5 cm)
Courtesy of the artist and Salon 94, New York

Glenn Ligon

Self-Portrait at Eleven Years Old, 2004 (detail on following spread)
Cotton base sheet with stenciled linen pulp painting
35 5/8 × 30 in. (90.5 × 76.2 cm)
Courtesy of the artist and Dieu Donné, New York

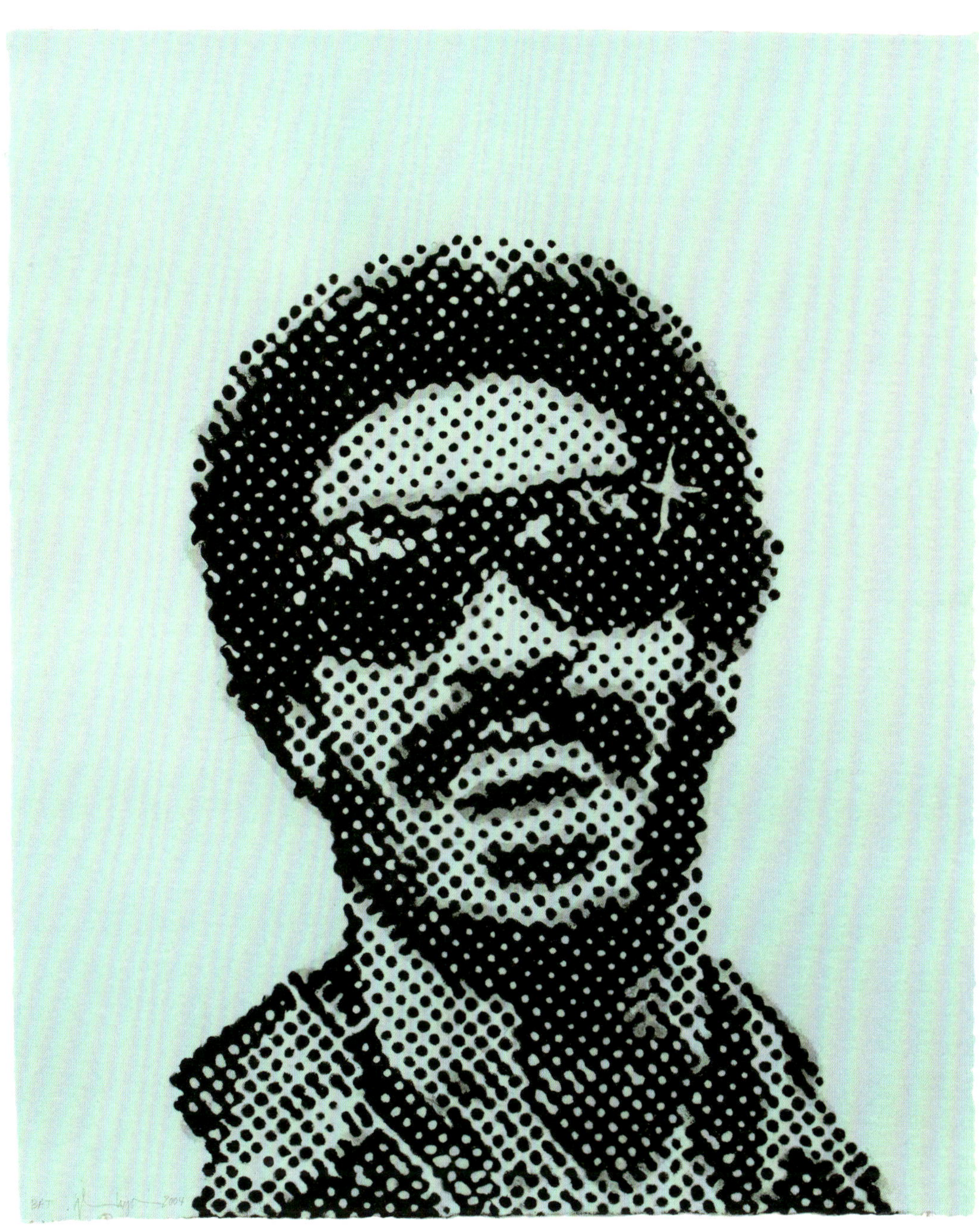

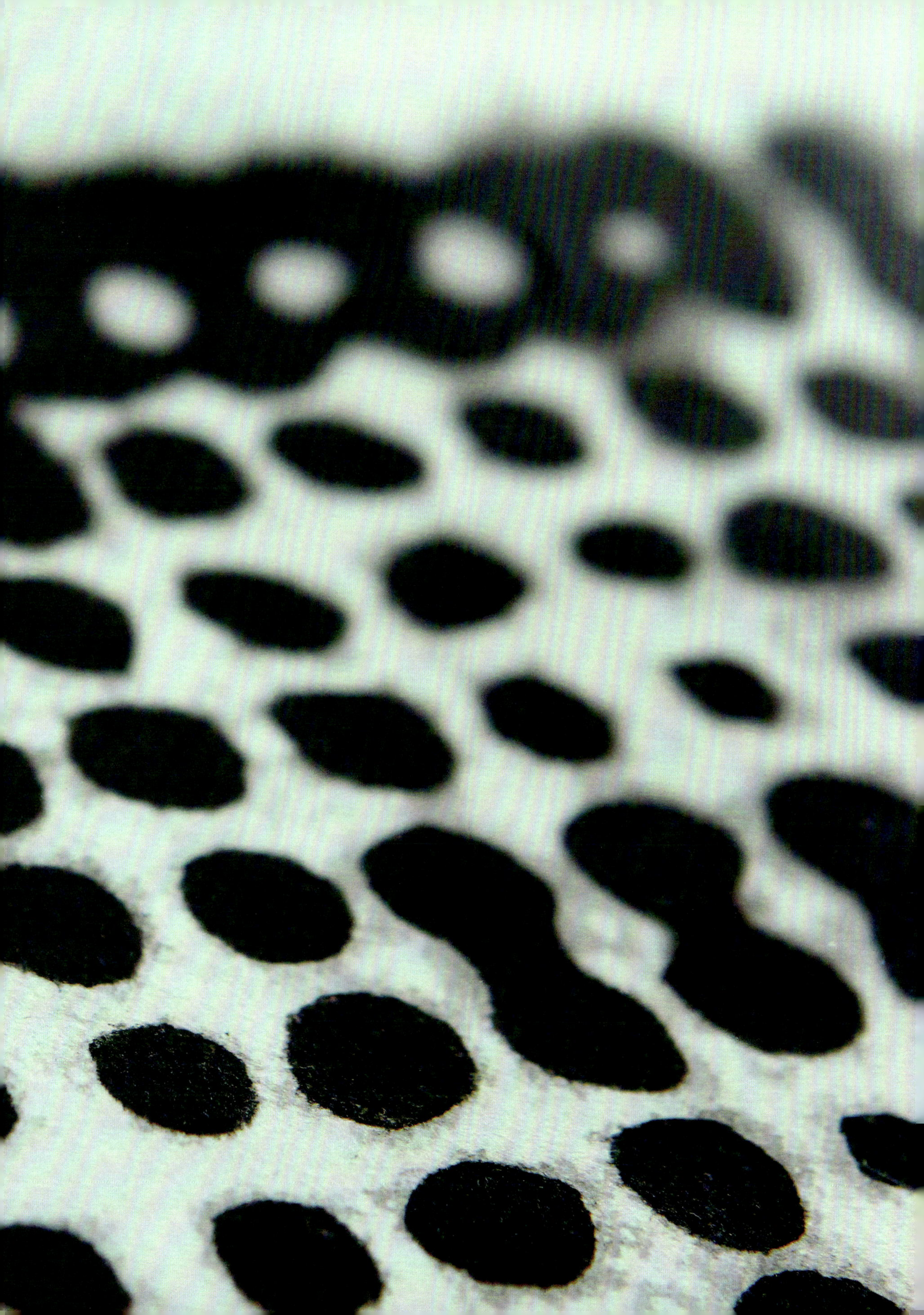

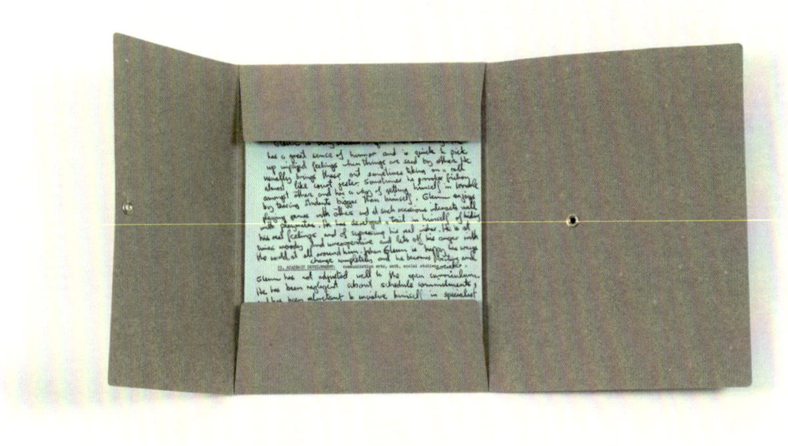

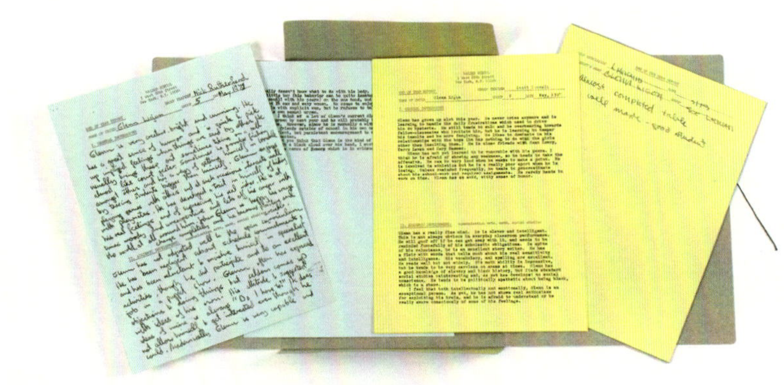

Glenn Ligon

End of Year Reports, 2003
Photocopy and screenprint on eight sheets of pigmented cotton and abaca paper in a handmade cotton paper portfolio
11 ½ × 9 ⅛ in. (29.2 × 23.2 cm)
Courtesy of the artist and Dieu Donné, New York

...ing games with others ...
... playmates. He has developed ...
real feelings and of ignorance ...
...es moody and uncooperative ...
...o world, at all around him. ...
change complete...

II. ACADEMIC DEVELOPMENT:

Glenn has not adjusted
He has been negligent
and has been reluctant
activities, though he
job in a puppet
objections to doing

Suzanne McClelland

Seven from "Internal Affairs," 2015 (detail on following spread)
Pigmented linen pulp paint on abaca and cotton handmade paper with handmade paper collage and silkscreened ink
40 ⅛ × 60 ⅜ in. (101.9 × 153.4 cm)
Courtesy of the artist, TEAM Gallery, New York, and Dieu Donné, New York

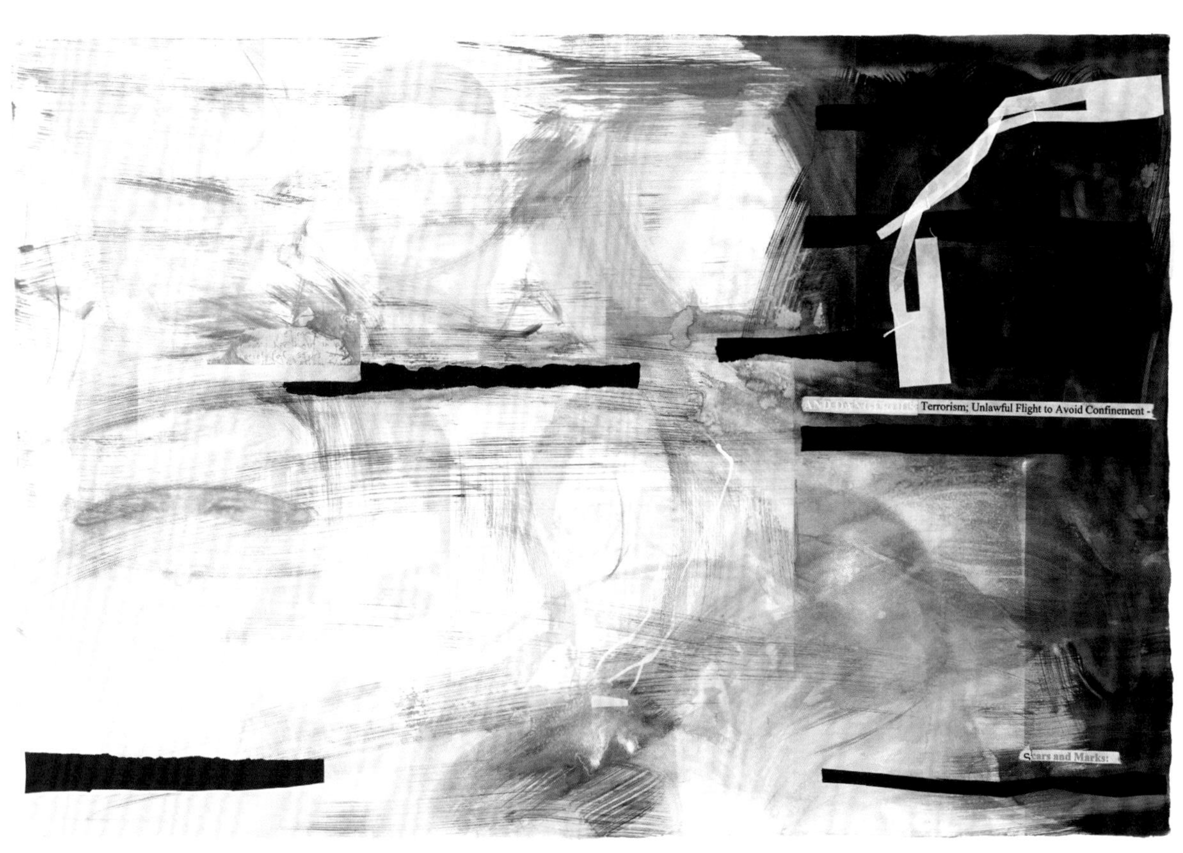
Terrorism; Unlawful Flight to Avoid Confinement -
Scars and Marks:

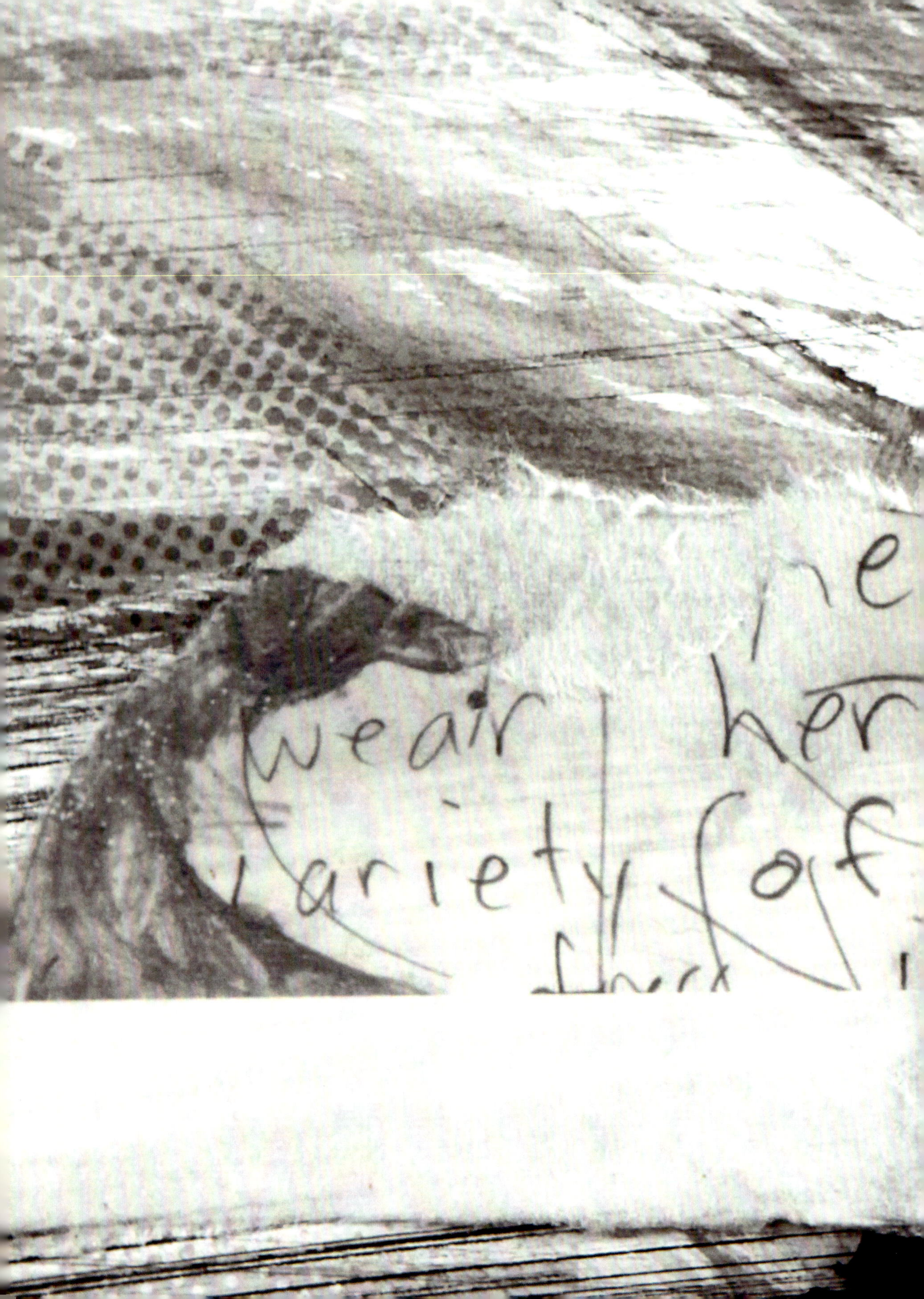
he
weair her
ariety of

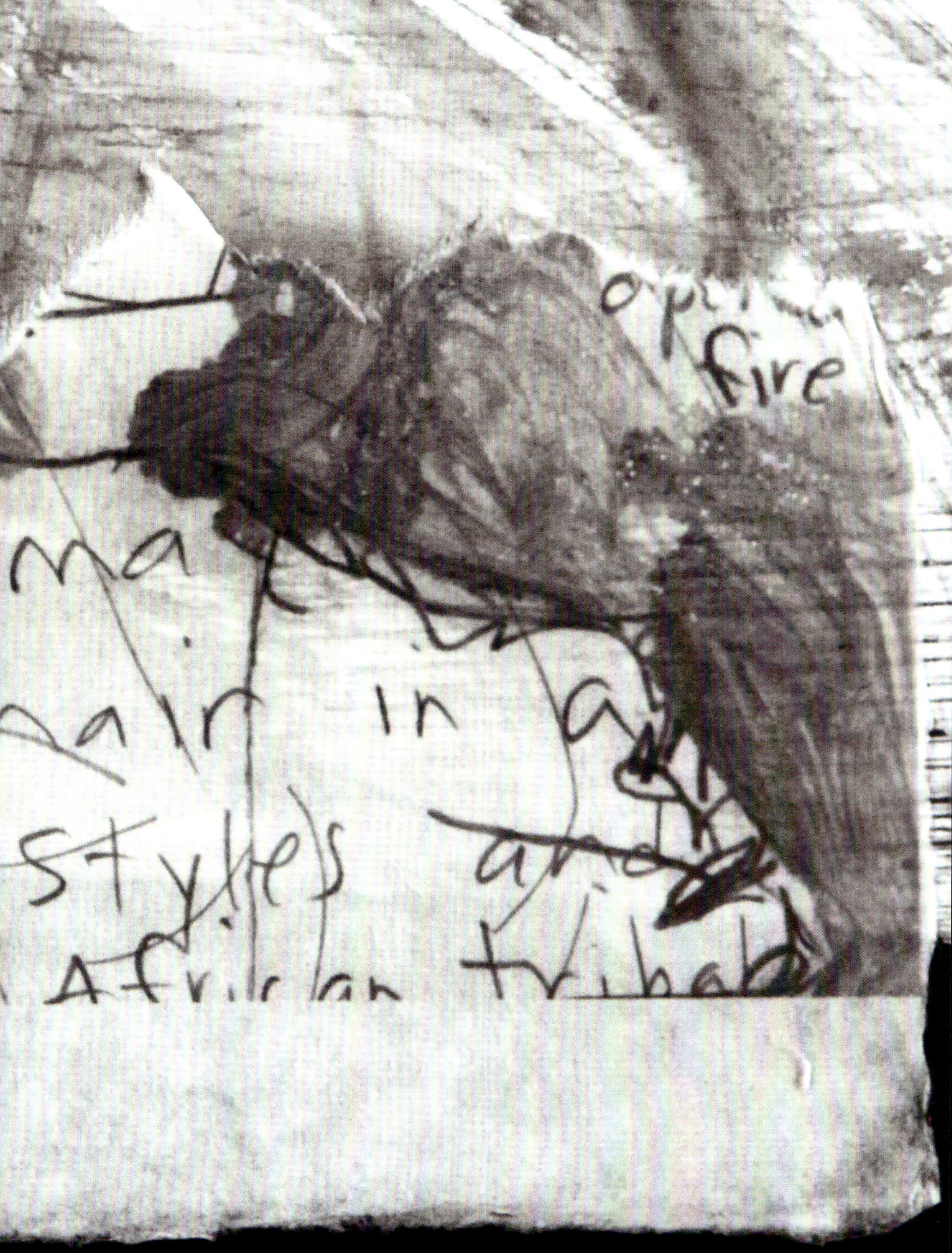

fire
ma
air in
styles
African

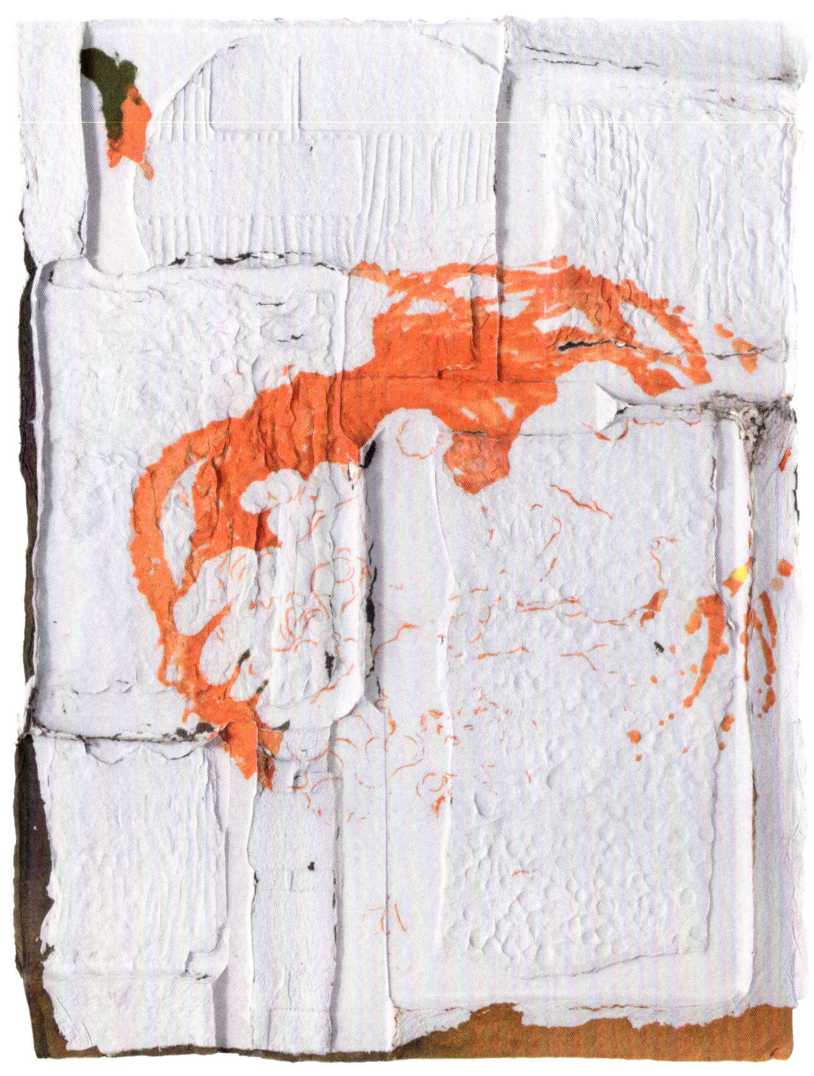

Arlene Shechet

Parallel Play: Swivel, 2012
Pigment and stenciled linen pulp on abaca base sheet
39 ⅛ × 31 × 1 in. (99.4 × 78.7 × 2.5 cm)
Courtesy of the artist and Dieu Donné, New York

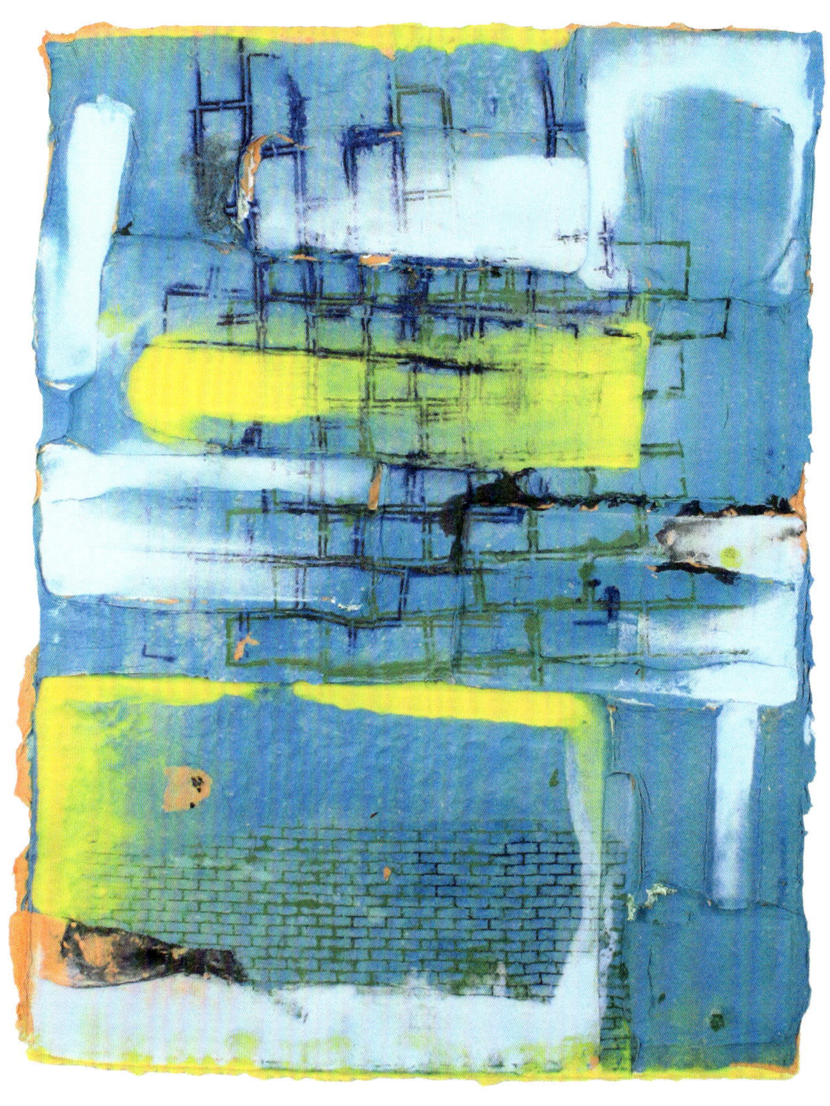

Parallel Play: Anymore, 2012 (detail on following spread)
Stenciled and painted linen pulp on cast cotton base sheet
40 3/8 × 30 5/8 × 1 in. (102.6 × 77.8 × 2.5 cm)
Courtesy of the artist

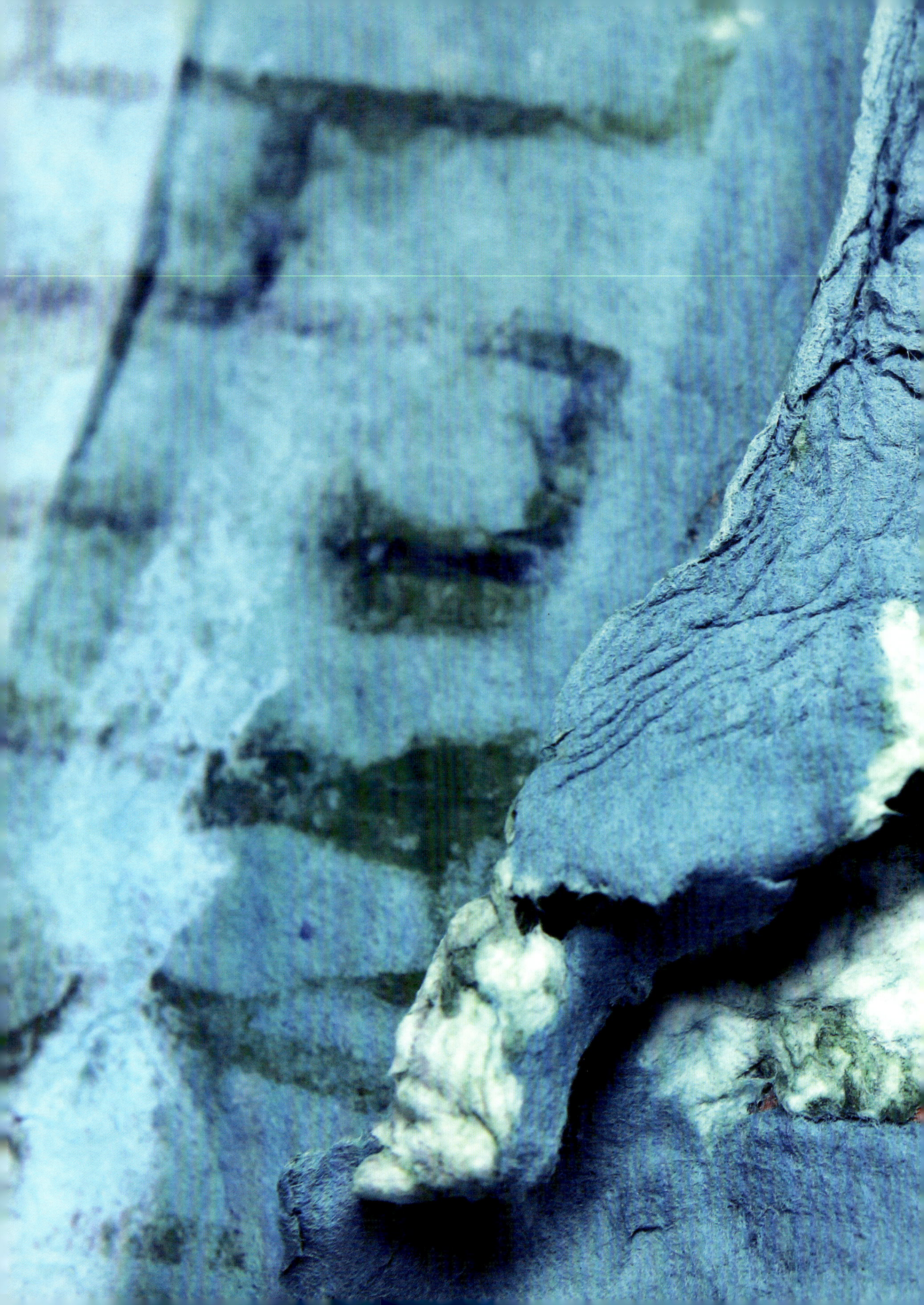

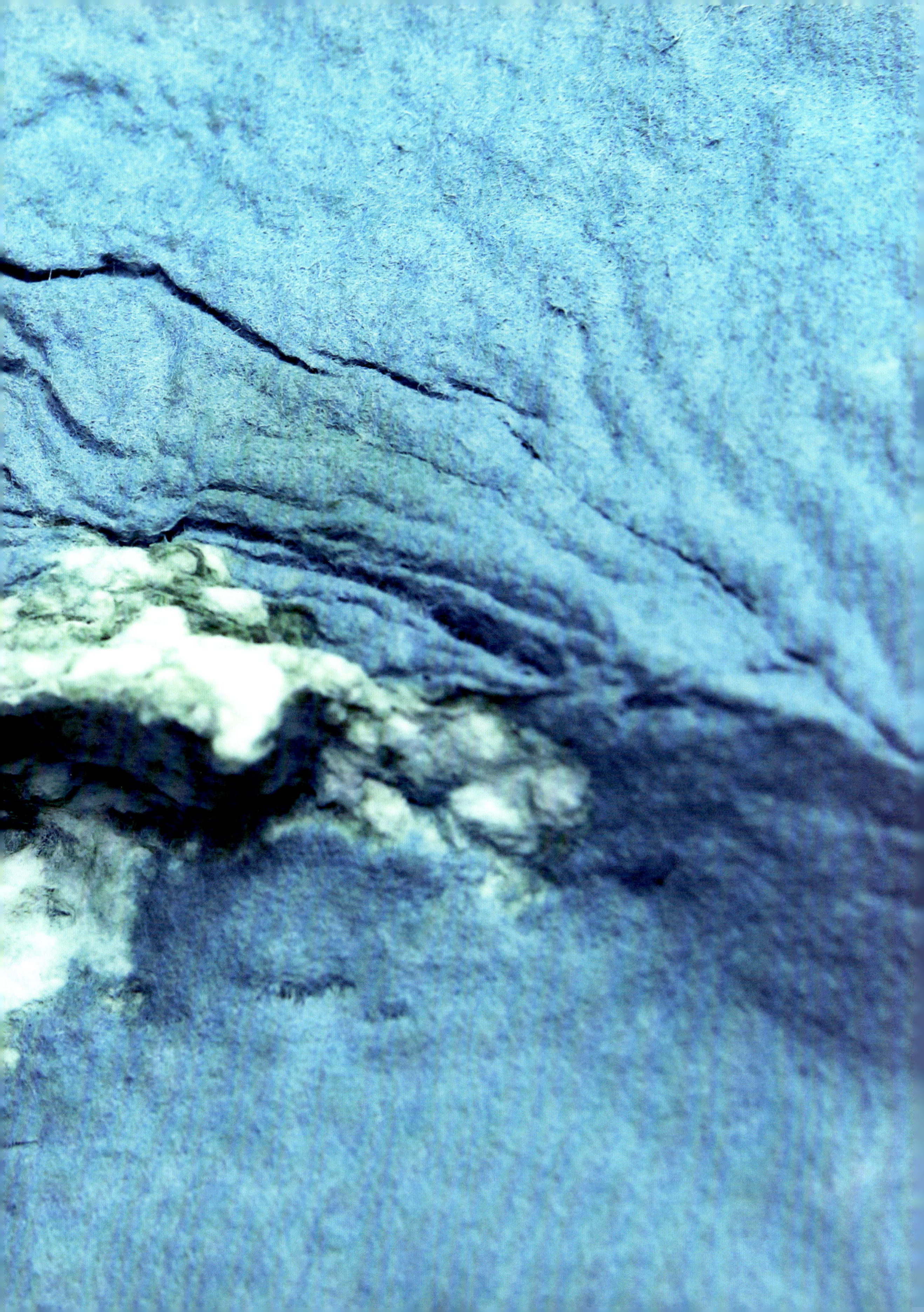

Kate Shepherd

Great Cousin Mary, 2011
Pigmented linen blowout on pigmented linen cotton base sheet
35 ⅜ × 24 ⅜ (89.9 × 61.9 cm)
Courtesy of the artist and Dieu Donné, New York

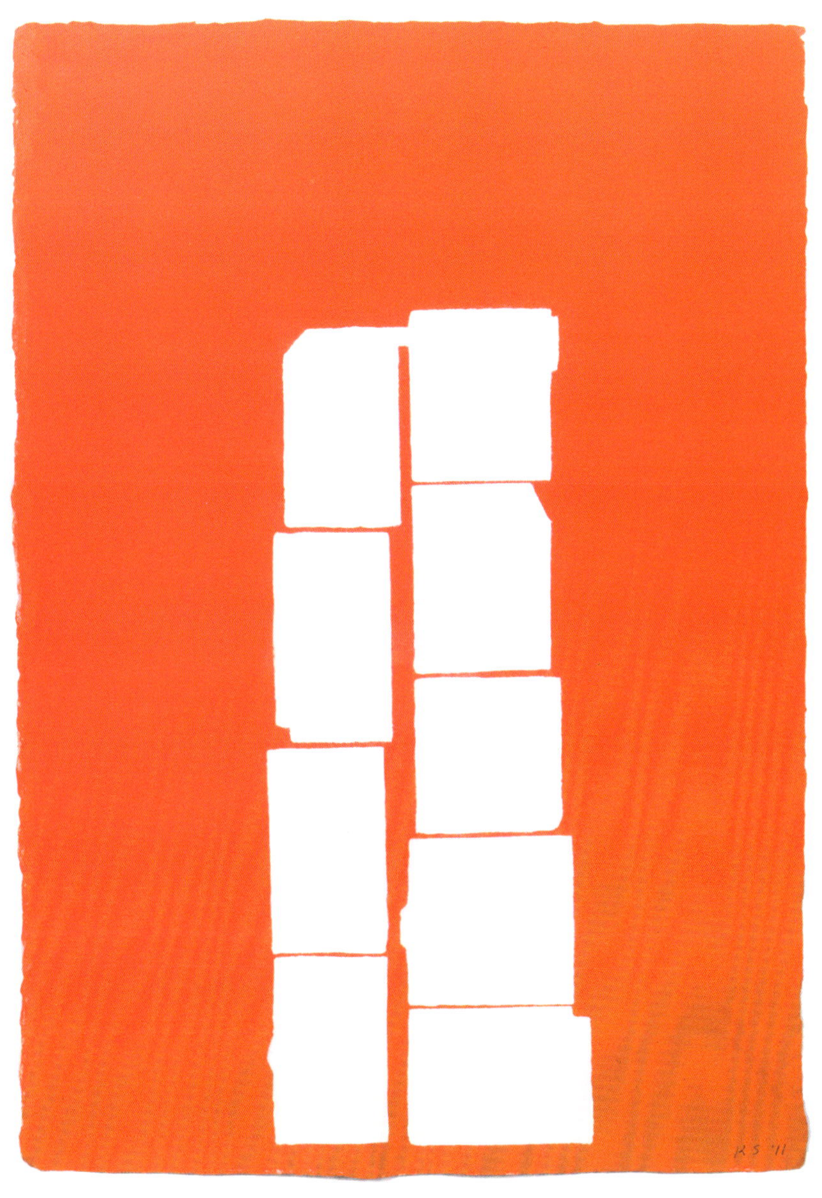

Dark Orange White Stacks, Notched (4, 5), 2011
Pigmented linen blowout on pigmented linen cotton base sheet
30 ⅜ × 21 ⅜ in. (77.2 × 54.3 cm)
Courtesy of the artist and Dieu Donné, New York

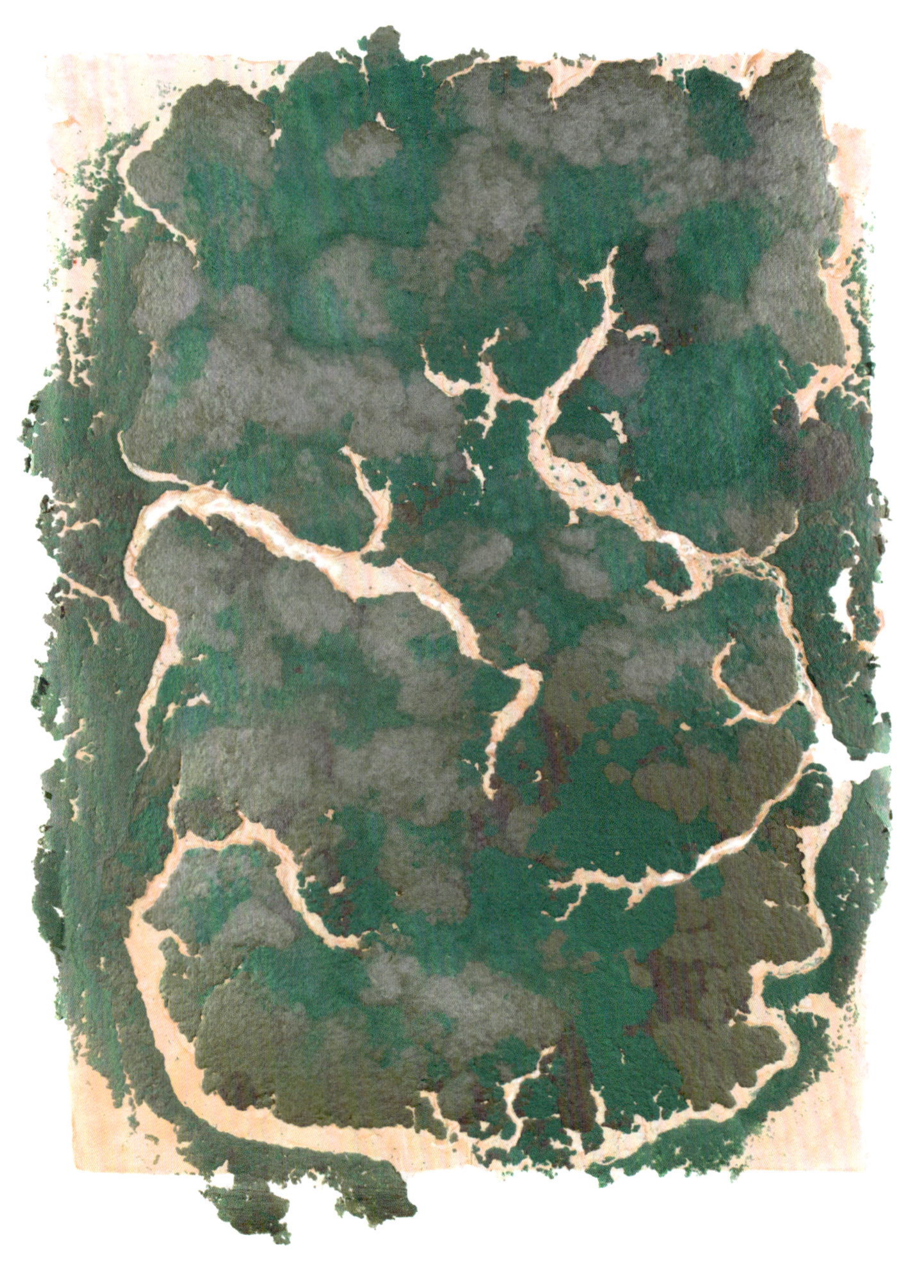

Molly Smith

Swamp, 2012 (detail on pp. 38–39)
Handmade cotton, abaca, linen, and recycled paper
43 ½ × 32 in. (110.5 × 81.3 cm)
Courtesy of the artist and Dieu Donné, New York

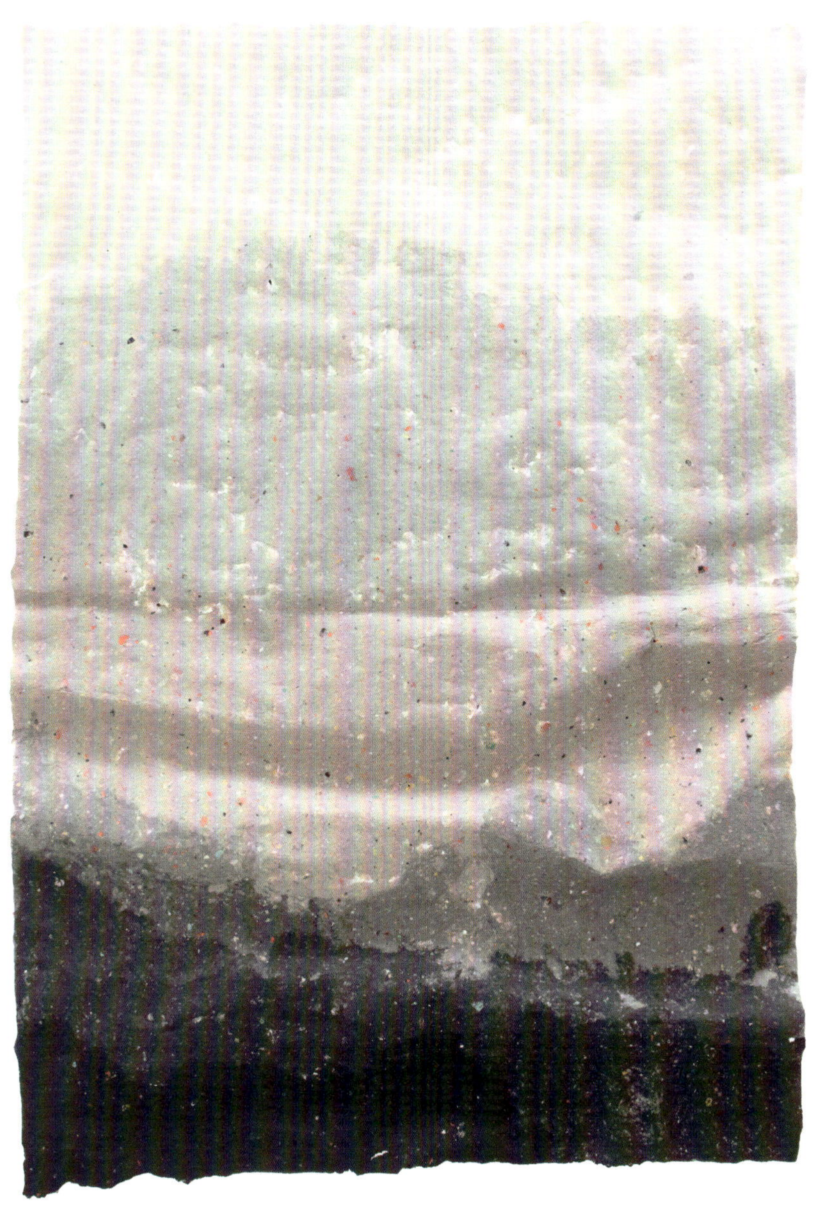

Dust, 2012 (detail on following spread)
Handmade cotton, abaca, linen, and recycled paper
58 ¼ × 39 ⅝ in. (147.8 × 100.6 cm)
Courtesy of the artist and Dieu Donné, New York

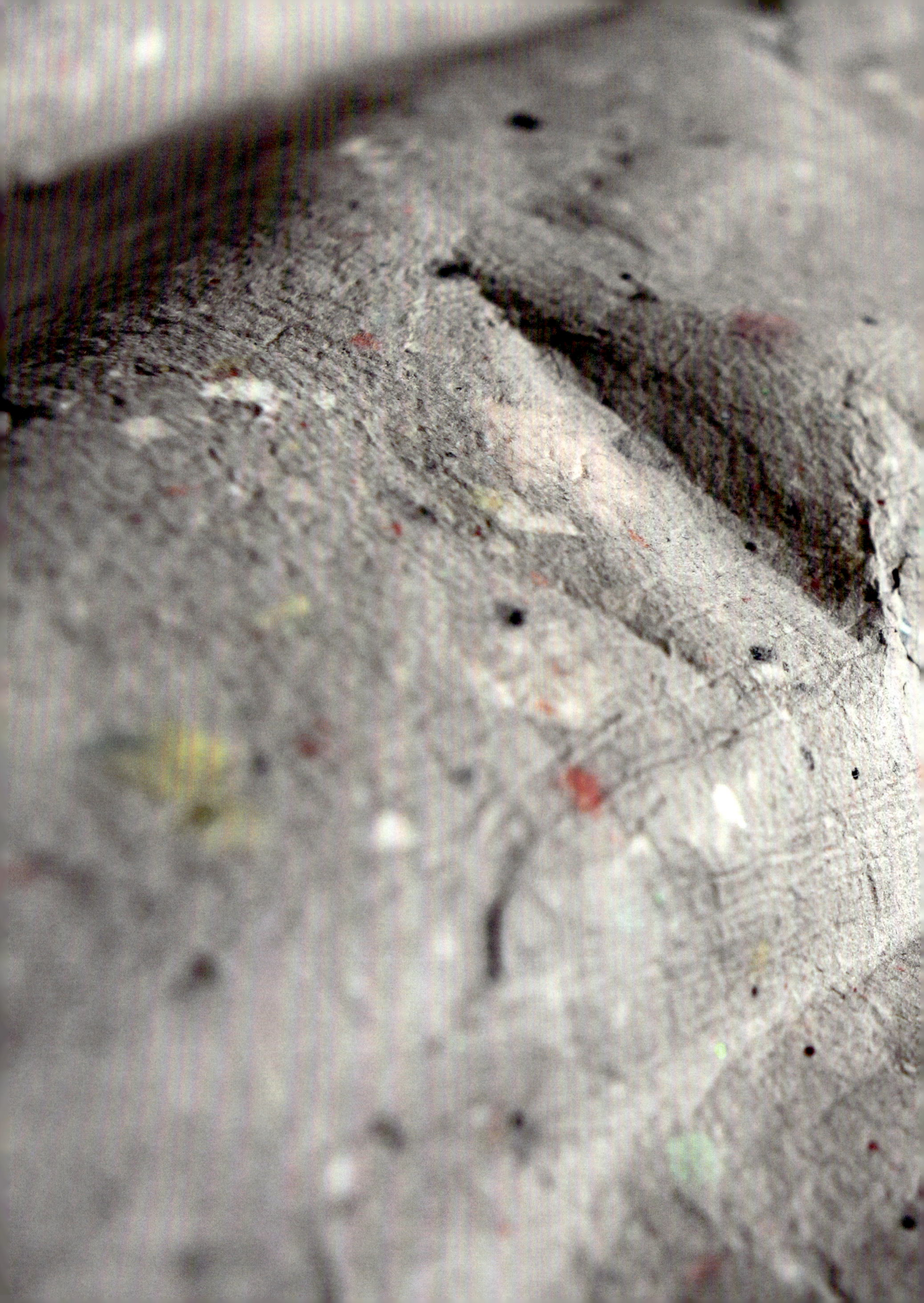

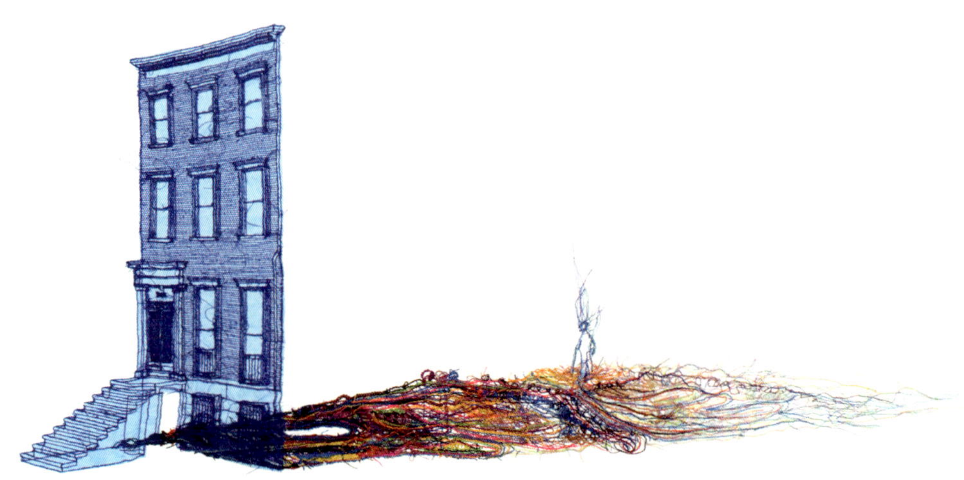

Do Ho Suh

Blueprint, 2013
Thread, cotton, and methylcellulose
30 × 40 in. (76.2 × 101.6 cm)
Collection of Miyoung Lee and Neil Simpkins, New York

Opposite: *Staircase*, 2013 (detail on following spread)
Thread, cotton, and methylcellulose
14 ¼ × 11 ⅜ in. (36.2 × 28.9 cm)
Courtesy of the artist and Dieu Donné, New York

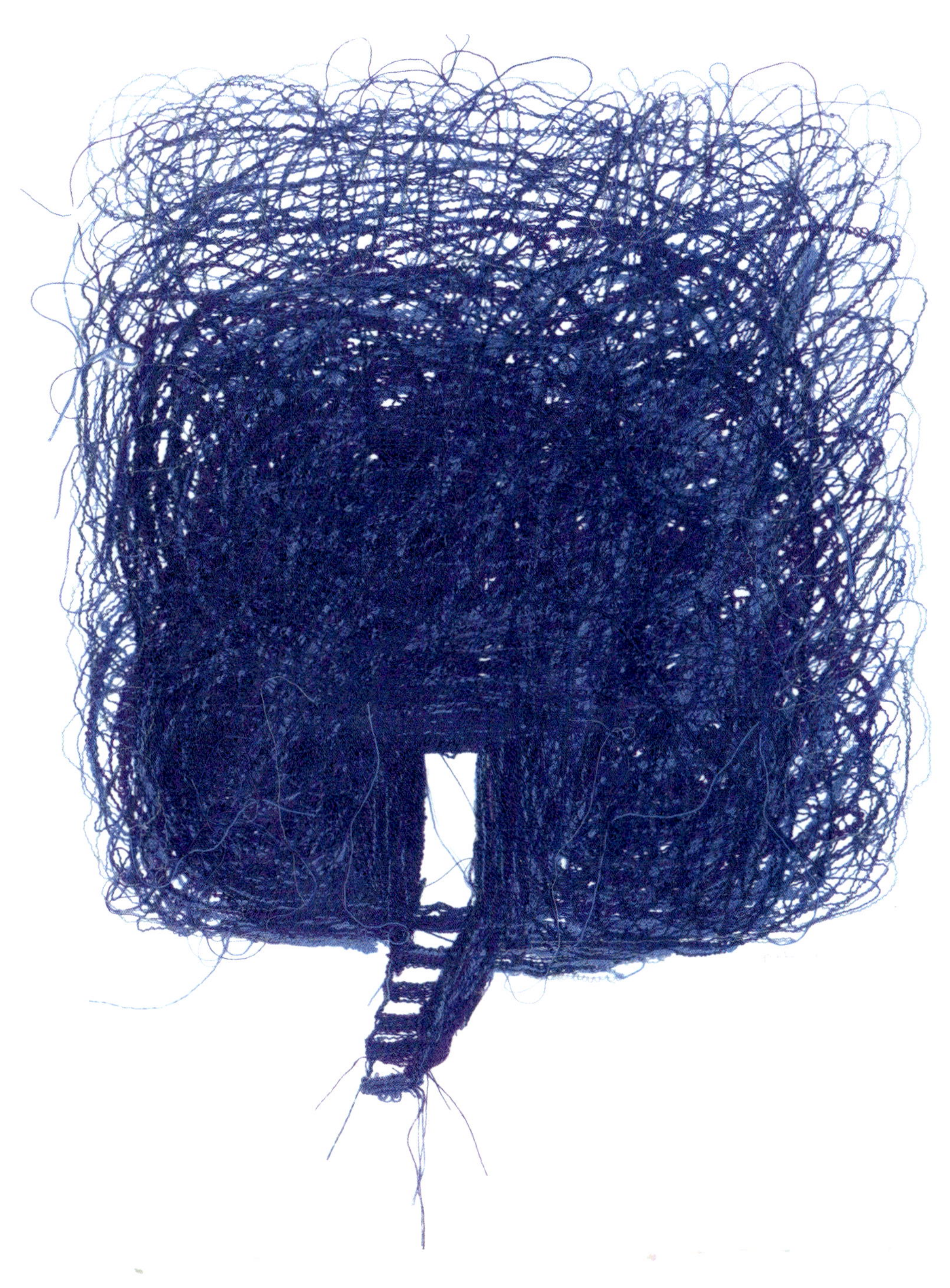

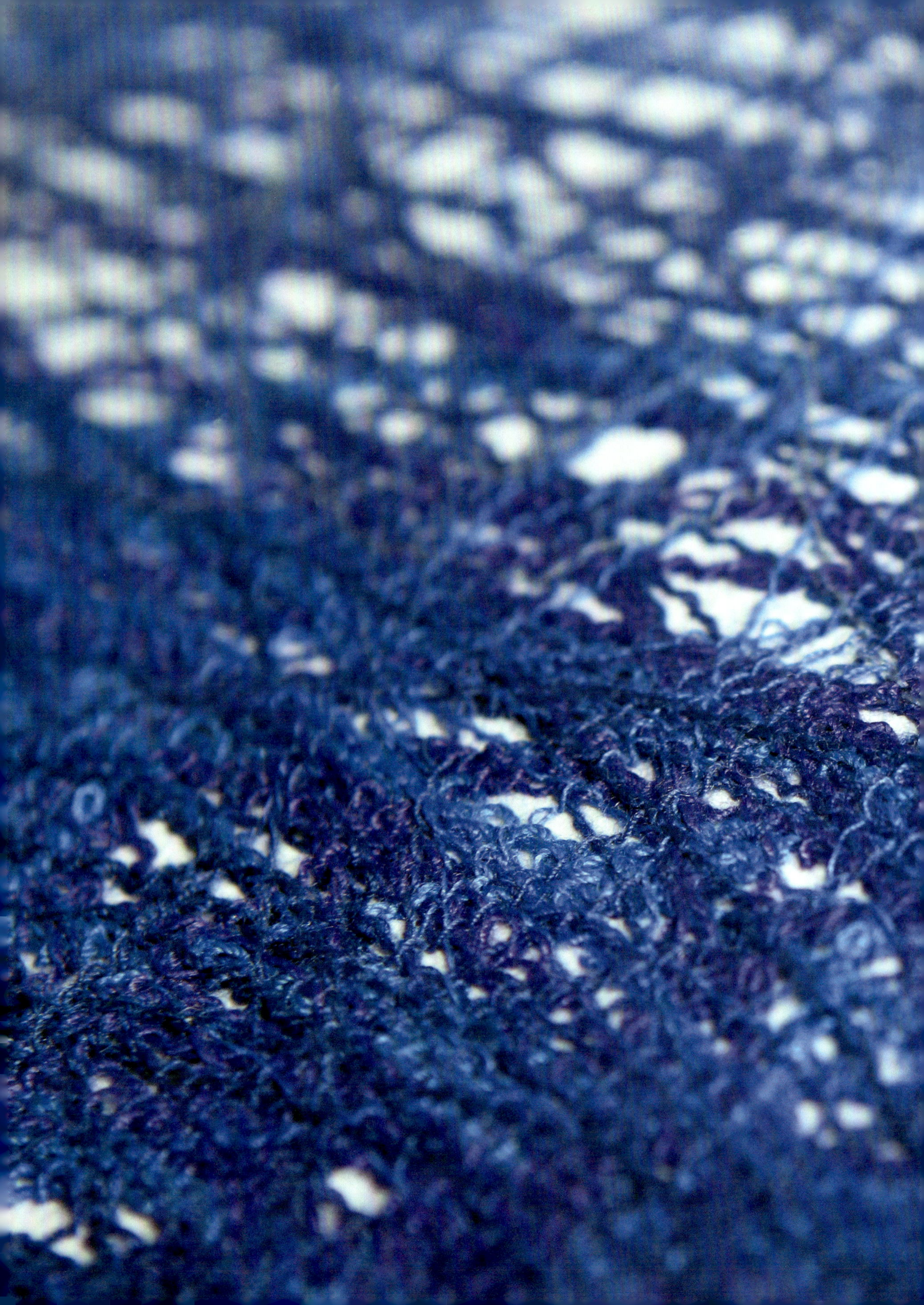

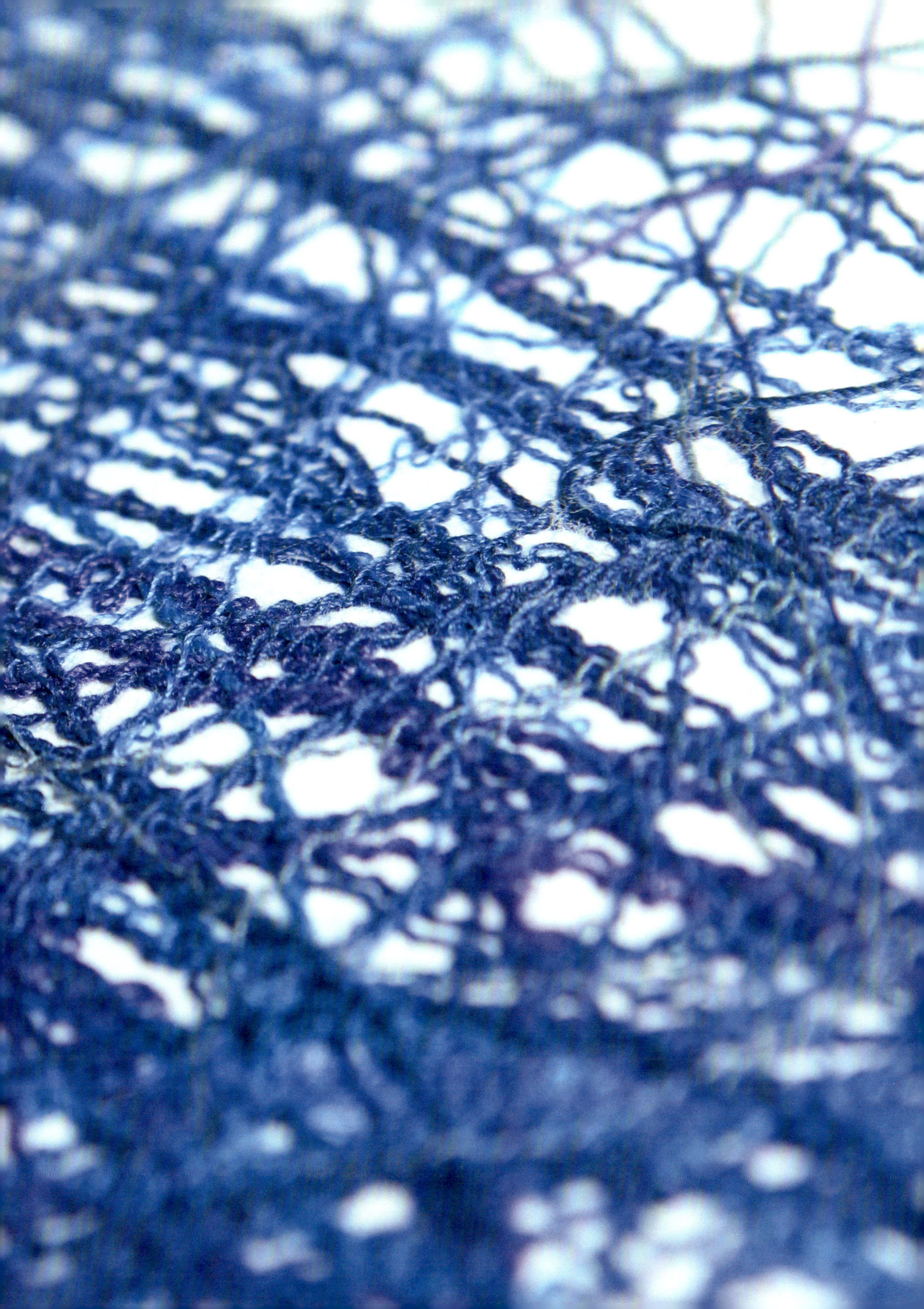

Mary Temple

Spring Light, 2007 (detail on following spread)
Cotton blowout on abaca base sheet
40 × 59 ¾ in. (101.6 × 151.6 cm)
Courtesy of the artist and Dieu Donné, New York

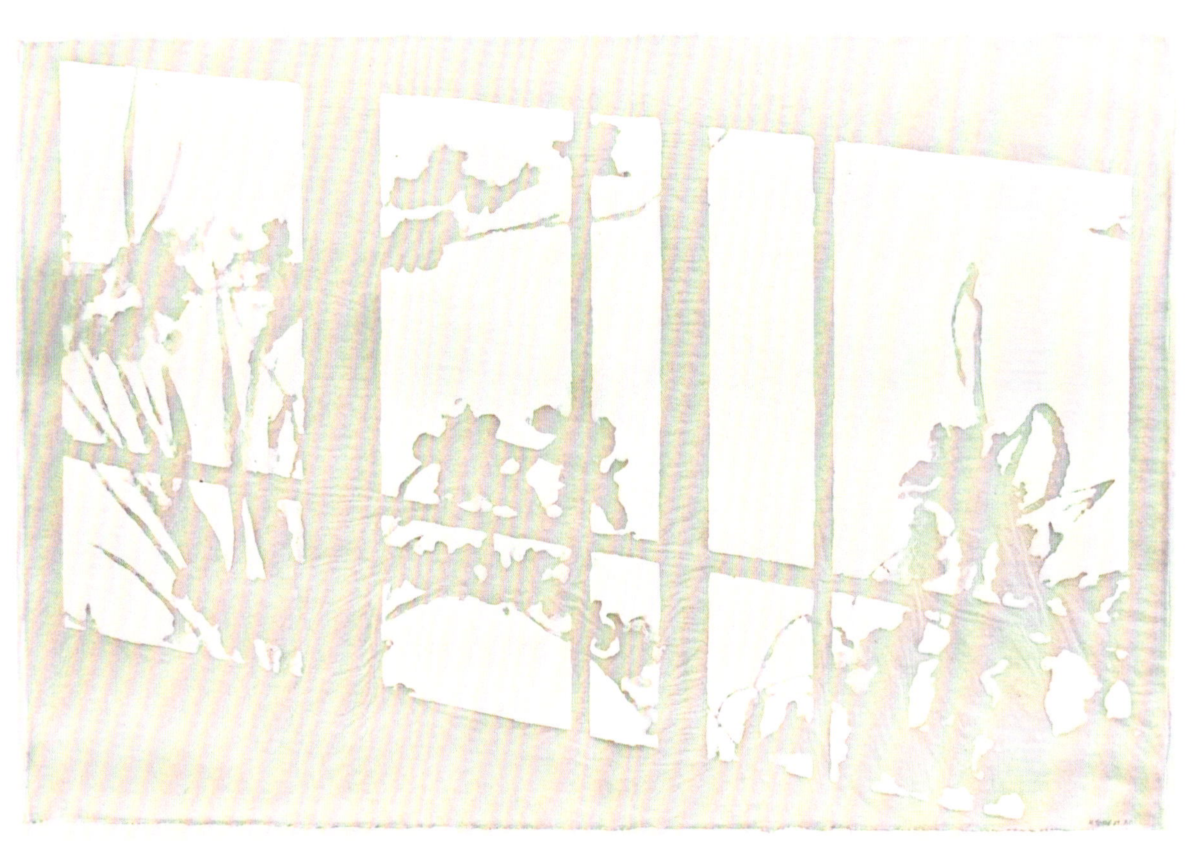

Richard Tuttle

The Triumph of Night, 2009 (detail on following spread)
Hand-cast cotton pulp and wire in painted wooden box
14 × 32 ⅛ × 6 ¼ in. (35.6 × 81.4 × 15.9 cm)
Courtesy of the artist and Dieu Donné, New York

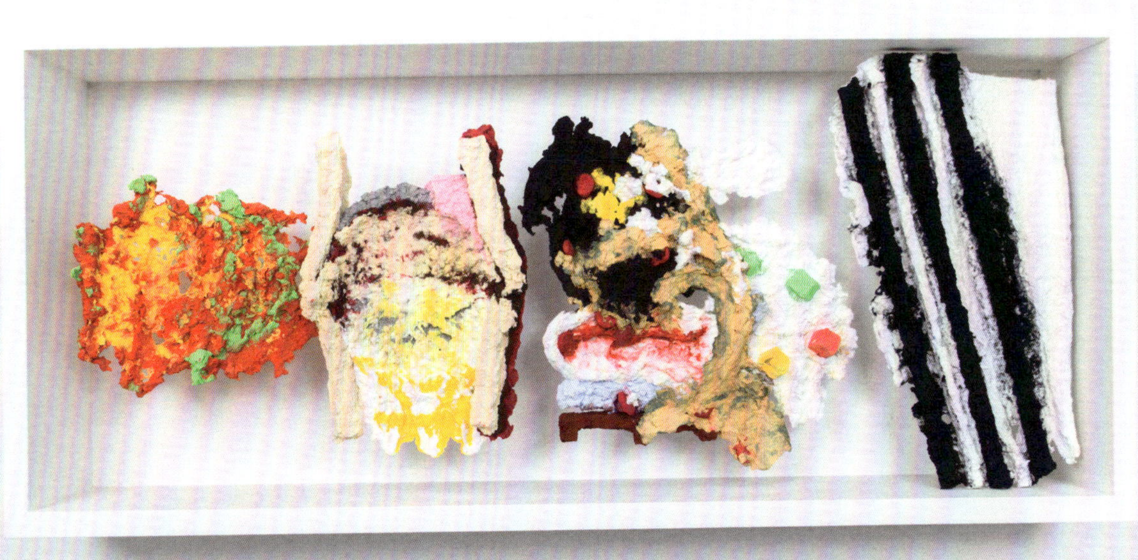

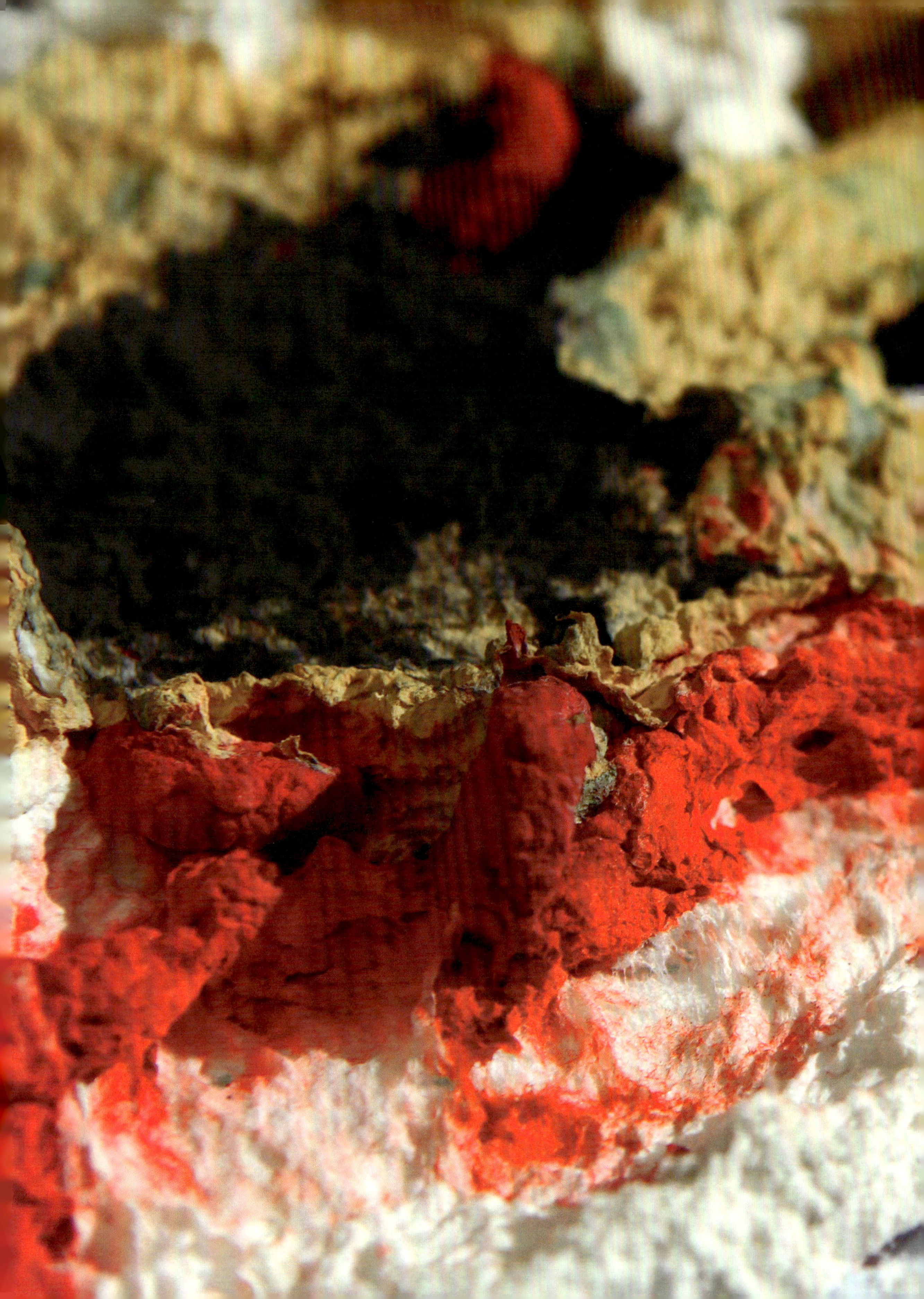

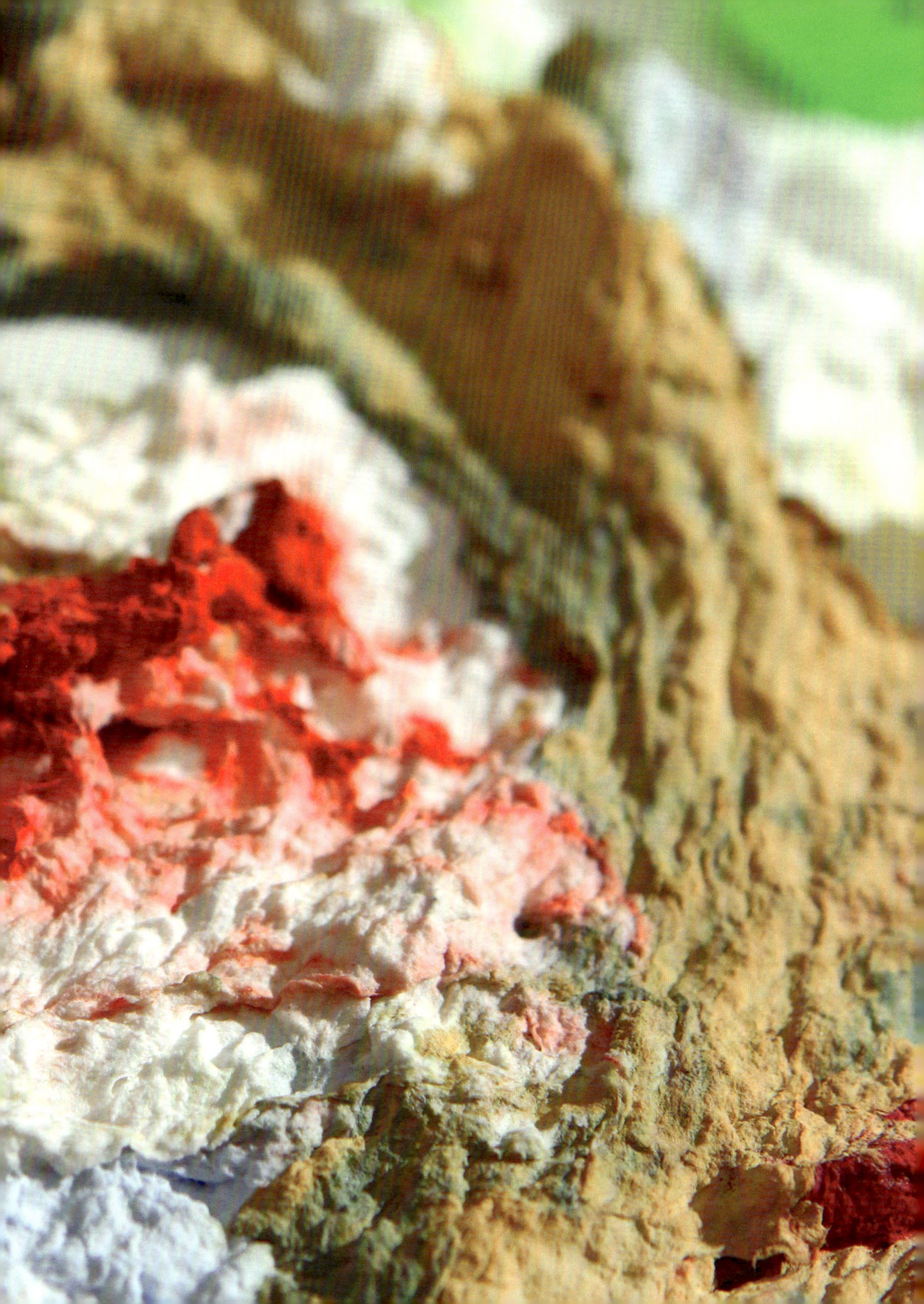

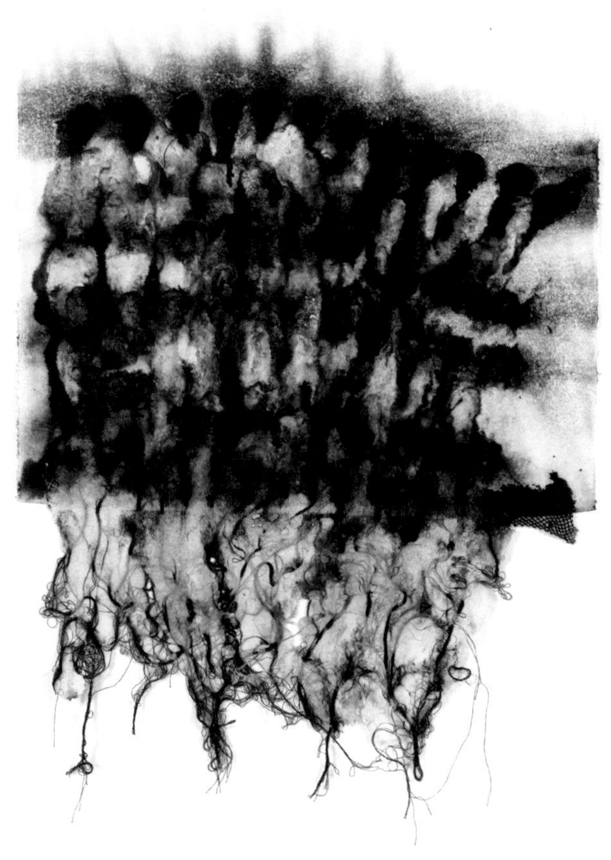

Ursula von Rydingsvard

Above: *Untitled*, 2010
Thread, pigment, fabric, and handmade paper
41 ½ × 22 ¼ in. (105.4 × 56.5 cm)
Courtesy of the artist and Dieu Donné, New York

Opposite: *Untitled*, 2010 (detail on following spread)
Thread, pigment, fabric, and handmade paper
42 ⅛ × 22 ⅛ in. (107 × 56.2 cm)
Courtesy of the artist and Dieu Donné, New York

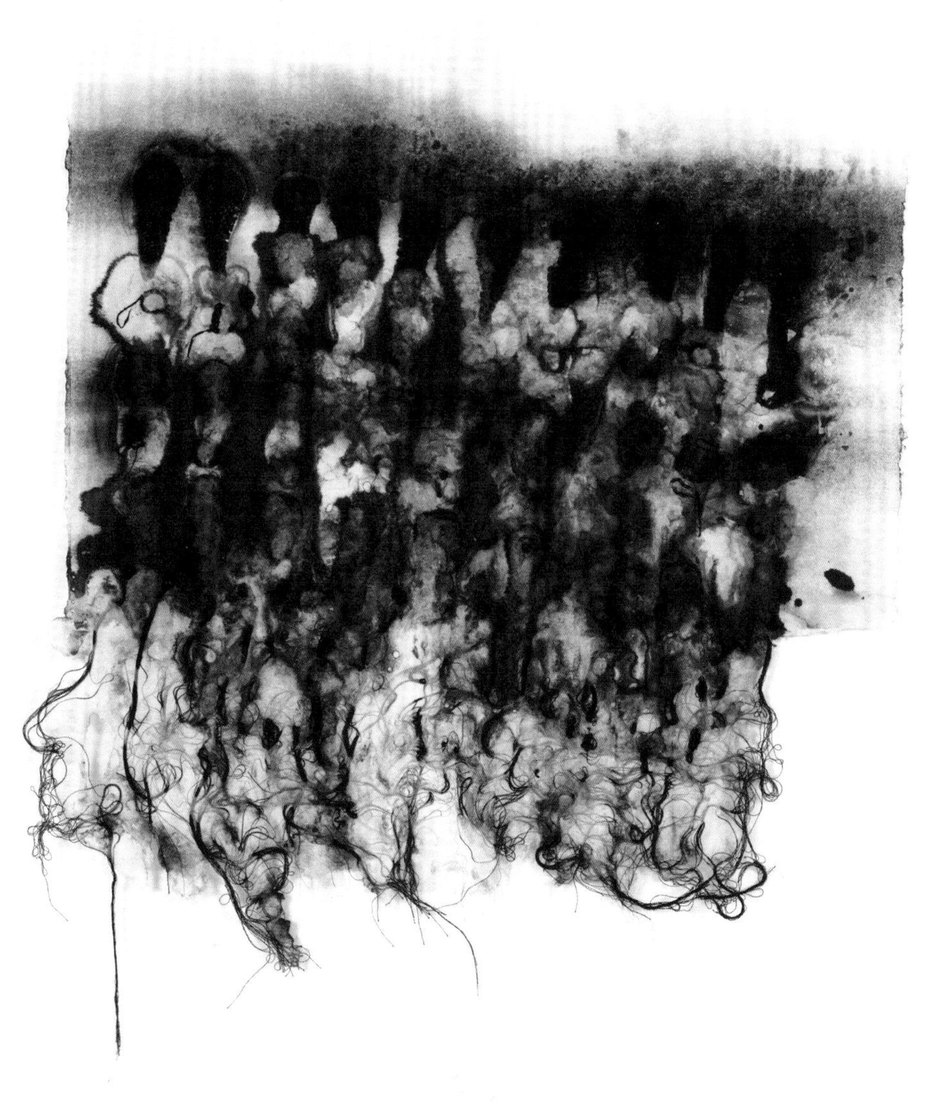

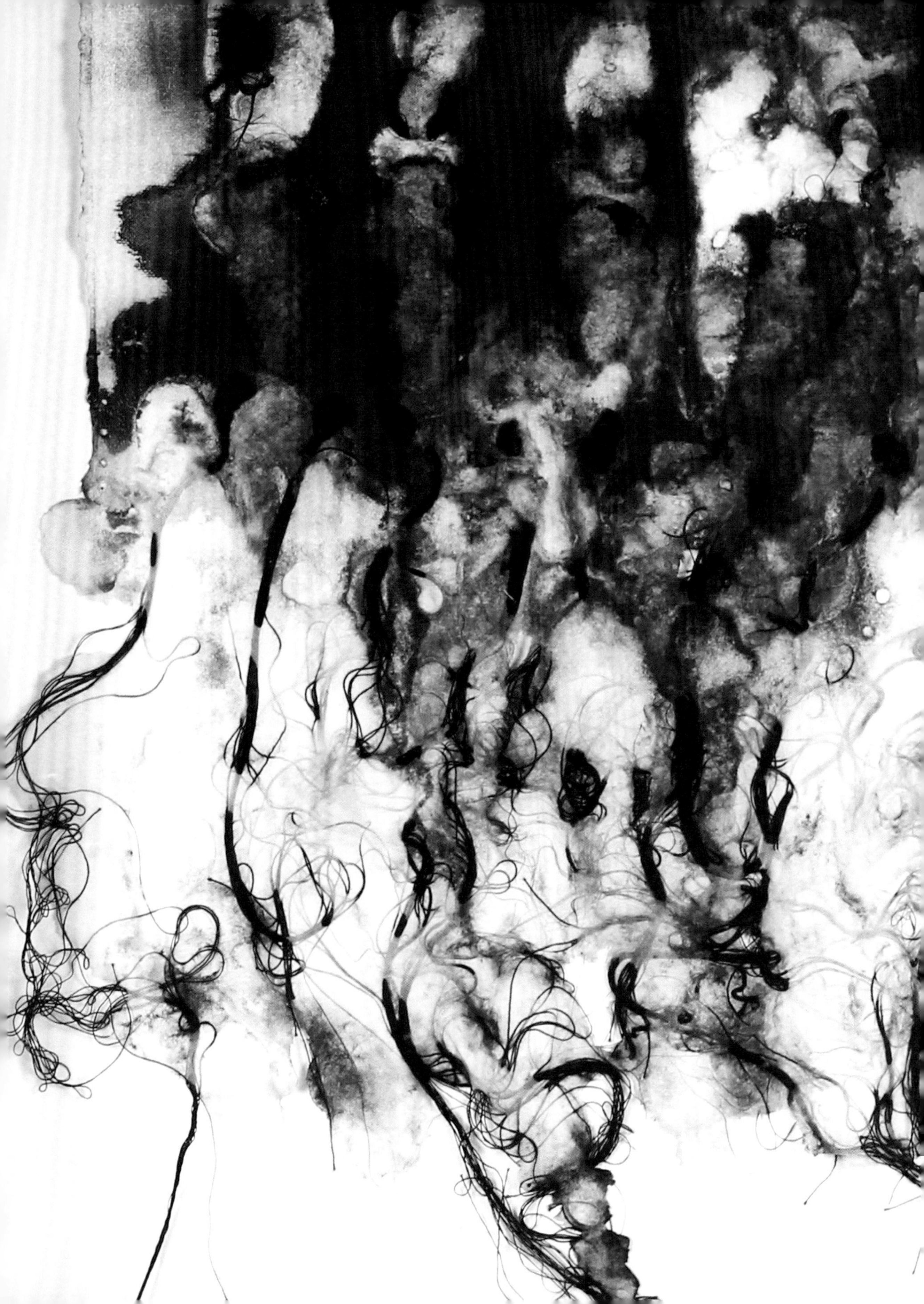

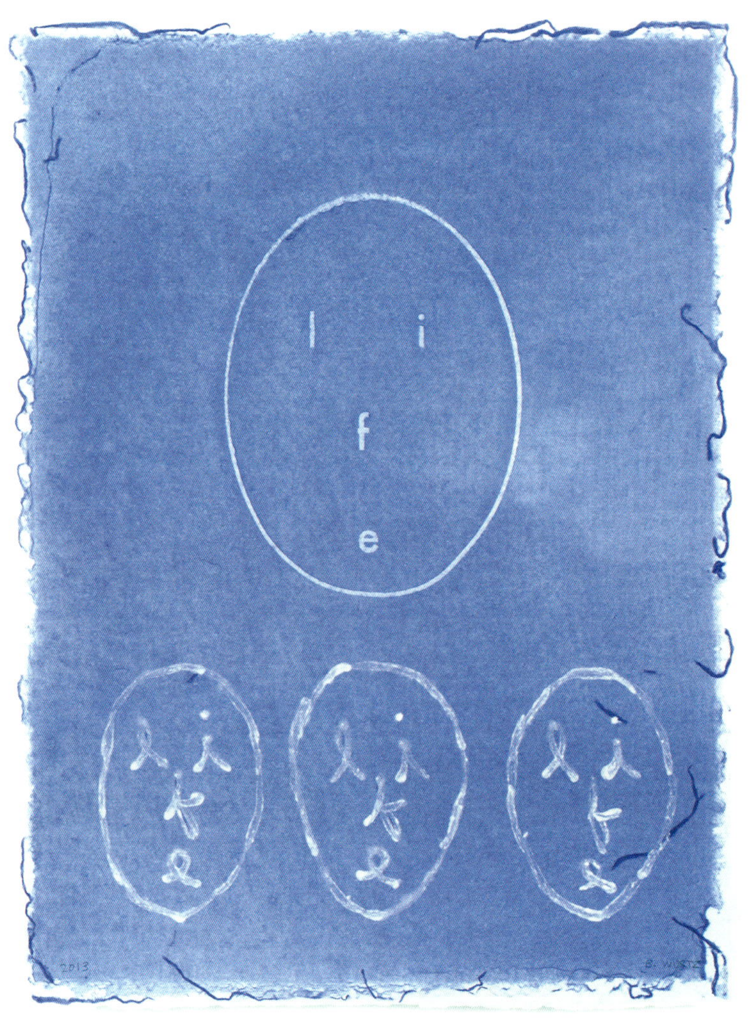

B. Wurtz

Untitled (7864), 2013 (detail opposite)
Watermarked, pigmented abaca with linen pulp paint
on cotton base sheet
24 ¼ × 18 ¼ in. (61.6 × 46.4 cm)
Courtesy of the artist and Dieu Donné, New York

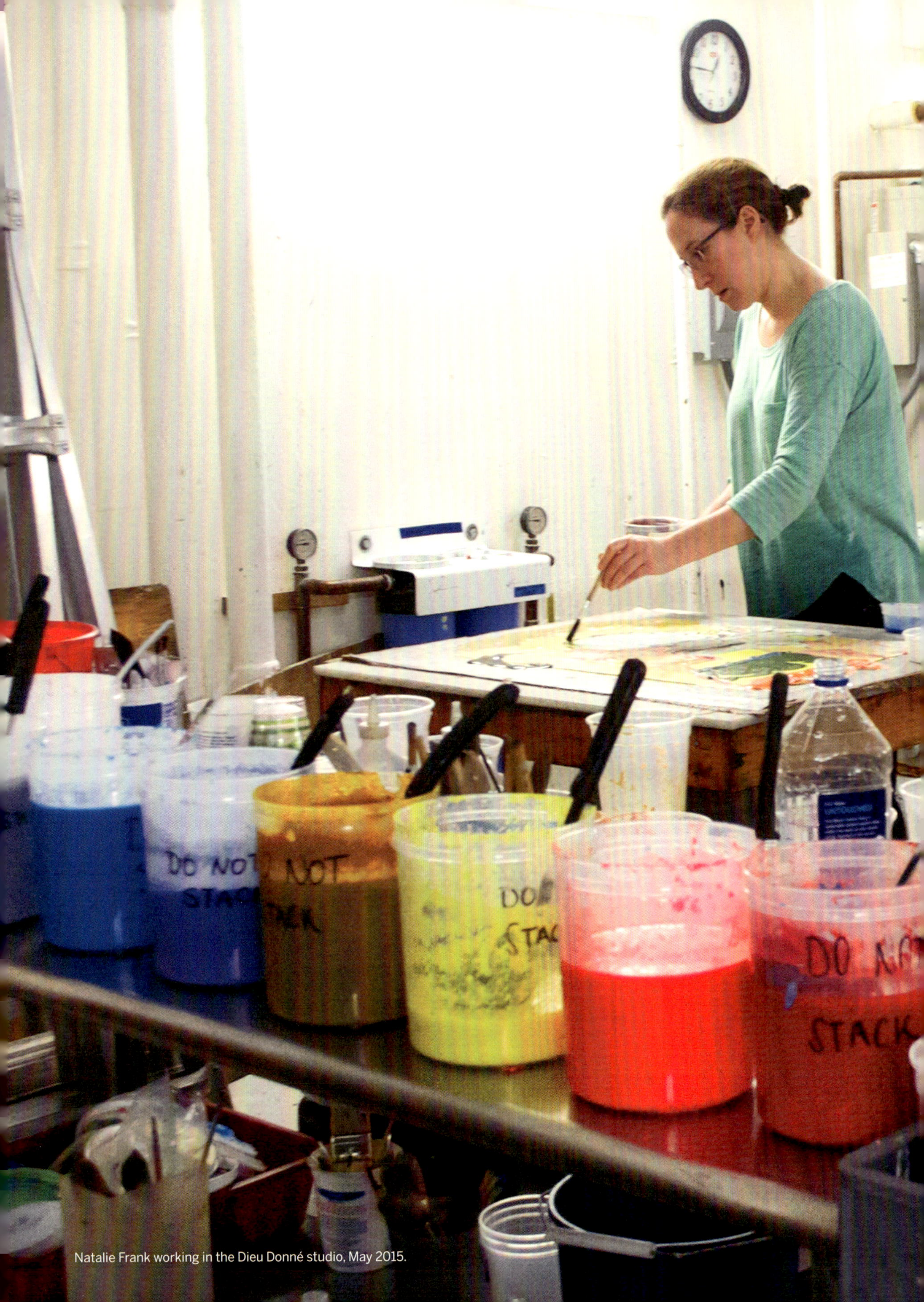

Natalie Frank working in the Dieu Donné studio, May 2015.

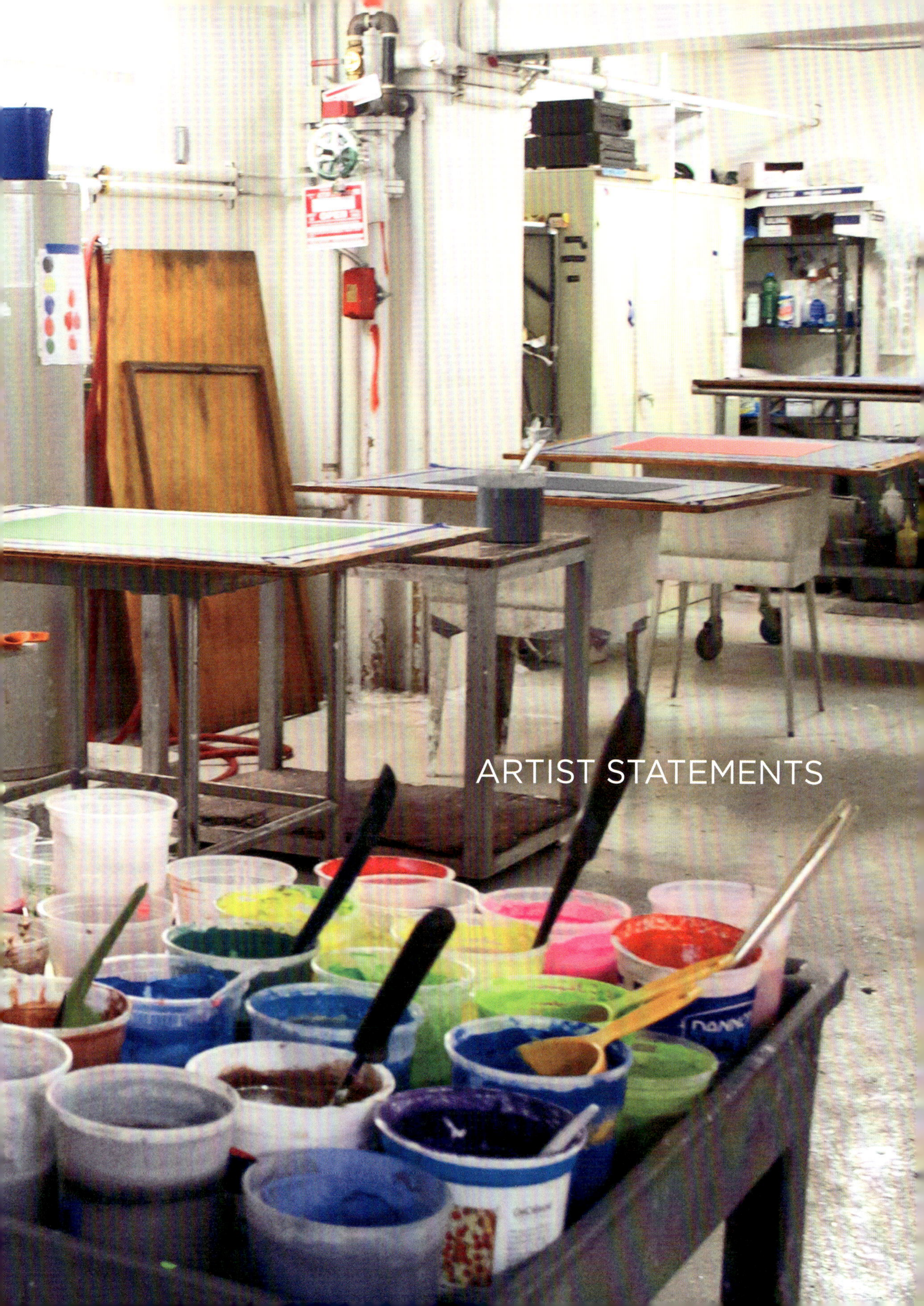

ARTIST STATEMENTS

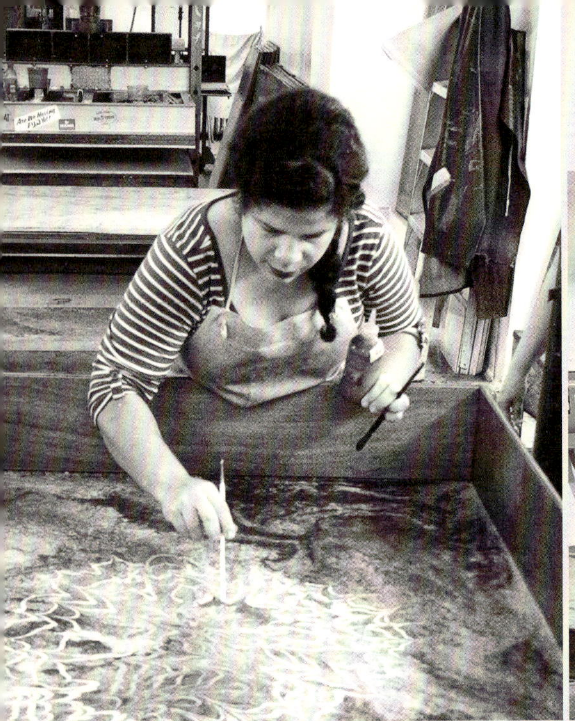

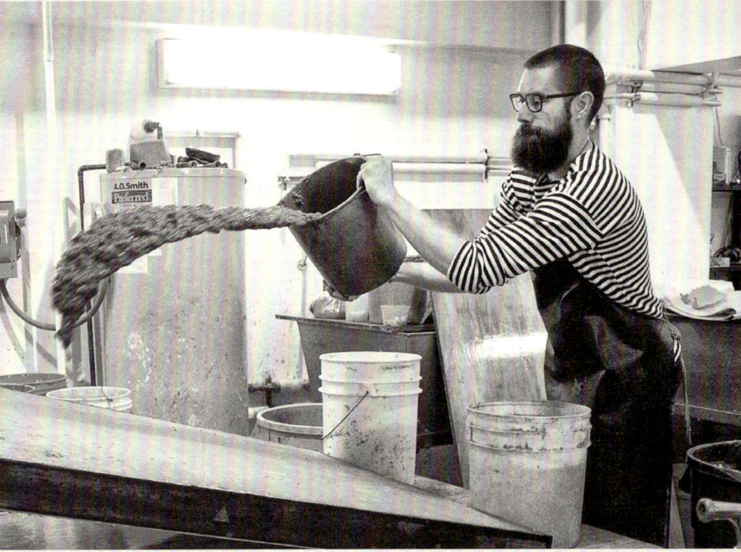

Firelei Báez

BORN 1981 IN THE DOMINICAN REPUBLIC
LIVES AND WORKS IN MIAMI, FL
WORKSPACE PROGRAM 2013
COLLABORATOR: AMY JACOBS

I followed an intuitive process, allowing the materials to inform the work I made in my residency, including *Amidst the future and present there is a memory table* (2013). I enjoy exploring new, unexpected ways of using materials, which is why I was drawn to pulp painting, marbling, and collaging freshly pulled sheets. All of these techniques are usually associated with surface, but in this body of work each gesture is structurally embedded in the form. The warp and pull of different kinds of paper was also a point of interest, since they allow for a more objectlike, corporeal experience of paper.

Amy was an amazing collaborator-slash-magician. She made the transition from working in my studio to working at Dieu Donné seamless. She knows the process so well and is open to play, which allowed me to invent as I went along and to just trust the materials, rather than trying to impose something else on them.

Ian Cooper

BORN 1978 IN NEW YORK CITY
LIVES AND WORKS IN NEW YORK CITY
WORKSPACE PROGRAM 2009
COLLABORATOR: AKEMI MARTIN

By extracting and reconfiguring set pieces and props from coming-of-age films and television programs, my work explores and unravels these media-constructed templates for the format of adolescence. Themes like isolation, longing, and escape are central to these tropes.

Chalice (2010) is derived from a poor quality paparazzi photograph of Blanket Jackson (son of the late pop star Michael Jackson), and is an extrapolation of the child's hat and hair as observed in *Star Magazine*. Upside-down and hollow, with a black mass of tangled, wilted hair that droops and drapes like the dead leaves of a neglected house plant, the baseball cap's brim is adorned with a paper pulp re-creation of the Puffy Paint gestures seen on Blanket's actual hat: a dripping rainbow with the letters "L O V E" scrawled below.

The tragic spectacle of Blanket's existence predates Michael's untimely death, and was visually emphasized by his father's enforced costuming while in public. Like some ad-hoc superhero, Blanket's masks and hats accompany his fright-wig-like hair in gestures reminiscent of the adolescent charade of subculture identification: boiled-down hallmarks of skater, hip-hop, or goth style: oversized, unkempt, color saturated, adorned. Compounding this charade, Blanket's inherent facelessness adds him to the motley crew company of such fictional personas as the Invisible Man, Orko, or the virtuosic metal guitarist Buckethead.

In *Chalice*, Blanket's hat and hair are realized in a slightly odd scale: an action further disconnecting the original source from reality. Whereas, Walt Disney designed buildings along his park's Main Street USA to be constructed in ¾ scale in an attempt to psychologically assuage the park's guests into feeling empowered, important, or special, the scale employed in *Chalice* is created in direct opposition to Disney's tactics. The 75 percent enlargement seeks to promote the off-kilter, alienating, awkward, and ultimately uncanny as the sculpture's crux lies in its highlighting the absence of the head itself. Located somewhere between the abject grizzle of a Native American trophy scalp, and the gimmickry of a novelty Rastafarian hat with felt dreadlocks, the sculpture maintains the role of an empty chalice, or a hollow cavity, as much as it appears as a discarded or forgotten dress-up disguise. It is decidedly without content, unfilled, and absent.

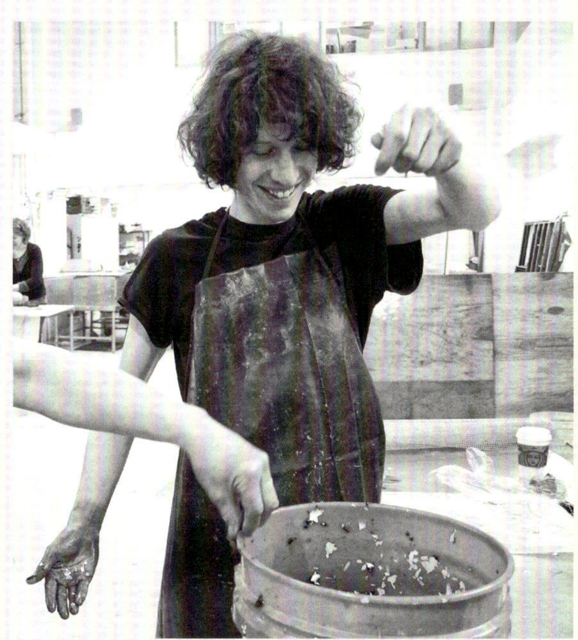

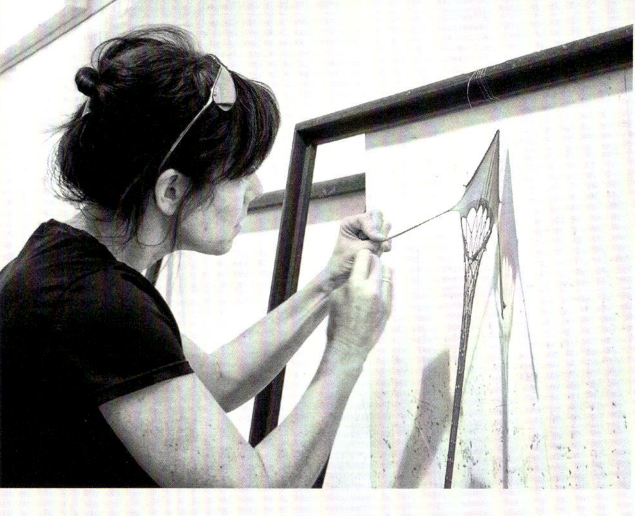

E.V. Day

BORN 1967 IN NEW YORK CITY
LIVES AND WORKS IN NEW YORK CITY
LAB GRANT PROGRAM 2008–09
COLLABORATOR: CATHERINE COX

When you're squeezing the paper pulp in the press, you've got so much pressure going down on this paper and you squeeze the water out and watch the fluid run like a pool of ink down to the drains in the floor. And you think, "We're getting a really good color!" But you don't know, maybe it all was squeezed out! The whole space is a fabulous studio, very Zen. It's not unlike what I'd imagine a cheese factory would be like—artisanal cheeses or tofu—because everything is very clean and there are screens that skim the paper pulp like curds. It feels really special, not like a print facility where you've got harsh inks and there's noise. The only noise you hear is the music playing while you're working with paper. We're fully focused on this one special process that you can't do anywhere else.

One of the things we worked on a lot was trying to select pigments. Pigments come in different forms: powder and liquid. And then different colors of pigment would react very differently with water. Once we got an idea of what we wanted, it was sort of this scientific baking exercise, in a way...how long to leave it in the oven, a little salt, a little pepper. With *Shazam (Black and Phosphorescence)*, made in 2009, I wanted this net to show great definition, but also wanted the ink to be flowing out, but not all washed away. And some lines would be so super crisp, you start to create a vocabulary with the pigment viscosity and the pressure strength of the press. And start to create goals within that language.

What's neat about this is that the paper is the object, like a sculpture. I can't just go buy paper and have it do what we did here in the studio. To me, this is a sculpture. It's a total object, sculpted with compression. It's not about an image on the surface. You can edition loaves of bread, but really each one is a little bit different.

David Kennedy Cutler

BORN 1979 IN SANDGATE, VT
LIVES AND WORKS IN NEW YORK CITY
WORKSPACE PROGRAM 2011
COLLABORATOR: PAUL WONG

In 2008, I began a ritual of photographing the streets surrounding my studio on rainy days. I took a picture of every oil rainbow I could find on my daily travels in Greenpoint, Brooklyn. Having learned that my studio was situated above the outer rim of one of the largest urban oil spills, I began to interpret these oil rainbows as manifestations of the unseen amalgamation of oil below. Like blossoms, they opened up, thirsty in the rain. In the barren industrial landscape of the easternmost section of Greenpoint, I began to regard the oil spill as my only local natural resource, and decided to tap into it, exploit it. Like Daniel Plainview in *There Will Be Blood*, I would become a prospector, an oilman, a profiteer, a maker of petroleum-based cultural artifacts.

Furthermore, I found myself interested not in the remediation of an environmental disaster, but concerned more with the essence of the accidents and apathy that led to a massive geologic displacement under my neighborhood. For against all rhetoric of efficiency, profit, and human ingenuity, the true manifestation (or monument) of our endeavors was the accident itself and the impossibility of containing it.

A residency at Dieu Donné then became a perfect metaphor for these slippery concerns. The essence of paper is to provide a "ground" on which to execute a performance of artifice, a transcription of meaning. The paper pulp itself reminded me of the ground (a muddy earthy slop), which is harnessed into the convenient rectangles or lots that we use to compartmentalize our world. Attempting to make the paper defy its own materiality inevitably led to accidents, which created revelatory form, such as *Mount*, which I made in 2011. Paul Wong provided me with the structure I needed: a perfectly crafted ground, meant to appear like asphalt or pavement.

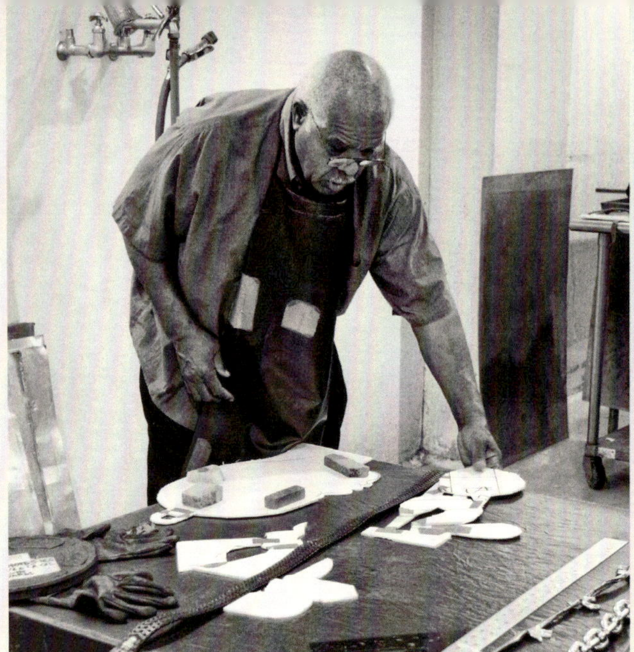

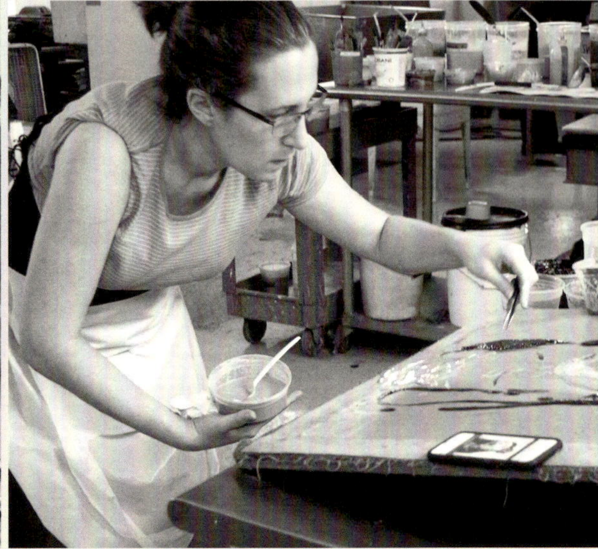

Melvin Edwards

BORN 1937 IN HOUSTON, TX
LIVES AND WORKS IN NEW YORK CITY; PLAINFIELD, NJ; AND DAKAR, SENEGAL
LAB GRANT PROGRAM 2000–01
COLLABORATOR: PAT ALMONRODE

What's interesting is we didn't necessarily end up using things in anticipated ways, but we certainly got very interesting things out of the process.

There are some references straight out of Angola—the working tools, for instance, and the importance of water in life and art. In my search to try to find things in my African heritage to use, well, utilitarian objects are all over the place. Only if you spend time there will you see how people use them. You know how you see a thing that's used for cooking, or for hair, and then you see somebody using it for a textile process, and it's the same tool. And if they can do that, then I can go straight to paper and ink, or to something else as I did for *Dakar Days*, *Sud foire*, and *in Gorée*.

You know how when we were young kids and we would play with our own shadows in relation to the sun? That means you're aesthetically aware of what reality and proportion are. On the other hand, the shadow can fix the moment. They are impressions of our existence... And then the tools that appear in the work...When anthropologists want to see early traces of humanity, they look for something that indicates a tool. That's as early as it gets. If there is no indication of a tool, there's no way to know we were there. But if it's something we cooked with or cut with, then, we were there.

Natalie Frank

BORN 1980 IN AUSTIN, TX
LIVES AND WORKS IN NEW YORK CITY
WORKSPACE PROGRAM 2015
COLLABORATOR: AMY JACOBS

During my residency, I fell in love with papermaking and pulp painting, specifically. There are freedoms inherent in this medium that I had never encountered—there is an unusual ability to make marks and forms with intense fluidity. I love the ways in which pulp can be used with various agents to become transparent, and also opaque, and can retain a sense of speed, which often feels embedded in the surface of the paper. I enjoyed layering and juxtaposing areas of rendered painting (with elements that I think of when working in oil: skin, hands, faces, eyes) with areas of pure pulp. I was able to play with effects specific to paper, such as marbling, swirling, and pure accident. The pulp can retain such bright and pure color, even when being mixed, manipulated, and poured. Unlike my past work in oil, gouache, and chalk pastel, pulp paints act in unexpected ways that often felt humorous to me!

While at Dieu Donné, I began experimenting with different ways to use the pulp and to paint with it and lay it down. In a series of portraits of women, I tried embedding threads, marbling, and using some of the bright forms of the paint in combinations with rendered areas that recall the possibilities of oil paint. Soon, I was finding immense pleasure in moving off of the page, usually 20 by 30 inches and then 30 by 40 inches as I became more confident. I was thinking of the paper as shaped canvases, using the pellons and tape to demarcate the absolute boundaries of size. Painting women and dogs kissing and dancing in the landscape and in interiors, I came to love the way that the color and the pulp as image itself could support the humor and playfulness and perversity of the imagery.

I came to Dieu Donné at a time when I had just finished a sustained project of drawings, with no expectation that I might fall in love with a medium outside of oil painting or drawing with gouache and chalk pastel. I feel with certainty that working with pulp painting has revealed new ideas and modes of working, which I have taken back into the studio. I am also sure that this practice will be a part of mine for the rest of my life. Anything and everything seemed possible.

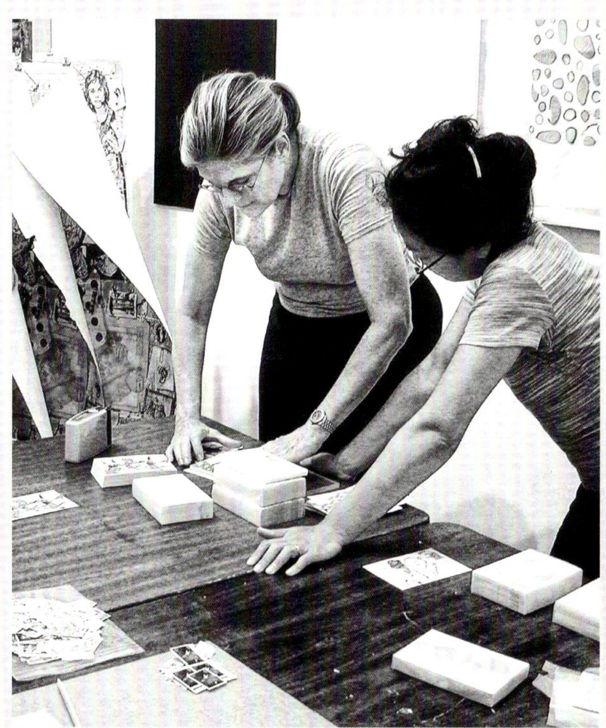

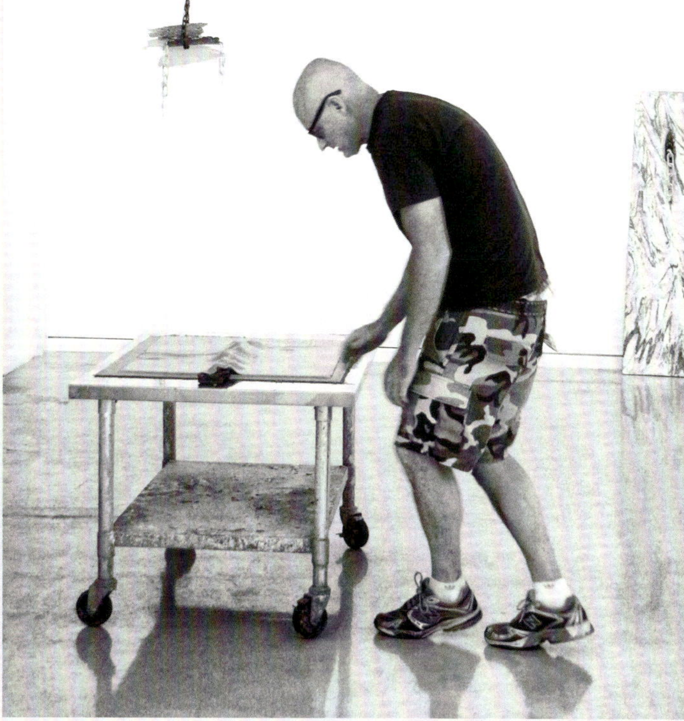

Jane Hammond

BORN IN 1950 IN BRIDGEPORT, CT
LIVES AND WORKS IN NEW YORK CITY
LAB GRANT PROGRAM 2000–02
COLLABORATORS: SUSAN GOSIN (DIEU DONNÉ PRESS) AND MINA TAKAHASHI

The process of making *Be Zany, Poised Harpists/Be Blue, Little Sparrows* (2002) from start to finish and the relationship of its poetry to artwork is one of my proudest accomplishments. The poems are all miraculous—but each in a very different sort of way—from the Zen-like koan of the first to the Baroque architecture of the final poem. That the book manages to be both internally varied and tight is its strength. When I think of it residing in the collections of the Met, MoMA, the Whitney, the Getty, and the Bibliothèque nationale in Paris—this is really a sublime reward.

Jim Hodges

BORN 1957 IN SPOKANE, WA
LIVES AND WORKS IN NEW YORK CITY
LAB GRANT PROGRAM 2001–02; PUBLISHING PROJECT 2010
COLLABORATOR: PAUL WONG

The entire experience working here was inspiring! I hope that what we made together will attract even more people to this perfect laboratory where ideas and materials mix in a sloshy slippery world of possibilities.

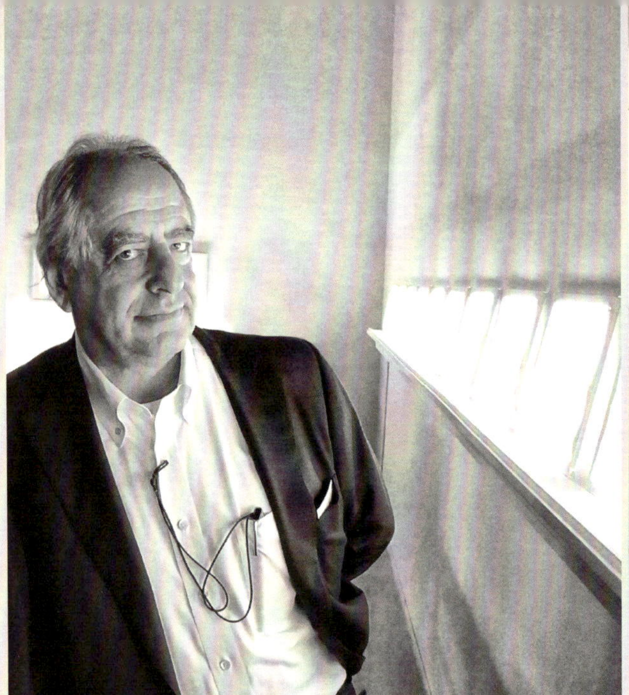

William Kentridge

BORN 1955 IN JOHANNESBURG, SOUTH AFRICA
LIVES AND WORKS IN JOHANNESBURG, SOUTH AFRICA
PUBLISHING PROJECTS 2002, 2006, AND 2009
COLLABORATORS: SUSAN GOSIN (DIEU DONNÉ PRESS) AND PAUL WONG

What can I do with this handmade paper that wouldn't be just a drawing on top of a sheet of paper? The solution that Sue Gosin suggested was, "Well, then, why don't you make a drawing inside the paper?" And a drawing inside of the paper is a watermark.

The first collaboration at Dieu Donné and the subsequent publishing project, which is this book, *Sheets of Evidence*, made in 2009, were both about having a drawing hidden inside of the paper.

It is a book of poems and images, but it is also very much a book about paper itself, and what's possible with different kinds of paper. So the work has to do with some sheets, which are transparent, and working with kinds of overlays and images.

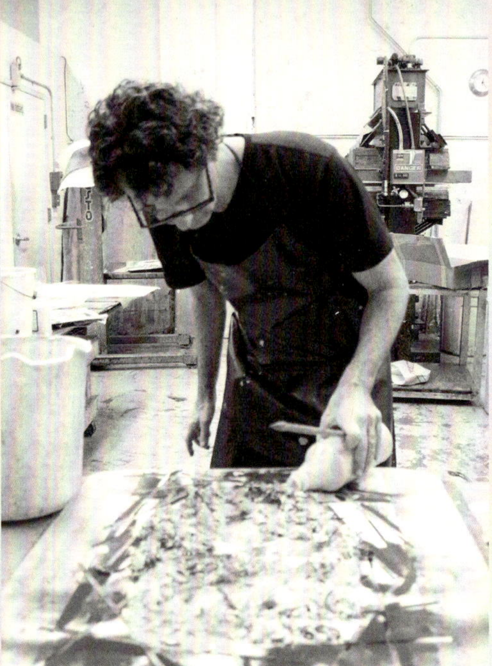

Jon Kessler

BORN 1957 IN YONKERS, NY
LIVES AND WORKS IN NEW YORK CITY
LAB GRANT PROGRAM 2007–08
COLLABORATOR: RACHEL GLADFELTER

I knew I had no interest in doing direct sculptural processes at Dieu Donné, I didn't want to start making latex molds. The things that interested me, initially, were the masher [beater] and the press, which are instruments of torture, with enormous, excessive force and violence. I was like, "OK, I'm going to use those," because those were the instincts I was drawing from in my own studio to make my kinetic sculpture. Otherwise, the intuition I've been drawing on here doesn't relate to my sculptural process, except for obvious things like using wire mesh and cutting into it. This whole new sense of the rip, the tear, the mash—thinking about the pulp as a kind of glue.

The pulp was like a post-Katrina, post-tsunami soup. Everything we were using had a fiber. The money, the hair, the photographs—each one of those things had a fiber with little fingers that were grasping on to the life raft.

We would always start out the same way. Rachel would press a sheet, and then I'd be staring at the proverbial blank page. In order to start somewhere, I would attack it with pulp. It was rare that I would say, "I need a specific color." Normally I would reach for what was already mixed up for other people's projects. And then I would introduce an image or text into that. Then we'd press it and see what we got.

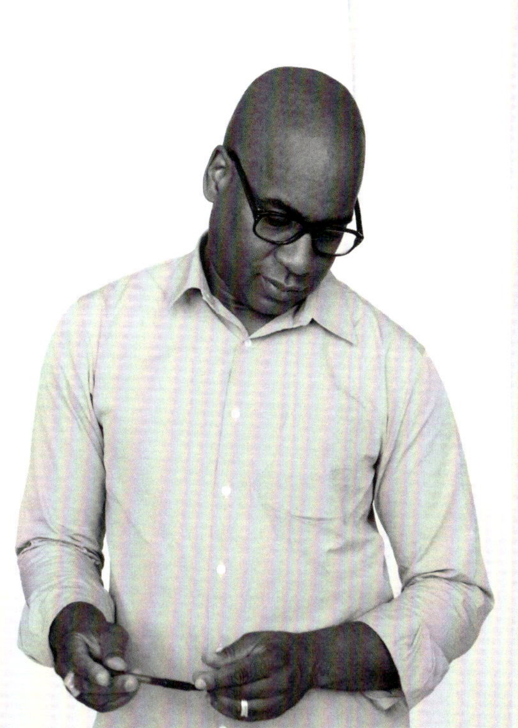

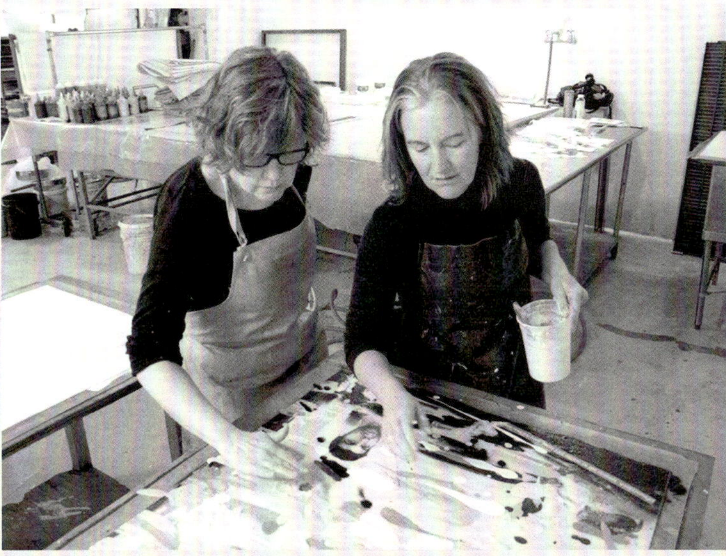

Glenn Ligon

BORN 1960 IN NEW YORK CITY
LIVES AND WORKS IN NEW YORK CITY
LAB GRANT PROGRAM 2003–04
COLLABORATOR: MEGAN MOORHOUSE

Remember when you were a kid and one album or song seemed to speak directly to your soul? The singer seemed to have made the record just for you. And you lived intensely in that album or song for a while, playing it everyday, buying posters of the singer, dressing like him or her, imitating her or his singing style in the bathroom mirror. That singer's image was your image and that is what *Self-Portrait at Eleven Years Old*, made in 2004 at Dieu Donné, is about. It is about how you can become so intensely identified with pop culture figures that they become part of how you see yourself in the world.

The difference between my studio practice and working with Dieu Donné is that in the studio it's just me. Working with Dieu Donné was much more collaborative because the technical aspects of the medium were new to me and I relied on the staff to figure out how to make things work. While I am used to endless revisions in the studio, I was much more conscious of getting my ideas to a certain level of polish before I presented them to Dieu Donné. Overall, it was incredibly easy, which is not the usual process for me. I have fifty more ideas for projects I want to do with them.

Suzanne McClelland

BORN 1959 IN JACKSONVILLE, FL
LIVES AND WORKS IN NEW YORK CITY
LAB GRANT PROGRAM 2014–16
COLLABORATOR: AMY JACOBS

Working with Amy, my studio collaborator, has been very enlightening. She was quick to respond to ideas, to describe what is possible, and to find technical and material solutions that would give each group of images a different weight. The linen delivers color with intensity. Very thin, translucent and smooth, it has an appearance of fragility; however it also has a kind of strength, more than one would think. Amy made beautiful gradations of pulp colors in linen as well as the warmer, softer cotton. She was always prepared to "jump in," so to speak.

Making a mark or gesture with the same material that the surface is made of, and having the two end up on the same physical plane was a pleasant surprise. Working flat into wet material is familiar to me but the hydraulic press would compress the cut papers and photographs into one surface. This created an optical distance in the image, which I appreciated, as seen in *Seven* (from "Internal Affairs"). I decided to use chance operations by dropping images into the wet pulp, avoiding the fussiness of cutting and pasting that goes along with traditional collage. I started this technique in my paintings; but with pulp, the surface remains seamless and it feels like gravity has more impact on the final form than in paintings. The "drop" creates the form that appears to float with printed images and text...once it falls in—it's done. There is no turning back or fixing anything—take it or leave it.

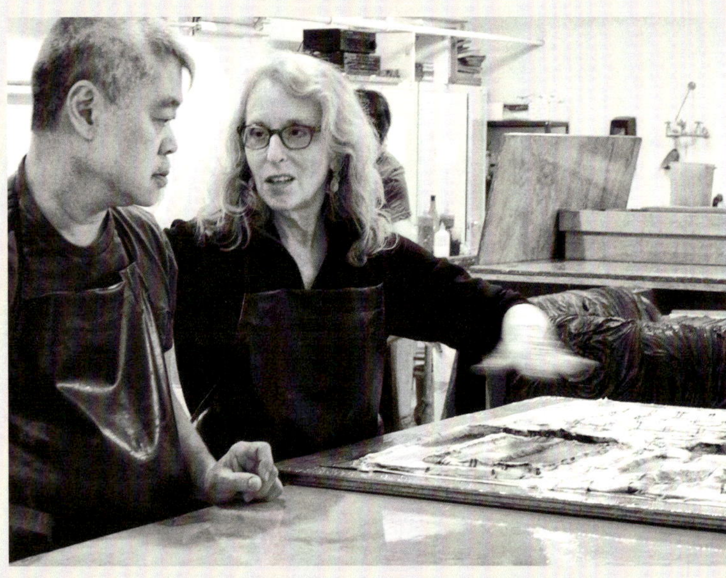

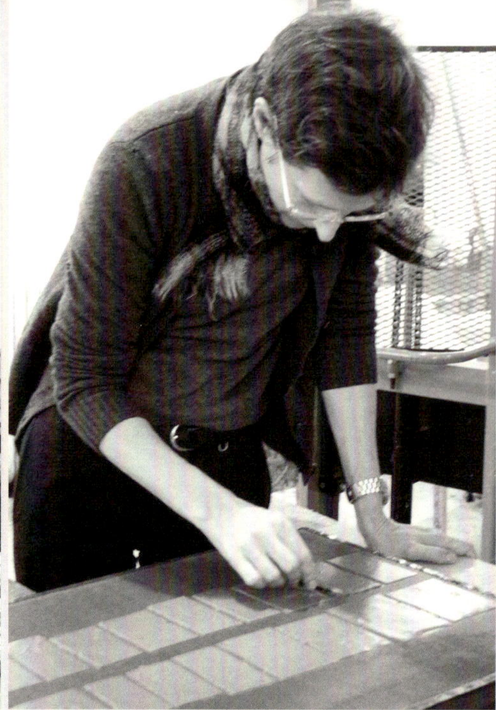

Arlene Shechet

BORN 1951 IN NEW YORK CITY
LIVES AND WORKS IN NEW YORK CITY AND WOODSTOCK, NY
WORKSPACE PROGRAM 1997, PUBLISHING PROJECT 2012
COLLABORATORS: AMY JACOBS, LISA SWITALSKI, AND PAUL WONG

I really like the idea of color and form being one thing. It's not that I've painted on the paper—it's that the color is the paper, and it goes pretty deep into that...In that way, it's very similar to working with the clay, where the glaze and the clay become one thing—one structure, surface, and form.

The thing about working with paper is the immediacy of that entire process. I love seeing it and responding...The fun of it is you are prepared, but then you don't know anything.

Sometimes the work we do on a given layer never shows up: you never know it's there, although I believe in the energy of it underneath. There is a certain physicality that is exciting to me.

Papermaking is a situation, and it doesn't have any answers, it just provides a forum. It creates a way to provide that lateral expansion of the practice without knowing where it's going to go and I'm hungry for that.

Kate Shepherd

BORN 1961 IN NEW YORK CITY
LIVES AND WORKS IN NEW YORK CITY
LAB GRANT PROGRAM 2005–06;
PUBLISHING PROJECT 2011
COLLABORATORS: RACHEL GLADFELTER,
MEGAN MOORHOUSE, AND PAUL WONG

Soon after starting to make work at Dieu Donné, I realized that I had to go with the flow of the paper pulp and its requisite processes. Having failed to make thin lines like those in my paintings, I came to realize that pulp was better suited to be used in blocks of color. I opted to work additively as though I was playing with wooden blocks and "build" with the shapes, one at a time, by spontaneously ripping paper with a straight edge. Just as the lines in my paintings connote three-dimensionality without rendering, the cut shapes could suggest a flattened non-perspectival version of sculptural forms.

When I retuned to the mill in 2011, I began a new strategy to create *Dark Orange with Stacks, Notched (4, 5) and Great Cousin Mary* that involved using the second layer of pulp as an overall wall of windows or architectural "face." Planar depth could still be suggested but in a flat way. The method used involved spontaneously cutting paper that I saw as a one-time template or "resist." I wanted the images to have a frightening although benign visage. I know a painting is finished when I find something human in it that I can latch onto.

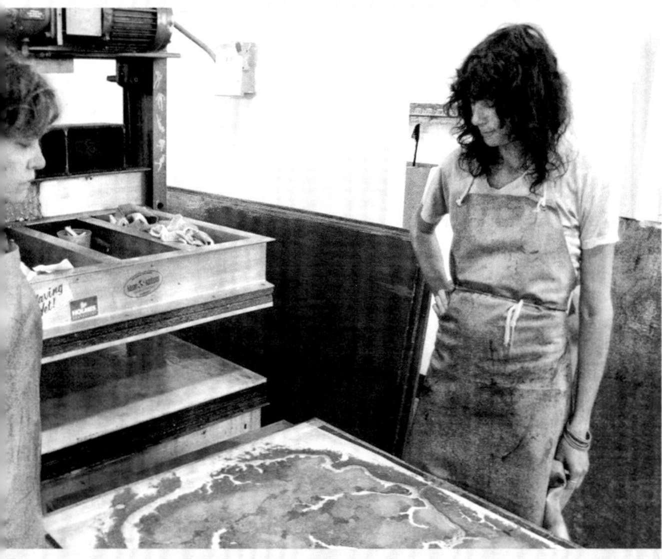

Molly Smith

BORN 1976 IN KANSAS CITY, MO
LIVES AND WORKS IN WORTHINGTON, MA
WORKSPACE PROGRAM 2012
COLLABORATOR: AMY JACOBS

I am drawn to forces acting upon matter. How elements play on materials is the very nature of papermaking and was a fitting extension of my process. Water controls the way the paper is created and pressure affects how it stays together. Papermaking has allowed me to let go of control, which has been a game I frequently play as an artist. I found that making paper requires me to stay present. I could have all my ingredients ready but until things happened in the moment, there was no way to determine the results so I had to be open to all possible outcomes. Accidents were welcome. In one of my first efforts, a very thick piece of paper was pressed quickly which caused it to split. This discovery led me to try similar effects in various pieces, *Swamp*, made in 2012, being one example. The results of drying were another exciting part of the development of each work. I enjoyed giving up expectations for what may result.

In my work, I repurpose objects and materials. Papermaking provides me many ways to transform discarded everyday materials into new forms. My color palette for the work I made at Dieu Donné was mostly created from leftover pulp from their walk-in refrigerator. It was, for me, another way to collaborate with chance. I also made paper pulp from recycled artwork and detritus from the classroom where I taught grade school art. It was wonderful how my collaborator, Amy Jacobs, did not ban the glitter-infused paper or the rusty metal from the wet studio. Amy saw the possibilities of experimenting with these unconventional materials in papermaking. Her matched curiosity and enthusiasm was crucial to my residency.

The Workspace residency came to me at just the right time. I was hoping to transition out of working with plaster in the hopes of finding a lighter and more ephemeral material that could still work sculpturally. Through the residency, I was able to explore how a three-dimensional piece could be made from something flat but still occupy a greater space by how it is manipulated. As I move across the country, my car provides me with the ability to make something out of nothing, wherever I am; a way of life that is my deepest desire as an artist.

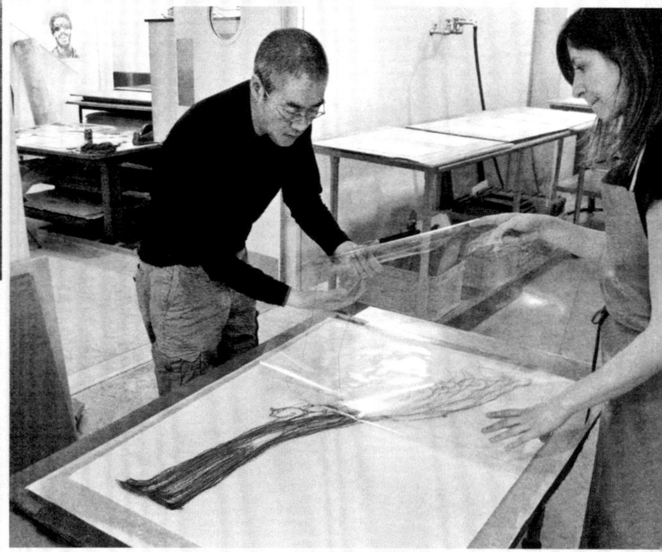

Do Ho Suh

BORN 1962 IN SEOUL, KOREA
LIVES AND WORKS IN NEW YORK CITY; LONDON, ENGLAND; AND SEOUL, KOREA
LAB GRANT PROGRAM 2006–13
COLLABORATORS: RACHEL GLADFELTER, AMY JACOBS, LISA SWITALSKI, AND PAUL WONG

I like that there is an unexpectedness to the thread drawings that is so different from my other works. There are all these little accidents. Sometimes, when the tension between the two threads in the sewing machine is not right, little loops of excess thread appear at the back of the sewing. In the beginning, I trimmed these excess threads, but I grew to like how they change the shapes of my drawings when they interact with water in the paper pulp.

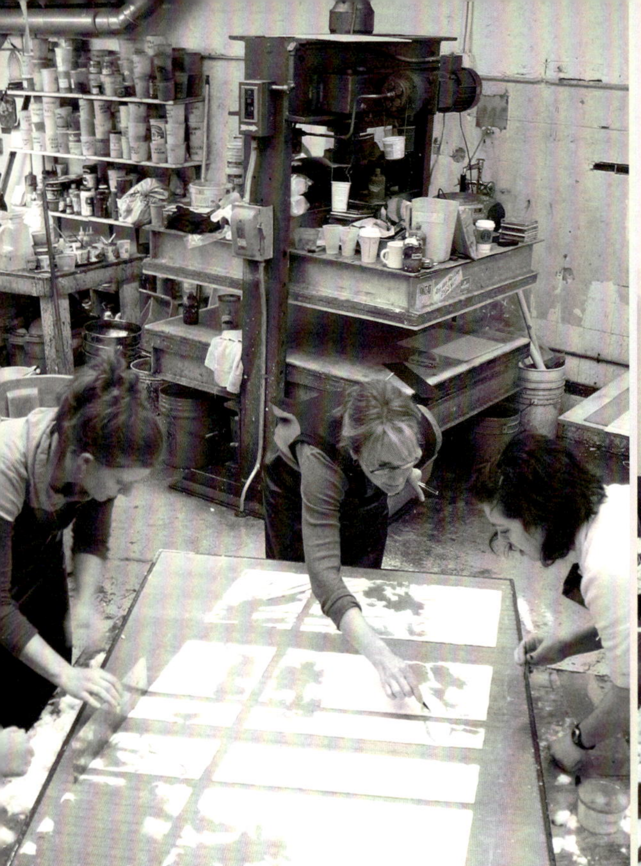

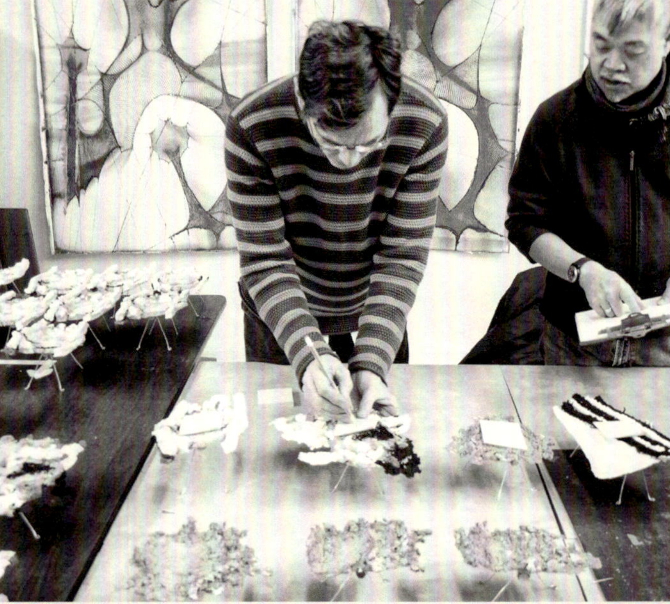

Mary Temple

BORN 1957 IN PHOENIX, AZ
LIVES AND WORKS IN NEW YORK CITY
WORKSPACE PROGRAM 2006
COLLABORATORS: CATHERINE COX AND RACHEL GLADFELTER

Key to papermaking for me is to allow the material to clearly influence the outcome—so that the final work seems inevitable and in agreement with paper's character. To that end, working with a master papermaker is crucial, because pulp can be charmingly adverse to persuasion. Dieu Donné's master papermakers' respect for the material is legendary. It was such a great experience to get to learn from them while working on these pieces, such as *Spring Light*, made in 2007 at Dieu Donné.

Richard Tuttle

BORN 1941 IN RAHWAY, NJ
LIVES AND WORKS IN NEW YORK CITY; MOUNT DESERT, ME; AND ABIQUIU, NM
PUBLISHING PROJECT 2002 AND 2009
COLLABORATOR: PAUL WONG

You have to have a very ethical relation to material and there is no higher ethical relationship than simultaneously using it and finding it.

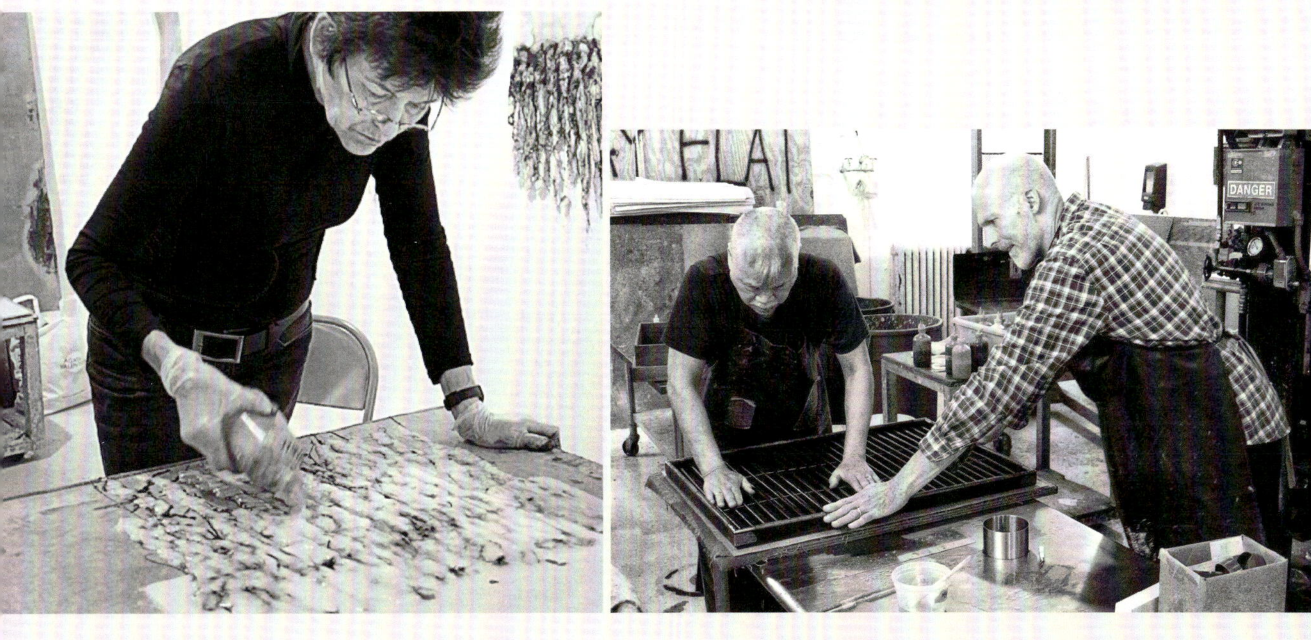

Ursula von Rydingsvard

BORN 1942 IN DEENSEN, GERMANY
LIVES AND WORKS IN NEW YORK CITY
LAB GRANT PROGRAM 2007–10
COLLABORATOR: PAUL WONG

Dieu Donné has opened up so many options for my working with paper. Just to be able to grab the pulp with my hands or to squirt it out of a bottle, or to place my huge array of fabrics, thin string, and knots on top of the wet pulp, dousing it with black ink—all felt like it had extraordinarily exciting possibilities. There's a physical engagement that I seem to need. Additionally, the abaca paper with its strong self-adhering powers has enabled me to make very lightweight reliefs, which I cast from my cedar sculptures. Dieu Donné is a treasure whose continued existence we should guard with great care.

B. Wurtz

BORN 1948 IN PASADENA, CA
LIVES AND WORKS IN NEW YORK CITY
LAB GRANT PROGRAM 2012–15
COLLABORATORS: LISA SWITALSKI AND PAUL WONG

My residency at Dieu Donné has been an absolutely wonderful experience. I have made work in the past using paper but never had the opportunity to actually make paper. I will never forget the thrill of seeing the whole paper pulp and water process for the first time.

The collaborative aspect of my time here has been great. I feel I have a very special relationship with the staff; we really work well together. I am so used to working completely by myself on my art that this situation has really opened me up to new possibilities. In other words, the art I have made at Dieu Donné would never have happened if I had just been on my own. Yet, it is also very much my art, and I attribute that partly to the staff having such a good understanding of what I am about.

The process of working on my new pieces at Dieu Donné has been fascinating. We have started out with ideas, but as we go along things change and alterations are made. That is exactly how I like to work—open to where making the art may lead me. The situation at Dieu Donné has been perfect in that respect.

Checklist of the Exhibition

Firelei Báez

Amidst the future and present there is a memory table, 2013
Pigmented abaca, cotton, and linen on abaca base sheet with radiograph opaque ink
39 ¾ × 60 ⅜ in. (101 × 153.4 cm)
Courtesy of the artist and Gallery Wendi Norris, San Francisco

Ian Cooper

Chalice, 2010
Handmade denim and cotton papers, commercial papers, fabric, cast paper pulp, trash bags, brush bristles, gloss medium, and jade adhesive
57 × 11 × 16 in. (144.8 × 27.9 × 40.6 cm)
Courtesy of the artist

David Kennedy Cutler

Mount, 2011
Archival inkjet on Japanese paper, metal-embedded data from compact discs, and pigmented cotton
81 × 18 × 17 in. (205.7 × 45.7 × 43.2 cm)
Courtesy of the artist and Derek Eller Gallery, New York

E.V. Day

Shazam (Black and Phosphorescence), 2009
Fishnet bodysuit pigment embossing on cotton base sheet
60 × 40 in. (152.4 × 101.6 cm)
Courtesy of the artist

Melvin Edwards

Dakar Days, 2006
Cotton blowout on pigmented abaca base sheet
21 ⅞ × 16 ⅞ in. (55.6 × 42.9 cm)
Courtesy of the artist and Dieu Donné, New York

in Gorée, 2006
Cotton blowout on pigmented abaca base sheet
22 ⅜ × 17 ⅛ in. (56.8 × 43.5 cm)
Courtesy of the artist and Dieu Donné, New York

Sud foire, 2006
Cotton blowout on pigmented abaca base sheet
21 ¾ × 16 in. (55.2 × 40.6 cm)
Courtesy of the artist and Dieu Donné, New York

Natalie Frank

Portrait (Woman I), 2015
Pigmented linen pulp on cotton base sheet
35 ⅜ × 28 in. (89.9 × 71.1 cm)
Collection of Sylvia Shepard. Courtesy of Dieu Donné, New York

Portrait (Woman II), 2015
Pigmented linen pulp on cotton base sheet
35 ½ × 27 ¾ in. (90.2 × 70.5 cm)
Courtesy of the artist and Dieu Donné, New York

Jane Hammond

Be Zany, Poised Harpists/Be Blue, Little Sparrows, 2002
Artist book with poems by Raphael Rubinstein
Raw Indian silk, letterpress, digital prints, photocopies, vintage postage stamps, hand-coloring, rubber stamping, and collage on a variety of archival materials in a slipcase of raw Indian silk
13 ¼ × 10 ½ × 2 in. (33.7 × 26.7 × 5.1 cm)
Edition of 30, plus 17 proofs, each with a one-of-a-kind book cover and a slipcase in one of four colors
Impression: 21/30
Copublished by Dieu Donné Press, New York and Dieu Donné, New York
Courtesy of the artist and Dieu Donné, New York

Jim Hodges

In Wet III, 2010
Pigmented and cast cotton
41 ⅜ × 19 ¾ × 1 in. (105.1 × 50.2 × 2.5 cm)
Courtesy of the artist and Dieu Donné, New York

William Kentridge

Sheets of Evidence, 2009
Artist book of eighteen watermarked drawings
12 ⅝ × 15 × 1 ¼ in. (32.1 × 38.1 × 3.2 cm)
Edition of 20, plus 10 proofs
Impression: proof 5/10
Copublished by Dieu Donné Press, New York and Dieu Donné, New York
Courtesy of the artist and Dieu Donné, New York

Jon Kessler

Me Hate, 2008
Pigment, paper pulp, mirror, yarn, horsehair, cotton, plastic bags, U.S. currency, and digital print on handmade paper
60 × 38 × 1 in. (152.4 × 96.5 × 2.5 cm)
Courtesy of the artist and Salon 94, New York

Suicide Bomber #1, 2008
Pigment, paper pulp, and digital print on handmade paper
55 × 36 × 1 in. (139.7 × 91.4 × 2.5 cm)
Courtesy of the artist and Salon 94, New York

Glenn Ligon

Self-Portrait at Eleven Years Old, 2004
Cotton base sheet with stenciled linen pulp painting
35 ⅝ × 30 in. (90.5 × 76.2 cm)
Edition of 20, plus 7 proofs (5 A.P., 1 B.A.T, and 1 H.C.)
Impression: proof 1/5
Courtesy of the artist and Dieu Donné, New York

End of Year Reports, 2003
Photocopy and screenprint on eight sheets of pigmented cotton and abaca paper in a handmade cotton paper portfolio
11 ½ × 9 ⅛ in. (29.2 × 23.2 cm)
Edition of 10, plus 2 proofs
Impression: proof 2/2
Courtesy of the artist and Dieu Donné, New York

Suzanne McClelland

Seven from "Internal Affairs," 2015
Pigmented linen pulp paint on abaca and cotton handmade paper with handmade paper collage and silkscreened ink
40 ⅛ × 60 ⅜ in. (101.9 × 153.4 cm)
Courtesy of the artist, TEAM Gallery, New York, and Dieu Donné, New York

Arlene Shechet

Parallel Play: Anymore, 2012
Stenciled and painted linen pulp on cast cotton base sheet
40 ⅜ × 30 ⅝ × 1 in. (102.6 × 77.8 × 2.5 cm)
Courtesy of the artist

Parallel Play: Swivel, 2012
Pigment and stenciled linen pulp on abaca base sheet
39 ⅛ × 31 × 1 in. (99.4 × 78.7 × 2.5 cm)
Courtesy of the artist and Dieu Donné, New York

Kate Shepherd

Dark Orange White Stacks, Notched (4, 5), 2011
Pigmented linen blowout on pigmented linen cotton base sheet
30 ⅜ × 21 ⅜ in. (77.2 × 54.3 cm)
Courtesy of the artist and Dieu Donné, New York

Great Cousin Mary, 2011
Pigmented linen blowout on pigmented linen cotton base sheet
35 ⅜ × 24 ⅜ in. (89.9 × 61.9 cm)
Courtesy of the artist and Dieu Donné, New York

Molly Smith

Dust, 2012
Handmade cotton, abaca, linen, and recycled paper
58 ¼ × 39 ⅝ in. (147.8 × 100.6 cm)
Courtesy of the artist and Dieu Donné, New York

Swamp, 2012
Handmade cotton, abaca, linen, and recycled paper
43 ½ × 32 in. (110.5 × 81.3 cm)
Courtesy of the artist and Dieu Donné, New York

Do Ho Suh

Blueprint, 2013
Thread, cotton, and methylcellulose
30 × 40 in. (76.2 × 101.6 cm)
Collection of Miyoung Lee and Neil Simpkins, New York

Staircase, 2013
Thread, cotton, and methylcellulose
14 ¼ × 11 ⅜ in. (36.2 × 28.9 cm)
Courtesy of the artist and Dieu Donné, New York

Mary Temple

Spring Light, 2007
Cotton blowout on abaca base sheet
40 × 59 ¾ in. (101.6 × 151.6 cm)
Courtesy of the artist and Dieu Donné, New York

Richard Tuttle

The Triumph of Night, 2009
Hand-cast cotton pulp and wire in painted wooden box
14 × 32 ⅛ × 6 ¼ in. (35.6 × 81.4 × 15.9 cm)
Edition of 10, plus 9 proofs
Impression: 2/10
Courtesy of the artist and Dieu Donné, New York

Ursula von Rydingsvard

Untitled, 2010
Thread, pigment, fabric, and handmade paper
41 ½ × 22 ¼ in. (105.4 × 56.5 cm)
Courtesy of the artist and Dieu Donné, New York

Untitled, 2010
Thread, pigment, fabric and handmade paper
42 ⅛ × 22 ⅛ in. (107 × 56.2 cm)
Courtesy of the artist and Dieu Donné, New York

B. Wurtz

Untitled (7864), 2013
Watermarked, pigmented abaca with linen pulp paint on cotton base sheet
24 ¼ × 18 ¼ in. (61.6 × 46.4 cm)
Courtesy of the artist and Dieu Donné, New York

Curator's Acknowledgments

BRIDGET DONLON

A few short years ago, I knew very little about paper or pulp. I only knew of some artists whose work had been transformed by residencies, at a place called Dieu Donné. I credit Jane Hammond, Kate Shepherd, and Ursula von Rydingsvard, three such artists that I have known since I was a gallerina fresh out of undergrad, with leading me to this extraordinary place that I have been proud to work in for nearly four years. I now know a whole lot more about paper—where fibers come from; what they do; how to use various techniques to achieve different creative ends; what a deckled edge looks like; and what the difference is between bleached and natural abaca. When I see an artist's work on commercially produced paper, I lament how improved it would be if it were instead on some handmade cotton or linen. In short, this place has turned me into a paper snob.

Working on *Pure Pulp* has been a joy—not only for the experience of collaborating with an incredibly supportive team at the Wellin Museum of Art—but also for the chance it provided to delve further into the history of the residency programs at Dieu Donné. Like most non-profit gigs, things never come to a stop and they hardly ever slow down. The annual cycle whirls on, bringing new artists to the studio and new projects to the walls. Taking the time to look back at the creative output from the recent history of artist residencies in the paper studio was a luxury and welcomed challenge. What stood out to me initially, and now in reflection, is the overwhelming diversity of work made possible from a few humble ingredients. It is the creativity of the artists and the depth of knowledge of our expert papermakers that give paper a seemingly infinite mutability. The experience at Dieu Donné is as democratic as it is generous—our kindergarten workshops are surprisingly similar to the orientation workshop we give our resident artists—and I have been proud to offer a contribution to the legacy of this wonderful place.

In particular, I want to thank the energetic interns that helped me with research and my colleagues at Dieu Donné: Amy Jacobs, Lisa Switalski, and Desiree Adams who are the best teammates a person could ever hope to work with; Paul Wong, whose reputation among artists as a master is well deserved, and I am grateful to him for being able to answer every question I had in my research on this exhibition with great, illuminating anecdotes; and most of all Kathleen Flynn for her unyielding support, encouragement, and guidance. It has been an absolute pleasure to work alongside these incredibly talented and hardworking individuals. I would also like to recognize all previous Dieu Donné studio collaborators—with a distinct mention to Pat Almonrode, Catherine Cox, Rachel Gladfelter, Akemi Martin, Megan Moorhouse, and Mina Takahashi for their additional collaborations with the exhibition artists—and members of the staff who have contributed to this labor of love over the past forty years.

I would like to acknowledge the Dieu Donné Board of Directors for their passionate dedication to this exceptional organization. My highest regards go to Susan Gosin for founding a place that has become such a significant institution in the field of contemporary art to such a broad range of individuals including students, craftsmen, and artists worldwide.

I have greatly enjoyed working with the staff at the Wellin Museum—Katherine Alcauskas, Megan Austin, Christopher Harrison, Amy Sylvester, and Susanna White—and have appreciated additional support from Jennifer Scanlan and Sarah Windham. I am so grateful to Tracy Adler for this opportunity. A mutual friend suggested we meet, and that initial wintry chat has turned into a project of huge significance to me both professionally and personally.

Many thanks to Jack Flam and Katy Rogers at the Dedalus Foundation, New York, and Teri Williams and Virginia Howell at the Robert C. Williams Museum of Papermaking at Georgia Tech, Atlanta, for extending this traveling exhibition to their venues.

My gratitude also goes to Miyoung Lee and Sylvia Shepard for lending works from their personal collections to this exhibition, and to Derek Eller Gallery, Gallery Wendi Norris, Rosemary Suh, Jessie Henson, Anne McIlleron, David Lawrence Mitchell, Andria Morales, and Heesun Shin for helping to coordinate loans and catalogue information.

This catalogue was made possible by the amazing team at SNAP Editions led by Sarah King and including Diane Armitage, Amy Chang, Louis Doulas, and Angelica Villa; through the stunning design by Tim Laun and Natalie Wedeking; and beautiful photography by John Bentham, Andrew Kist, and Jason Mandella. I am thrilled to thank Richard Tuttle for his contribution, a text that gives me more to think about each time I read it, and the multitalented Rachel Wolff for her exemplary interview with my colleagues.

I am indebted to Casey Ruble for a myriad of reasons but, most relevantly here, for her crucial feedback and coaching during the early stages of writing my essay.

Above all, I thank each artist in this exhibition for taking on the challenge of working in pulp and finding such exquisite ways to use it. The most difficult part of curating this exhibition was not having enough room to include everything.

Thank you to my immediate, extended, and constructed family, especially Dad, Joel, and David.

This is for Dorothy Donlon and Samantha Smith: two strong women—one I knew my whole life, the other for just a short time—whom I was lucky to have as personal cheerleaders. Each would have been more excited than anybody else (except, perhaps, one another) to see this exhibition and read this catalogue.

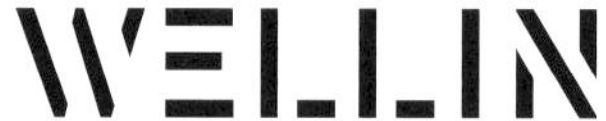

Ruth and Elmer Wellin Museum of Art
Hamilton College

Tracy L. Adler
Director

Megan Austin
Manager of Educational Programming and Outreach

Katherine D. Alcauskas
Collections and Exhibitions Specialist

Christopher Harrison
Building Manager and Preparator

Amber Spadea
Andrew W. Mellon Educator for School and Community Programs

Amy Sylvester
Office Assistant

Matt Makuch
Museum Security Administrator

Alexander D'Acunto
Lead Security Officer

Right: Hamilton College alumni with Amy Jacobs (center) in the Dieu Donné studio during an event hosted by the Wellin Museum of Art, December 2014.

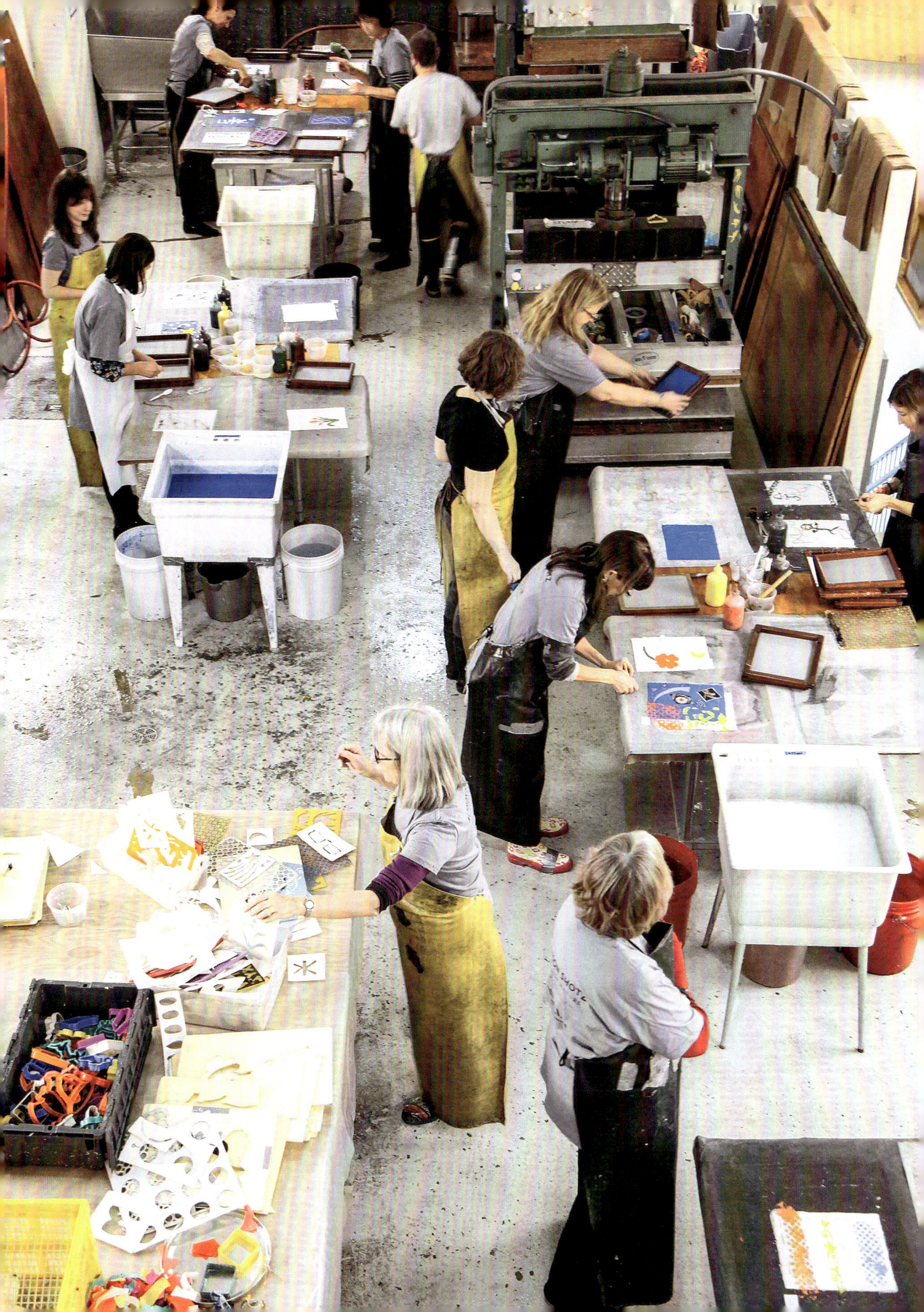

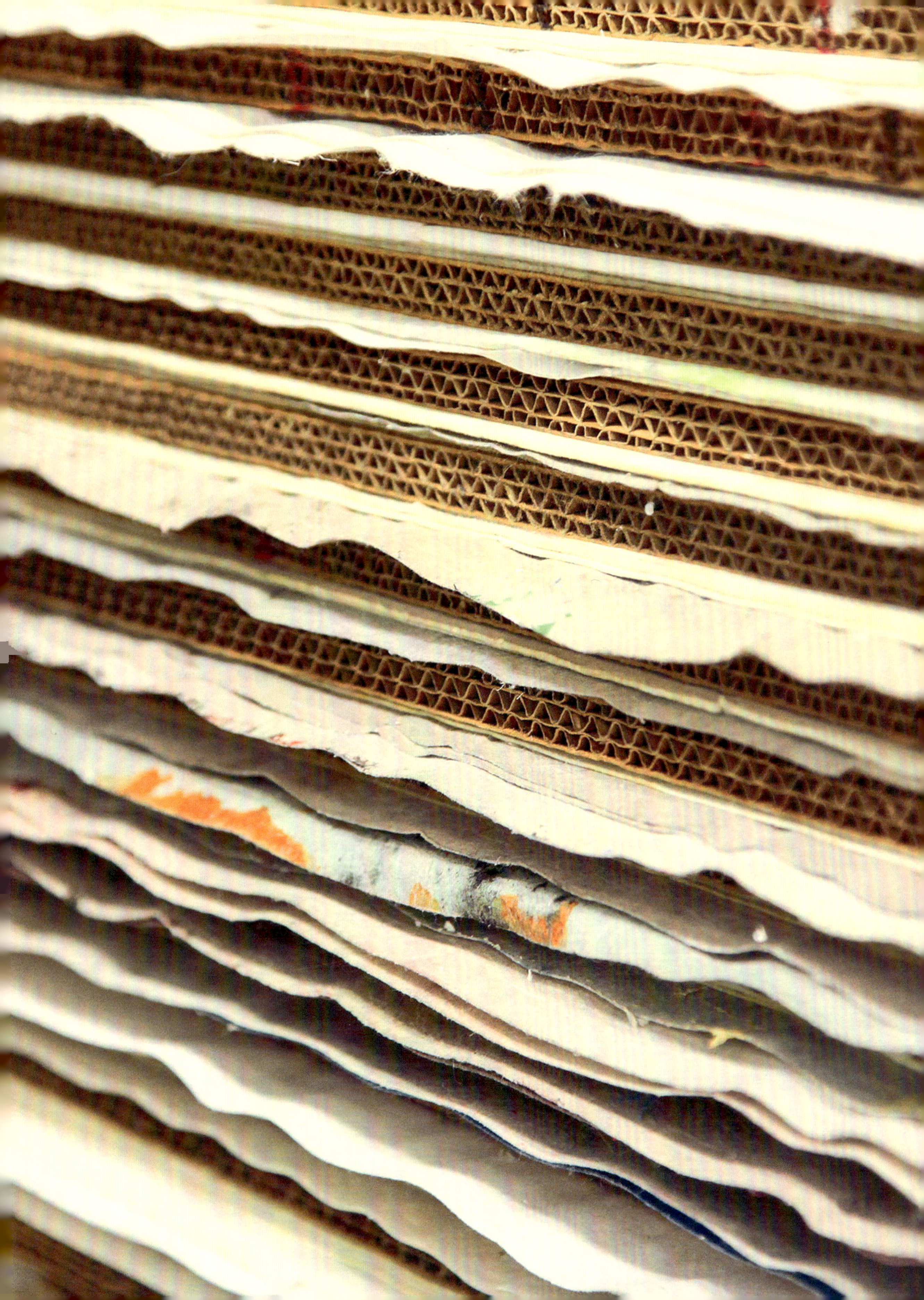